D1421722

THE SPREAD OF
NUCLEAR WEAPONS
AN ENDURING DEBATE

With new chapters on Iran, Iraq, and North Korea,
and on the prospects for global nuclear disarmament

Scott D. Sagan
Kenneth N. Waltz

W. W. Norton & Company   New York • London

W. W. Norton & Company has been independent since its founding in 1923, when William Warder Norton and Mary D. Herter Norton first published lectures delivered at the People's Institute, the adult education division of New York City's Cooper Union. The firm soon expanded its program beyond the Institute, publishing books by celebrated academics from America and abroad. By midcentury, the two major pillars of Norton's publishing program—trade books and college texts—were firmly established. In the 1950s, the Norton family transferred control of the company to its employees, and today—with a staff of four hundred and a comparable number of trade, college, and professional titles published each year—W. W. Norton & Company stands as the largest and oldest publishing house owned wholly by its employees.

Editor: Roby Harrington
Project Editor: Rachel Mayer
Editorial Assistant: Caitlin Cummings
Marketing Manager, Political Science: Sasha Levitt
Production Manager: Ashley Horna

Composition: Westchester Book Composition
Manufacturing: R. R. Donnelley

The text of this book is composed in Palatino with the display set in Univers.

Library of Congress Cataloging-in-Publication Data

Sagan, Scott Douglas.
    The spread of nuclear weapons : an enduring debate / Scott D. Sagan,
Kenneth N. Waltz. — [3rd ed.].
        p. cm.
    Includes bibliographical references and index.
    ISBN 978-0-393-92010-9 (pbk.)
        1. Nuclear weapons. 2. Arms race. 3. Nuclear nonproliferation.
    4. Nuclear terrorism. 5. Ballistic missile defenses.   I. Waltz, Kenneth Neal,
    1924– II. Title.
    U264.S233 2013
    327.1'747—dc23
                                                                    2012017369

W. W. Norton & Company, Inc., 500 Fifth Avenue, New York, NY 10110-0017
wwnorton.com

W. W. Norton & Company Ltd., Castle House, 75/76 Wells Street, London W1T 3QT

1 2 3 4 5 6 7 8 9 0

Contents

Acknowledgments

We thank Roby Harrington from W. W. Norton for once again encouraging us to pit our ideas against one another, and Caitlin Cummings for coordinating the editing and production of this third edition of our debate. Kenneth Waltz thanks the Institute of War and Peace Studies of Columbia University for its generous support. Scott Sagan thanks Stanford University's Center for International Security and Cooperation and the Carnegie Corporation of New York for their support, and Jane Esberg and Reid Pauly for their great work as research assistants. We both want to express our gratitude to Mira Rapp-Hooper for her extraordinary help with Chapter 6 and with other manuscript revisions and updates.

Finally, we both thank our many students and colleagues whose comments on our work have improved our thinking on this subject and prevented us from making unnecessary mistakes. All remaining errors in the book, of course, are the fault of the other author.

Scott D. Sagan   Kenneth N. Waltz
Palo Alto, CA   New York, NY

Preface

This book is about one of today's most critical international issues: the spread of nuclear weapons. If one looks even briefly at the history of the spread of nuclear weapons, two facts are clear. First, nuclear weapons have spread slowly but surely around the globe. One new government has developed a nuclear weapon approximately every five years since the end of the Second World War. Second, many more countries than the nine current nuclear states could build the bomb should they choose to do so. Scholars estimate that at least seventeen governments have actively explored building the bomb in the past, and a number of new potential nuclear powers have appeared on the horizon. Iran claims to want only civilian nuclear power, but most foreign governments and international scholars believe that Tehran is covertly working toward a nuclear weapons capability. Saudi government officials claim that if the Islamic Republic of Iran develops a nuclear bomb, Saudi Arabia will do so as well. In Tokyo, some leading politicians no longer rule out acquisition of nuclear weapons by Japan. And North Korea has tested nuclear weapons twice and is widely suspected to have secretly sold or traded nuclear weapons–related technology to Syria.

This book, however, is not about who is likely to get the bomb next nor about the technical and political processes by which states may develop nuclear weapons. There are many articles, books, and government reports on these subjects. The purpose of this book is to address an even more fundamental uncertainty about our nuclear future: What are the likely consequences of the spread of nuclear weapons? The answer is by no means clear or simple. Indeed, as readers will discover, we disagree about this central issue. Kenneth Waltz argues that fear of the spread of nuclear weapons is exaggerated; "more may be better" since new nuclear states will use their weapons to deter other countries from attacking them. Scott Sagan argues that the spread of nuclear weapons will make the world less stable; "more will be worse" since some new nuclear states will engage in preventive wars, fail to build survivable forces, use their arsenals as shields behind which to commit acts of aggression, or have serious nuclear weapons accidents.

In the first two chapters, we present our central arguments and develop the logic and evidence that support each argument. In the third and fourth chapters we respond to each other's criticisms, showing where, on occasion, there is common ground and where, more often, strong disagreements remain. In the fifth chapter, we look in more detail at the contemporary case of confrontation between nuclear powers in an area of historical enmity and conflict: South Asia. In the sixth chapter, we explain our differing views on the most recent cases of successful, attempted, and prospective nuclear weapons acquisition: North Korea, Iraq, and Iran. The concluding chapter critically examines the likely causes and potential consequences of the Obama administration's embrace of the goal of creating "a world without nuclear weapons." Is a world free of nuclear weapons a real possibility? Would such a world be a less dangerous and more peaceful place? Or would it encourage conventional wars and nuclear weapons use by the first state to reacquire nuclear arms in the future?

Disagreements about these issues will take up much of this book, but here we point out some important matters of agreement between us. First, we both believe that theories are a necessary aid to understanding international politics. Although many scholars and policymakers claim to present "just the facts" or to judge situations purely on "a case by case basis," most individuals still have theories that guide their views, even if they are not well developed or clearly presented.

Both of us lay out the assumptions and logic behind our positions and show how these concepts can provide insights into the question of nuclear proliferation.

Second, both of us believe that intellectual debates are useful. We believe that ideas are improved through debate and by repeatedly testing these ideas against evidence. We have found this debate to be stimulating and have discovered that our disagreements have sharpened our arguments and have led to improved understanding even when many divergent opinions remain. In the polarized Washington environment today, reasoned and civil debate appears to be increasingly rare. We hope that our readers will find our debate, with disagreements expressed in a frank but respectful manner, to be refreshing and thought provoking.

Third, we believe that political scientists should try to help improve government policy. We study international politics because we believe it matters and that it influences all of our lives. We also write about international politics because we believe that strong scholarship can influence policymaking by challenging underlying beliefs, discovering and interpreting new evidence, and providing new ideas and arguments.

Fourth, and finally, we obviously agree that nuclear weapons have not been fired in anger in the sixty-seven years since the end of the Second World War. Kenneth Waltz reminds readers of this crucial point and maintains that the fact that many of his theories and arguments contained within this book are as relevant today as they were in 1995, when the first edition of this book was published, is noteworthy. Scott Sagan reminds readers that new nuclear states have appeared and maintains that this creates even more daunting nuclear dangers than those that we overcame, with skill and luck, during the Cold War. Thus our disagreements continue. The debate endures.

THE SPREAD OF
NUCLEAR WEAPONS

AN ENDURING DEBATE

Chapter 1

MORE MAY BE BETTER

Kenneth N. Waltz

What will the spread of nuclear weapons do to the world? I say "spread" rather than "proliferation" because so far nuclear weapons have proliferated only vertically as the major nuclear powers have added to their arsenals. Horizontally, they have spread slowly across the world, and the pace is not likely to change much. Short-term candidates for admission to the nuclear club are not numerous, and they are not likely to rush into the nuclear business. One reason is that the United States works with some effect to keep countries from doing that.

Nuclear weapons will nevertheless spread, with a new member occasionally joining the club. Membership grew to twelve in the first fifty years of the nuclear age, and that number included three countries that suddenly found themselves in the nuclear military business as successor states to the Soviet Union. Membership in the club then dropped to eight as South Africa, Kazakhstan, Belarus, and Ukraine liquidated their weapons, and rose to nine when North Korea developed its first weapon. A 50 percent growth of membership in the next decade would be surprising. Since rapid changes in international conditions can be unsettling, the slowness of the spread of nuclear

This is a revised version of my article "Toward Nuclear Peace," in D. Brito and M. Intrilligator, eds., *Strategies for Managing Nuclear Proliferation* (Lexington, MA: Lexington Books, 1982) and The Spread of Nuclear Weapons: More May Be Better, Adelphi Paper 171 (London: International Institute for Strategic Studies, 1981).

weapons is fortunate. Someday the world will be populated by fifteen or eighteen nuclear-weapon states (hereafter referred to as nuclear states). What the further spread of nuclear weapons will do to the world is therefore a compelling question.

THE MILITARY LOGIC OF SELF-HELP SYSTEMS

The world has enjoyed more years of peace since 1945 than had been known in modern history, if peace is defined as the absence of general war among the major states of the world. The Second World War followed the first one within twenty-one years. Almost sixty years have elapsed since the Allies' victory over the Axis powers. Conflict marks all human affairs. In the past half century, conflict has generated hostility among states and has at times issued in violence among the weaker and smaller ones. Even though the more-powerful states of the world were occasionally direct participants, war was confined geographically and limited militarily. Remarkably, general war was avoided in a period of rapid and far-reaching change: decolonization; the rapid economic growth of some states; the formation and tightening of blocs, and the eventual dissolution of one of them; the development of new technologies; and the emergence of new strategies for fighting guerrilla wars and deterring nuclear ones. The prevalence of peace, together with the fighting of circumscribed wars, indicates a high ability of the postwar international system to absorb changes and to contain conflicts and hostility.

Presumably, features found in the postwar system that were not present earlier account for the world's recent good fortune. The biggest changes in the postwar world were, first, the shift from multipolarity to bipolarity and ultimately to unipolarity, and, second, the introduction of nuclear weapons. In this chapter I concentrate on the latter.

States coexist in a condition of anarchy. Self-help is the principle of action in an anarchic order, and the most important way in which states must help themselves is by providing for their own security. Therefore, in weighing the chances for peace, the first questions to ask are questions about the ends for which states use force and about the strategies and weapons they employ. The chances of peace rise if states can achieve their most important ends without using force. War becomes less likely as the costs of war rise in relation to possible gains. Strategies bring ends and means together. How nuclear weapons affect the chances for peace is seen by examining the different implications of defense and deterrence.

How can one state dissuade another state from attacking? One way to counter an intended attack is to build fortifications and to muster forces that look forbiddingly strong. To build defenses so patently strong that no one will try to destroy or overcome them would make international life perfectly tranquil. I call this the defensive ideal. The other way to counter an intended attack is to build retaliatory forces able to rain unacceptable punishment upon a would-be aggressor. "To deter" means to stop people from doing something by frightening them. In contrast to dissuasion by defense, dissuasion by deterrence operates by frightening a state out of attacking, not because of the difficulty of launching an attack and carrying it home, but because the expected reaction of the opponent may result in one's own severe punishment. Defense and deterrence are often confused. One used to hear statements like this: "A strong defense in Europe will deter a Soviet attack." What was meant was that a strong defense would dissuade the Soviet Union from attacking. Deterrence is achieved not through the ability to defend but through the ability to punish. Purely deterrent forces provide no defense. The message of the strategy is this: "Although we are defenseless, if you attack we may punish you to an extent that more than cancels your gains." Second-strike nuclear forces serve that kind of strategy. Purely defensive forces provide no deterrence. They offer no means of punishment. The message of the strategy is this: "Although we cannot strike back at you, you will find our defenses so difficult to overcome that you will dash yourself to pieces against them." The Maginot line was to serve that kind of strategy.[1]

Do nuclear weapons increase or decrease the chances of war? The answer depends on whether nuclear weapons permit and encourage states to deploy forces in ways that make the active use of force more or less likely and in ways that promise to be more or less destructive. If nuclear weapons make the offense more effective and the blackmailer's threat more compelling, then nuclear weapons are bad for the world— the more so the more widely diffused nuclear weapons become. If defense and deterrence are made easier and more reliable by the spread of nuclear weapons, we may expect the opposite result. To maintain their security, states must rely on the means they can generate and the arrangements they can make for themselves. It follows that the quality of international life varies with the ease or the difficulty states experience in making themselves secure.

Weapons and strategies change the situation of states in ways that make them more or less secure. If weapons are not well suited for conquest, neighbors have more peace of mind. We should expect war to become less likely when weaponry is such as to make conquest more difficult, to discourage pre-emptive and preventive war, and to make coercive threats less credible. Do nuclear weapons have these effects? Some answers can be found by considering how nuclear deterrence and nuclear defense improve the prospects for peace.

First, war can be fought in the face of deterrent threats, but the higher the stakes and the closer a country moves toward winning them, the more surely that country invites retaliation and risks its own destruction. States are not likely to run major risks for minor gains. War between nuclear states may escalate as the loser uses larger and larger warheads. Fearing that, states will want to draw back. Not escalation but de-escalation becomes likely. War remains possible, but victory in war is too dangerous to fight for. If states can score only small gains, because large ones risk retaliation, they have little incentive to fight.

Second, states act with less care if the expected costs of war are low and with more care if they are high. In 1853 and

1854 Britain and France expected to win an easy victory if they went to war against Russia. Prestige abroad and political popularity at home would be gained, if not much else. The vagueness of their expectations was matched by the carelessness of their actions. In blundering into the Crimean War, they acted hastily on scant information, pandered to their people's frenzy for war, showed more concern for an ally's whim than for the adversary's situation, failed to specify the changes in behavior that threats were supposed to bring, and inclined toward testing strength first and bargaining second.[2] In sharp contrast, the presence of nuclear weapons makes states exceedingly cautious. Think of Kennedy and Khrushchev in the Cuban missile crisis. Why fight if you can't win much and might lose everything?

Third, the deterrent deployment of nuclear weapons contributes more to a country's security than does conquest of territory. A country with a deterrent strategy does not need territory as much as a country relying on conventional defense. A deterrent strategy makes it unnecessary for a country to fight for the sake of increasing its security, and thus removes a major cause of war.[3]

Fourth, deterrent effect depends both on capabilities and on the will to use them. The will of the attacked, striving to preserve its own territory, can be presumed to be stronger than the will of the attacker, striving to annex someone else's territory. Knowing this, the would-be attacker is further inhibited.[4]

Fifth, certainty about the relative strength of adversaries also makes war less likely. From the late nineteenth century onward, the speed of technological innovation increased the difficulty of estimating relative strengths and predicting the course of campaigns. Since World War II, technological advance has been even faster, but short of a ballistic missile defense breakthrough, this has not mattered. It did not disturb the American-Soviet military equilibrium, because one side's missiles were not made obsolete by improvements in the other side's missiles. In 1906, the British Dreadnought, with the greater range and fire power of its guns, made older battleships obsolete. This does not happen to missiles. As Bernard

Brodie put it, "Weapons that do not have to fight their like do not become useless because of the advent of newer and superior types."[5] They may have to survive their like, but that is a much simpler problem to solve.

Many wars might have been avoided had their outcomes been foreseen. "To be sure," Georg Simmel wrote, "the most effective presupposition for preventing struggle, the exact knowledge of the comparative strength of the two parties, is very often only to be obtained by the actual fighting out of the conflict."[6] Miscalculation causes wars. One side expects victory at an affordable price, while the other side hopes to avoid defeat. Here the differences between conventional and nuclear worlds are fundamental. In the former, states are too often tempted to act on advantages that are wishfully discerned and narrowly calculated. In 1914, neither Germany nor France tried very hard to avoid a general war. Both hoped for victory even though they believed the opposing coalitions to be quite evenly matched. In 1941, Japan, in attacking the United States, could hope for victory only if a series of events that were possible but unlikely took place. Japan hoped to grab resources sufficient for continuing its war against China and then to dig in to defend a limited perimeter. Meanwhile, the United States and Britain would have to deal with Germany, supposedly having defeated the Soviet Union and therefore reigning supreme in Europe. Japan could then hope to fight a defensive war until America, her purpose weakened, became willing to make a compromise peace in Asia.[7]

Countries more readily run the risks of war when defeat, if it comes, is distant and is expected to bring only limited damage. Given such expectations, leaders do not have to be crazy to sound the trumpet and urge their people to be bold and courageous in the pursuit of victory. The outcome of battles and the course of campaigns are hard to foresee because so many things affect them. Predicting the result of conventional wars has proved difficult.

Uncertainty about outcomes does not work decisively against the fighting of wars in conventional worlds. Countries armed with conventional weapons go to war knowing that even in defeat their suffering will be limited. Calculations about nuclear war are made differently. A nuclear world calls for a different kind of reasoning. If countries armed with nuclear weapons go to war with each other, they do so knowing that their suffering may be unlimited. Of course, it also may not be, but that is not the kind of uncertainty that encourages anyone to use force. In a conventional world, one is uncertain about winning or losing. In a nuclear world, one is uncertain about surviving or being annihilated. If force is used, and not kept within limits, catastrophe will result. That prediction is easy to make because it does not require close estimates of opposing forces. The number of one's cities that can be severely damaged is equal to the number of strategic warheads an adversary can deliver. Variations of number mean little within wide ranges. The expected effect of the deterrent achieves an easy clarity because wide margins of error in estimates of the damage one may suffer do not matter. Do we expect to lose one city or two, two cities or ten? When these are the pertinent questions, we stop thinking about running risks and start worrying about how to avoid them. In a conventional world, deterrent threats are ineffective because the damage threatened is distant, limited, and problematic. Nuclear weapons make military miscalculation difficult and politically pertinent prediction easy.

WHAT WILL THE SPREAD OF NUCLEAR WEAPONS DO TO THE WORLD?

Contemplating the nuclear past gives ground for hoping that the world will survive if further nuclear powers join today's eight. This hope is called into question by those who believe that the infirmities of some new nuclear states and the delicacy of their nuclear forces will work against the preservation of peace and for the fighting of nuclear wars. The likelihood of avoiding destruction as more states become members of the nuclear club is often coupled with the question of *who* those states will be. What are the likely differences in situation and behavior of new as compared to old nuclear powers?

Nuclear Weapons and Domestic Stability

What are the principal worries? Because of the importance of controlling nuclear weapons—of keeping them firmly in the hands of reliable officials—rulers of nuclear states may become more authoritarian and ever more given to secrecy. Moreover, some potential nuclear states are not politically strong and stable enough to ensure control of the weapons and control of the decision to use them. If neighboring, hostile, unstable states are armed with nuclear weapons, each will fear attack by the other. Feelings of insecurity may lead to arms races that subordinate civil needs to military necessities. Fears are compounded by the danger of internal coups, in which the control of nuclear weapons may be the main object and the key to political power. Under these fearful circumstances, it may be impossible to maintain governmental authority and civil order. The legitimacy of the state and the loyalty of its citizenry may dissolve because the state is no longer thought to be capable of maintaining external security and internal order. The first fear is that states become tyrannical; the second, that they lose control. Both fears may be realized either in different states or in the same state at different times.[8]

What can one say? Four things primarily. First, possession of nuclear weapons may slow arms races down, rather than speed them up, a possibility considered later. Second, for less-developed countries to build nuclear arsenals requires a long lead time. Nuclear weapons require administrative and technical teams able to formulate and sustain programs of considerable cost that pay off only in the long run. The more unstable a government, the shorter the attention span of its leaders. They have to deal with today's problems and hope for the best tomorrow. Governments may come and go in unpredictable fashion, but unless a minimum of continuity is maintained, nuclear programs cannot be sustained. Beneath what may be a chaotic political surface, a potential nuclear country must have a certain social-political equilibrium.

Third, although highly unstable states are unlikely to initiate nuclear projects, such projects, begun in stable times, may continue through periods of political turmoil and succeed in producing nuclear weapons. A nuclear state may be unstable or may become so. But what is hard to comprehend is why, in an internal struggle for power, the contenders would start using nuclear weapons. Who would they aim at? How would they use them as instruments for maintaining or gaining control? I see little more reason to fear that one faction or another in a less-developed country will fire atomic weapons in a struggle for political power than that they will be used in a crisis of succession. One or another nuclear state will experience uncertainty of succession, fierce struggles for power, and instability of regime. Those who fear the worst have not shown how those events might lead to the use of nuclear weapons. Strikingly, during the Cultural Revolution, which lasted from 1966 to 1976, one group or another managed to keep control of China's nuclear weapons. One can hardly imagine a greater instability than the chaos the Cultural Revolution inflicted on China for a decade. Fourth, the possibility of one side in a civil war firing a nuclear warhead at its opponent's stronghold nevertheless remains. Such an act would produce a national tragedy, not an international one. This question then arises: Once the weapon is fired, what happens next? The domestic use of nuclear weapons is, of all the uses imaginable, least likely to lead to escalation and to global tragedy.

Nuclear Weapons and Regional Stability

Nuclear weapons are not likely to be used at home. Are they likely to be used abroad? As nuclear weapons spread, what new causes may bring effects different from, and worse than, those known earlier in the nuclear age? This section considers five ways in which the new world is expected to differ from the old and then examines the prospects for, and the consequences of, new nuclear states using their weapons for blackmail or for fighting offensive wars.

In what ways may the actions and interactions of new nuclear states differ from those of old nuclear powers? First, new nuclear states may come in hostile pairs and share a common border. Where states are bitter enemies one may fear that they will be unable to resist using their nuclear weapons against each other. This is a worry about the future that the past does not disclose. The Soviet Union and the United States, and the Soviet Union and China, were hostile enough; and the latter pair shared a long border. Nuclear weapons caused China and the Soviet Union to deal cautiously with each other. But bitterness among some potential nuclear states, it is said, exceeds that felt by the old ones. Playing down the bitterness sometimes felt by the United States, the Soviet Union, and China requires a creative reading of history. Moreover, those who believe that bitterness causes wars assume a close association that is seldom found between bitterness among nations and their willingness to run high risks.

Second, many fear that states that are radical at home will recklessly use their nuclear weapons in pursuit of revolutionary ends abroad. States that are radical at home, however, may not be radical abroad. Few states have been radical in the conduct of their foreign policy, and fewer have remained so for long. Think of the Soviet Union and the People's Republic of China. States coexist in a competitive arena. The pressures of competition cause them to behave in ways that make the threats they face manageable, in ways that enable them to get along. States can remain radical in foreign policy only if they are overwhelmingly strong—as none of the new nuclear states will be— or if their acts fall short of damaging vital interests of other nuclear powers.

States that acquire nuclear weapons will not be regarded with indifference. States that want to be freewheelers have to stay out of the nuclear business. A nuclear Iraq, for example, would have to show caution, even in rhetoric, lest it suffer retaliation in response to someone else's anonymous attack on a third state. That state, ignorant of who attacked, might claim that its intelligence agents had identified Iraq as the culprit and take the opportunity to silence it by striking a heavy conventional blow. Nuclear weapons induce caution in any state, especially in weak ones.

Third, some new nuclear states may have governments and societies that are not well rooted. If a country is a loose collection of hostile tribes, if its leaders form a thin veneer atop a people partly nomadic, if the state has a history of authoritarian rule, its leaders may be freer of constraints than, and have different values from, those who rule older and more fully developed polities. Idi Amin and Muammar Qaddafi, rulers of Uganda and Libya, fit these categories, and they were favorite examples of the kinds of rulers who supposedly could not be trusted to manage nuclear weapons responsibly. Despite wild rhetoric aimed at foreigners, however, both of these "irrational" rulers became cautious and modest when punitive actions against them might have threatened their ability to rule. Even though Amin lustily slaughtered members of tribes he disliked, he quickly stopped goading Britain when it seemed that it might intervene militarily. Qaddafi showed similar restraint. He and Egypt's Anwar Sadat were openly hostile. In July of 1977, both launched commando attacks and air raids, including two large air strikes by Egypt on Libya's el Adem air-base. However, neither side let the attacks get out of hand. Qaddafi showed himself to be forbearing and amenable to mediation by other Arab leaders. Shai Feldman used these and other examples to argue that Arab leaders are deterred from taking inordinate risks, not because they engage in intricate rational calculations but simply because they, like other rulers, are "sensitive to costs."[9] Saddam Hussein further illustrated the point during, and even prior to, the war of 1991. He invaded Kuwait only after the United States had given many indications that it would not oppose him or use military force to liberate a Kuwait conquered by Iraq. During the war, he launched missiles against Israel. But Iraq's missiles were so lightly armed that little risk was run of prompting attacks more punishing than what Iraq was already suffering. Deterrence worked for the United States and for Israel as it has for every other nuclear state.

Many Westerners write fearfully about a future in which Third World countries have nuclear weapons. They seem to view the people of these nations in the old imperialist manner, as "lesser breeds without the law." As ever, with ethnocentric views, speculation takes the place of evidence. How do we know that a nuclear-armed and newly hostile Egypt, or a nuclear-armed and still-hostile Syria, would not strike to destroy Israel? Would either do so at the risk of Israeli bombs falling on some of its own cities? Almost a quarter of Egypt's people live in four cities: Cairo, Alexandria, El-Giza, and Shoubra el-Kheima. More than a quarter of Syria's live in three: Damascus, Aleppo, and Homs.[10] What government would risk sudden losses of such proportion, or indeed of much lesser proportion? Rulers want to have a country that they can continue to rule. Some Arab country might wish that some other Arab country would risk its own destruction for the sake of destroying Israel, but why should one think that any country would be willing to do so? Despite ample bitterness, Israelis and Arabs have limited their wars and accepted constraints placed on them by others. Arabs did not marshal their resources and make an all-out effort to destroy Israel in the years before Israel could strike back with nuclear warheads. We cannot expect countries to risk more in the presence of nuclear weapons than they did in their absence.

Fourth, while some worry about nuclear states coming in hostile pairs, others worry that they won't come in hostile pairs. The simplicity of relations when one party can concentrate its anxieties on a single other, and the ease of calculating forces and estimating the dangers they pose, may be lost. Early in the Cold War, the United States deterred the Soviet Union, and in due course, the Soviet Union deterred the United States. As soon as additional states joined the nuclear club, however, the question of who deterred whom could no longer be easily answered. The Soviet Union had to worry lest a move made in Europe might cause France and Britain to retaliate, thus possibly setting off American forces as well. Such worries at once complicated calculations and strengthened deterrence. Somebody might have retaliated, and that was all a would-be attacker needed to know. Nuclear weapons restore the clarity and simplicity lost as bipolar situations are replaced by multipolar ones.

Fifth, in some of the new nuclear states, civil control of the military may be shaky. Nuclear weapons may fall into the hands of military officers more inclined than civilians are to put them to offensive use. This again is an old worry. I can see no reason to think that civil control of the military was secure in the Soviet Union, given the occasional presence of military officers in the Politburo and some known and some surmised instances of military intervention in civil affairs at critical times.[11] In the People's Republic of China, military and civil branches of government are not separated but fused. Although one may prefer civil control, preventing a highly destructive war does not require it. What is required is that decisions be made that keep destruction within bounds, whether those decisions are made by civilians or soldiers. Soldiers may be more cautious than civilians.[12] Generals and admirals do not like uncertainty, and they do not lack patriotism. They do not like to fight conventional wars under unfamiliar conditions. The offensive use of nuclear weapons multiplies uncertainties. Nobody knows what a nuclear battlefield would look like, and nobody knows what would happen after the first city was hit. Uncertainty about the course that a nuclear war might follow, along with the certainty that the destruction would be immense, strongly inhibits the first use of nuclear weapons.

Examining the supposedly unfortunate characteristics of new nuclear states removes some of one's worries. One wonders why their civil and military leaders should be less interested in avoiding their own destruction than leaders of other states have been.[13] Nuclear weapons have never been used in a world in which two or more states had them. Still, one's feeling that something awful will emerge as new nuclear powers are added to the present group is not easily quieted. The fear remains that one state or another will fire its new nuclear weapons in a coolly calculated preemptive strike, or fire them in a moment of panic, or use them to launch a preventive war. These possibilities are examined in the next section. Nuclear weapons, so it is feared, may also be set off anonymously, or used to back a policy of blackmail, or be used in a combined conventional-nuclear attack.

Some have feared that a radical Arab state might fire a nuclear warhead anonymously at an Israeli city in order to block a peace settlement.[14] But the state firing the warhead could not be certain of remaining unidentified. Even if a country's leaders persuaded themselves that chances of retaliation were low, who would run the risk? Nor would blackmail be easy, despite one instance of seeming success. In 1953, the Soviet Union and China may have been convinced by President Dwight D. Eisenhower and Secretary of State John Foster Dulles that they would widen the Korean War and raise the level of violence by using nuclear weapons if a settlement were not reached. In Korea, we had gone so far that the threat of going farther was plausible. The blackmailer's threat is not a cheap way of working one's will. The threat is incredible unless a considerable investment has already been made. On January 12, 1954, Dulles gave a speech that seemed to threaten massive retaliation in response to bothersome actions by others, but the successful siege of Dien Bien Phu by Ho Chi Minh's forces in the spring of that year showed the limitations of such threats. Using American nuclear weapons to force the lifting of the siege was discussed in both the United States and France. But using nuclear weapons to serve distant and doubtful interests would have been a monstrous policy, too horrible to carry through. Nuclear weapons deter adversaries from attacking one's vital—and not one's minor—interests.

Although nuclear weapons are poor instruments for blackmail, would they not provide a cheap and decisive offensive force when used against a conventionally armed enemy? Some people once thought that South Korea, and earlier, the Shah's Iran, wanted nuclear weapons for offensive use. Yet one can say neither why South Korea would have used nuclear weapons against fellow Koreans while trying to reunite them nor how it could have used nuclear weapons against the North, knowing that China and the Soviet Union might have retaliated. And what goals might a conventionally strong Iran have entertained that would have tempted it to risk using nuclear weapons? A country that launches a strike has to fear a punishing blow from someone. Far from lowering the expected cost of aggression, a nuclear offense, even against a nonnuclear state, raises the possible costs of aggression to incalculable heights because the aggressor cannot be sure of the reaction of other states.

Nuclear weapons do not make nuclear war likely, as history has shown. The point made when discussing the internal use of nuclear weapons bears repeating. No one can say that nuclear weapons will never be used. Their use is always possible. In asking what the spread of nuclear weapons will do to the world, we are asking about the effects to be expected if a larger number of relatively weak states get nuclear weapons. If such states use nuclear weapons, the world will not end. The use of nuclear weapons by lesser powers would hardly trigger their use elsewhere.

Deterrence by Small Nuclear Forces

How hard is it for minor nuclear powers to build deterrent forces? In the following section, I answer this question.

The Problems of Preventive and Preemptive Strikes[15]

The first danger posed by the spread of nuclear weapons would seem to be that each new nuclear state may tempt an older one to strike and destroy an embryonic nuclear capability before it can become militarily effective. As more countries acquire nuclear weapons, and as more countries gain nuclear competence through power projects, the difficulties and dangers of making preventive strikes increase. Because of America's nuclear arsenal, the Soviet Union could hardly have destroyed the budding forces of Britain and France; but the United States could have struck the Soviet Union's early nuclear facilities, and the United States or the Soviet Union could have struck China's. Long before Israel struck Iraq's reactor, preventive strikes were treated as more than abstract possibilities. When Francis P. Matthews was President Harry S. Truman's secretary of the Navy, he made a speech that seemed to favor our waging a preventive war. The United States, he urged, should be willing to pay "even the price of instituting a war to compel cooperation for peace."[16] Moreover, preventive strikes against nuclear installations can be made by nonnuclear states and have sometimes been threatened. Thus President Nasser warned Israel in 1960 that Egypt would attack if it were sure that Israel was building a bomb. "It is inevitable," he said, "that we should attack the base of aggression even if we have to mobilize four million to destroy it."[17]

The uneven development of the forces of potential and of new nuclear states creates occasions that permit strikes and may invite them. Two stages of nuclear development should be distinguished. First, a country may be in an early stage of nuclear development and be obviously unable to make nuclear weapons. Second, a country may be in an advanced stage of nuclear development, and whether or not it has some nuclear weapons may not be surely known. All of the present nuclear countries went through both stages, yet until Israel struck Iraq's nuclear facility in June of 1981, no one had launched a preventive strike.

A number of causes combined may account for the reluctance of states to strike in order to prevent adversaries from developing nuclear forces. A preventive strike is most promising during the first stage of nuclear development. A state could strike without fearing that the country it attacked would be able to return a nuclear blow. But would one country strike so hard as to destroy another country's potential for future nuclear development? If it did not, the country struck could resume its nuclear career. If the blow struck is less than devastating, one must be prepared either to repeat it or to occupy and control the country. To do either would be forbiddingly difficult.

In striking Iraq, Israel showed that a preventive strike can be made, something that was not in doubt. Israel's act and its consequences, however, made clear that the likelihood of its useful accomplishment is low. Israel's action only increased the determination of Arabs to produce nuclear weapons. Israel's strike, far from foreclosing Iraq's nuclear career, gained Iraq support from some other Arab states to pursue it. Despite Israeli prime minister Menachem Begin's vow to strike as often as need be, the risks in doing so would have risen with each occasion.

A preemptive strike launched against a country that may have a small number of warheads is even less promising than a preventive strike during the first stage. If the country attacked has even a rudimentary nuclear capability, one's own severe punishment becomes possible. Nuclear forces are seldom delicate because no state wants delicate forces, and nuclear forces can easily be made sturdy. Nuclear warheads are fairly small and light; they are easy to hide and to move. Even the Model-T bombs dropped on Hiroshima and Nagasaki were small enough to fit into a World War II bomber. Early in the nuclear age, people worried about atomic bombs being concealed in packing boxes and placed in the holds of ships to be exploded when a signal was given. Now, more than ever, people worry about terrorists stealing nuclear warheads because various states have so many of them. Everybody seems to believe that terrorists are capable of hiding bombs.[18] Why should states be unable to do what terrorist gangs are thought to be capable of?

It was sometimes claimed that a small number of bombs in the hands of minor powers would create greater dangers than additional thousands in the hands of the United States or the Soviet Union. Such statements assume that preemption of a small force is easy. Acting on that assumption, someone may be tempted to strike; fearing this, the state with the small number of weapons may be tempted to use the few weapons it has rather than risk losing them. Such reasoning would confirm the thought that small nuclear forces create extreme dangers. But since protecting small forces by hiding and moving them is quite easy, the dangers evaporate.

Requirements of Deterrence

To be effective, deterrent forces, whether big or small ones, must meet three requirements. First, at least a part of a state's nuclear forces must appear to be able to survive an attack and launch one of its own. Second, survival of forces must not require early firing in response to what may be false alarms. Third, command and control must be reliably maintained; weapons must not be susceptible to accidental or unauthorized use.[19]

The first two requirements are closely linked both to each other and to measures needed to ensure that deterrent forces cannot be preempted. If states can deploy their forces in ways that preclude preemption—and we have seen that they can—then their forces need not be rigged for hair-trigger response. States can retaliate at their leisure.

This question then arises: May dispersing forces for the sake of their survival make command and control hard to maintain? Americans think so because we think in terms of large nuclear arsenals. Small nuclear powers neither have them nor need them. Lesser nuclear states may deploy, say, ten real weapons and ten dummies, while permitting other countries to infer that numbers are larger. An adversary need only believe that some warheads may survive its attack and be visited on it. That belief is not hard to create without making command and control unreliable. All nuclear countries live through a time when their forces are crudely designed. All countries have so far been able to control them. Relations between the United States and the Soviet Union, and later among the United States, the Soviet Union, and China, were at their bitterest just when their nuclear forces were in early stages of development and were unbalanced, crude, and presumably hard to control. Why should we expect new nuclear states to experience greater difficulties than the ones old nuclear states were able to cope with?

Although some of the new nuclear states may be economically and technically backward, they will either have expert and highly trained scientists and engineers or they will not be able to produce nuclear weapons. Even if they buy or steal the weapons, they will have to hire technicians to maintain and control them. We do not have to wonder whether they will take good care of their weapons. They have every incentive to do so. They will not want to risk retaliation because one or more of their warheads accidentally struck another country.

Hiding nuclear weapons and keeping them under control are tasks for which the ingenuity of numerous states is adequate. Means of delivery are neither difficult to devise nor hard to procure. Bombs can be driven in by trucks from neighboring countries. Ports can be torpedoed by small boats lying offshore. A thriving arms trade in ever more sophisticated military equipment provides ready access to what may be wanted, including planes and missiles suited to the delivery of nuclear warheads.

Lesser nuclear states can pursue deterrent strategies effectively. Deterrence requires the ability to inflict unacceptable damage on another country. "Unacceptable damage" to the Soviet Union was variously defined by Robert McNamara as requiring the ability to destroy a fifth to a fourth of its population and a half to two-thirds of its industrial capacity.

American estimates of what is required for deterrence were absurdly high. To deter, a country need not appear to be able to destroy a fourth or a half of another country, although in some cases that might be easily done. Would Libya try to destroy Israel's nuclear weapons at the risk of two bombs surviving to fall on Tripoli and Bengazi? And what would be left of Israel if Tel Aviv and Haifa were destroyed?

The weak can deter one another. But can the weak deter the strong? Raising the question of China's ability to deter the Soviet Union in the old days highlights the issue. The population and industry of most states are concentrated in a relatively small number of centers. This was true of the Soviet Union. A major attack on the top ten cities of the Soviet Union would have mashed 25 percent of its industrial capacity and 25 percent of its urban population. Geoffrey Kemp in 1974 concluded that China could probably have struck on that scale.[20] And I emphasize again, China needed only to appear to be able to do that. A low probability of carrying a highly destructive attack home is sufficient for deterrence. A force of an imprecisely specifiable minimum capacity is nevertheless needed.

In a 1979 study, Justin Galen (pseud.) wondered whether the Chinese had a force capable of deterring the Soviet Union. He estimated that China had sixty to eighty medium-range and sixty to eighty intermediate-range missiles of doubtful reliability and accuracy and eighty obsolete bombers. He rightly pointed out that the missiles might miss their targets even if fired at cities and that the bombers might not get through the Soviet Union's defenses. Moreover, the Soviet Union might have been able to preempt an attack, having almost certainly "located virtually every Chinese missile, aircraft, weapons storage area and production facility." [21] But surely Soviet leaders put these things the other way around. To locate virtually all missiles and aircraft is not good enough. Despite inaccuracies a few Chinese missiles might have hit Russian cities, and some bombers might have got through. Not much is required to deter. What political-military objective is worth risking Vladivostok, Novosibirsk, and Tomsk, with no way of being sure that Moscow would not go as well?

The Credibility of Small Deterrent Forces

The credibility of weaker countries' deterrent threats has two faces. The first is physical. Will such countries be able to construct and protect a deliverable force? We have found that they can quite readily do so. The second is psychological. Will deterrent threats that are physically feasible be psychologically plausible? Will an adversary believe that the retaliation that is threatened will be carried out?

Deterrent threats backed by second-strike nuclear forces raise the possible costs of an attack to such heights that war becomes unlikely. But deterrent threats may not be credible. In a world where two or more countries can make them, the prospect of mutual devastation may make it difficult, or irrational, to execute threats should the occasion for doing so arise. Would it not be senseless to risk suffering further destruction once a deterrent force had failed to deter? Believing that it would be, an adversary may attack counting on the attacked country's unwillingness to risk initiating a devastating exchange by its own retaliation. Why retaliate once a threat to do so has failed? If one's policy is to rely on forces designed to deter, then an attack that is nevertheless made shows that one's reliance was misplaced. The course of wisdom may be to pose a new question: What is the best policy once deterrence has failed? One gains nothing by destroying an enemy's cities. Instead, in retaliating, one may prompt the enemy to unleash more warheads. A ruthless aggressor may strike believing that the leaders of the attacked country are capable of following such a "rational" line of thought. To carry the threat out may be "irrational." This old worry achieved new prominence as the strategic capabilities of the Soviet Union approached those of the United States in the mid-1970s. The Soviet Union, some feared, might believe that the United States would be self-deterred.[22]

Much of the literature on deterrence emphasizes the problem of achieving the credibility on which deterrence depends and the danger of relying on a deterrent of uncertain credibility. One early solution of the problem was Thomas Schelling's notion of "the threat that leaves something to chance."[23] No state can know for sure that another state will refrain from retaliating even when retaliation would be irrational. No state can bet heavily on another state's common sense. Bernard Brodie put the thought more directly, while avoiding the slippery notion of rationality. Rather than ask what it may be rational or irrational for governments to do, the question he repeatedly asked was this: How do governments behave in the presence of awesome dangers? His answer was, very carefully.

To ask why a country should carry out its deterrent threat if deterrence fails is to ask the wrong question. The question suggests that an aggressor may attack believing that the attacked country may not retaliate. This invokes the conventional logic that analysts find so hard to forsake. In a conventional world, a country can sensibly attack if it believes that success is possible. In a nuclear world, a would-be attacker is deterred if it believes that the attacked may retaliate. Uncertainty of response, not certainty, is required for deterrence because, if retaliation occurs, one risks losing so much. In a nuclear world, we should look less at the retaliator's conceivable inhibitions and more at the challenger's obvious risks.

One may nevertheless wonder whether retaliatory threats remain credible if the strategic forces of the attacker are superior to those of the attacked. Will an unsuccessful defender in a conventional war have the courage to unleash its deterrent force, using nuclear weapons first against a country having superior strategic forces? Once more this asks the wrong question. The would-be attacker will ask itself, not whose forces are numerically superior, but whether a grossly provocative act might bring nuclear warheads down on itself. When vital interests are at stake, all of the parties involved are strongly constrained to be moderate because one's immoderate behavior makes the nuclear threats of others credible. With deterrent forces, the question is not whether one country has more than another but whether it has the capability of inflicting "unacceptable damage" on another, with "unacceptable" sensibly defined. Given second-strike capabilities, it is not the balance of forces but the possibility that they may be used that counts. The balance or imbalance of strategic forces affects neither the calculation of danger nor the question of whose will is the stronger. Second-strike forces have to be seen in absolute terms.

Emphasizing the importance of the "balance of resolve," to use Glenn Snyder's apt phrase, raises questions about what a deterrent force covers and what it does not.[24] In answering these questions, we can learn something from the experience of the Cold War. The United States and the Soviet Union limited their provocative acts, all the more carefully when major values for one side or the other were at issue. This can be seen both in what they did and in what they did not do. Whatever support the Soviet Union gave to North Korea's attack on the South in June of 1950 was given after Secretary of State Acheson, the Joint Chiefs of Staff, General MacArthur, the chairman of the Senate Foreign Relations Committee, and others explicitly excluded both South Korea and Taiwan from America's defense perimeter. The United States, to take another example, could fight for years on a large scale in Southeast Asia because neither success nor failure mattered much internationally. Victory would not have made the world one of American hegemony. Defeat would not have made the world one of Soviet hegemony. No vital interest of either superpower was at stake, as both Kissinger and Brezhnev made clear at the time.[25] One can fight without fearing escalation only where little is at stake. That is where the deterrent does not deter.

Actions at the periphery can safely be bolder than actions at the center. In contrast, where much is at stake for one side, the other side moves with care. Trying to win where winning would bring the central balance into question threatens escalation and becomes too risky to contemplate. The United States was circumspect when East European crises loomed in the mid-1950s. Thus Secretary of State Dulles assured the Soviet Union, when Hungarians rebelled in October of 1956, that we would not interfere with Soviet efforts to suppress them. And the Soviet Union's moves in the center of Europe were carefully controlled. Its probes in Berlin were tentative, reversible, and ineffective. Strikingly, the long border between Eastern and Western Europe—drawn where borders earlier proved unstable—was free even of skirmishes through all of the years after the Second World War.

Contemplating American and Soviet postwar behavior, and interpreting it in terms of nuclear logic, suggests that deterrence extends to vital interests beyond the homeland more easily than most have thought. The United States cared more about Western Europe than the Soviet Union did. The Soviet

Union cared more about Eastern Europe than the United States did. Communicating the weight of one side's concern as compared to the other side's was easily enough done when the matters at hand affected the United States and the Soviet Union directly. For this reason, West European anxiety about the coverage it got from American strategic forces, while understandable, was grossly exaggerated. The United States might have retaliated if the Soviet Union had made a major military move against a NATO country, and that alone was enough to deter the Soviet Union.

Because the use of nuclear weapons could lead to catastrophe for all of the parties involved, nuclear weapons create their own credibility. No one wants to risk their being used against them. Much of the nuclear literature is devoted to the problem of credibility, a problem that is easily solved.

The Problem of Extended Deterrence

How far from the homeland does deterrence extend? One answers that question by defining the conditions that must obtain if deterrent threats are to be credited. First, the would-be attacker must be made to see that the deterrer considers the interests at stake to be vital. One cannot assume that countries will instantly agree on the question of whose interests are vital. Nuclear weapons, however, strongly incline them to grope for de facto agreement on the answer rather than to fight over it.

Second, political stability must prevail in the area that the deterrent is intended to cover. If the threat to a regime is in good part from internal factions, then an outside power may risk supporting one of them even in the face of deterrent threats. The credibility of a deterrent force requires both that interests be seen to be vital and that it is an attack from outside that threatens them. Given these conditions, the would-be attacker provides both the reason to retaliate and the target for retaliation.

The problem of stretching a deterrent, which agitated the western alliance, is not a problem for lesser nuclear states. Their problem is not to protect others but to protect themselves. Many fear that lesser nuclear states will be the first ones to break the nuclear taboo and that they will use their weapons irresponsibly. I expect the opposite. Weak states easily establish their credibility. They are not trying to stretch their deterrent forces to cover others, and their vulnerability to conventional attack lends credence to their nuclear threats. Because in a conventional war they can lose so much so fast, it is easy to believe that they will unleash a deterrent force even at the risk of receiving a nuclear blow in return. With deterrent forces, the party that is absolutely threatened prevails.[26] Use of nuclear weapons by lesser states, or by any state, will come only if survival is at stake. This should be called not irresponsible but responsible use.

An opponent who attacks what is unambiguously mine risks suffering great distress if I have second-strike forces. This statement has important implications for both the deterrer and the deterred. Where territorial claims are shadowy and disputed, deterrent writs do not run. As Steven J. Rosen has said, "It is difficult to imagine Israel committing national suicide to hold on to Abu Rudeis or Hebron or Mount Hermon."[27] Establishing the credibility of a deterrent force requires moderation of territorial claims on the part of the would-be deterrer. For modest states, weapons whose very existence works strongly against their use are just what is wanted.

In a nuclear world, conservative would-be attackers will be prudent, but will would-be attackers be conservative? A new Hitler is not unimaginable. Would the presence of nuclear weapons have moderated Hitler's behavior? Hitler did not start World War II in order to destroy the Third Reich. Indeed, he was dismayed by British and French declarations of war on Poland's behalf. After all, the western democracies had not come to the aid of a geographically defensible and militarily strong Czechoslovakia. Why then should they have declared war on behalf of an indefensible Poland and against a Germany made stronger by the incorporation of Czechoslovakia's armor? From the occupation of the Rhineland in 1936 to the invasion of Poland in 1939, Hitler's calculations were realistically made. In those years, Hitler would have been deterred from acting in ways that immediately threatened massive death and widespread destruction in Germany. And, even if Hitler had not been deterred, would his generals have obeyed his commands? In a nuclear world, to act in blatantly offensive ways is madness. Under the circumstances, how many generals would obey the commands of a madman? One man alone does not make war.

To believe that nuclear deterrence would have worked against Germany in 1939 is easy. It is also easy to believe that in 1945, given the ability to do so, Hitler and some few around him would have fired nuclear warheads at the United States, Great Britain, and the Soviet Union as their armies advanced, whatever the consequences for Germany. Two considerations work against this possibility: the first applies in any world; the second in a nuclear world. First, when defeat is seen to be inevitable, a ruler's authority may vanish. Early in 1945, Hitler apparently ordered the initiation of gas warfare, but his generals did not respond.[28] Second, no country will press a nuclear nation to the point of decisive defeat. In the desperation of defeat, desperate measures may be taken, and the last thing anyone wants to do is to make a nuclear nation desperate. The unconditional surrender of a nuclear nation cannot be demanded. Nuclear weapons affect the deterrer as well as the deterred.

Arms Races among New Nuclear States

One may believe that old American and Soviet military doctrines set the pattern that new nuclear states will follow. One may also believe that they will suffer the fate of the United States and the former Soviet Union, that they will compete in building larger and larger nuclear arsenals while continuing to accumulate conventional weapons. These are doubtful beliefs. One can infer the future from the past only insofar as future situations may be like past ones. For three main reasons, new nuclear states are likely to decrease, rather than to increase, their military spending.

First, nuclear weapons alter the dynamics of arms races. In a competition of two or more parties, it may be hard to say who is pushing and who is being pushed, who is leading and who is following. If one party seeks to increase its capabilities, it may seem that others must too. The dynamic may be built into the competition and may unfold despite a mutual wish to resist it. But need this be the case in a strategic competition among nuclear countries? It need not be if the conditions of competition make deterrent logic dominant. Deterrent logic dominates if the conditions of competition make it nearly impossible for any of the competing parties to achieve a first-strike capability. Early in the nuclear age, the implications of deterrent strategy were clearly seen. "When dealing with the absolute weapon," as William T. R. Fox put it, "arguments based on relative advantage lose their point."[29] The United States has sometimes designed its forces according to that logic. Donald A. Quarles, when he was President Eisenhower's secretary of the Air Force, argued that "sufficiency of air power" is determined by "the force required to accomplish the mission assigned." Avoidance of total war then does not depend on the "relative strength of the two opposed forces." Instead, it depends on the "absolute power in the hands of each, and in the substantial invulnerability of this power to interdiction." [30] In other words, if no state can launch a disarming attack with high confidence, force comparisons are irrelevant. Strategic arms races are then pointless. Deterrent strategies offer this great advantage: Within wide ranges neither side need respond to increases in the other side's military capabilities.

Those who foresee nuclear arms racing among new nuclear states fail to make the distinction between war-fighting and war-deterring capabilities. War-fighting forces, because they threaten the forces of others, have to be compared. Superior forces may bring victory to one country; inferior forces may bring defeat to another. Force requirements vary with strategies and not just with the characteristics of weapons. With war-fighting strategies, arms races become hard to avoid. Forces designed for deterrence need not be compared. As Harold

Brown said when he was secretary of defense, purely deterrent forces "can be relatively modest, and their size can perhaps be made substantially, though not completely, insensitive to changes in the posture of an opponent."[31] With deterrent strategies, arms races make sense only if a first-strike capability is within reach. Because thwarting a first strike is easy, deterrent forces are quite cheap to build and maintain.

Second, deterrent balances are inherently stable. This is another reason for new nuclear states to decrease, rather than increase, their military spending. As Secretary Brown saw, within wide limits one state can be insensitive to changes in another state's forces. French leaders thought this way. France, as President Valéry Giscard d'Estaing said, "fixes its security at the level required to maintain, regardless of the way the strategic situation develops in the world, the credibility—in other words, the effectiveness—of its deterrent force."[32] With deterrent forces securely established, no military requirement presses one side to try to surpass the other. Human error and folly may lead some parties involved in deterrent balances to spend more on armaments than is needed, but other parties need not increase their armaments in response, because such excess spending does not threaten them. The logic of deterrence eliminates incentives for strategic-arms racing. This should be easier for lesser nuclear states to understand than it was for the United States and the Soviet Union. Because most of them are economically hard-pressed, they will not want to have more than enough.

Allowing for their particular situations, the policies of nuclear states confirm these statements. Britain and France are relatively rich countries, and they have tended to overspend. Their strategic forces were nevertheless modest enough when one considers that they thought that deterring the Soviet Union would be more difficult than deterring states with capabilities comparable to their own. China, of course, faced the same task. These three countries, however, have shown no inclination to engage in nuclear arms races. From 1974, when India tested its peaceful bomb, until 1998, when it resumed testing, India was content to have a nuclear military capability that may or may not have produced deliverable warheads, and Israel long maintained its own ambiguous status. New nuclear states are likely to conform to these patterns and aim for a modest sufficiency rather than vie with one another for a meaningless superiority.

Third, because strategic nuclear arms races among lesser powers are unlikely, the interesting question is not whether they will be run but whether countries having strategic nuclear weapons can avoid running conventional races. No more than the United States will new nuclear states want to rely on executing the deterrent threat that risks all. Will not their vulnerability to conventional attack induce them at least to maintain their conventional forces?

American policy since the early 1960s again teaches lessons that mislead. From President John F. Kennedy and Secretary Robert S. McNamara onward, the United States followed a policy of flexible response, emphasizing the importance of having a continuum of forces that would enable the United States to fight at any level from irregular to strategic nuclear warfare. A policy that decreases reliance on deterrence by placing more emphasis on conventional forces would seem to increase the chances that wars will be fought. Americans wanted to avoid nuclear war in Europe. Europeans wanted to avoid any war in Europe. Flexible response weakened Europeans' confidence in America's deterrent forces. Their worries were well expressed by a senior British general: "McNamara is practically telling the Soviets that the worst they need expect from an attack on West Germany is a conventional counterattack."[33] Why risk one's own destruction if one is able to fight on the ground and forego the use of strategic weapons? The policy of flexible response seemed to lessen reliance on deterrence and to increase the chances of fighting a war, although not nearly as much as the unnamed British general thought.

Large conventional forces neither add to nor subtract from the credibility of second-strike nuclear forces. Smaller nuclear states are likely to understand this more easily than the United States and the Soviet Union did, if only because few of them can afford to combine deterrent with large war fighting forces.

Throughout the Cold War, the United States and the Soviet Union missed a basic point about the effects of nuclear weapons. Nuclear weapons negate the advantages of conventional superiority because escalation in the use of conventional force risks receiving a nuclear strike. With nuclear weapons, not only is a small second-strike force equivalent to a large second-strike force, but small conventional forces are equivalent to large conventional forces because large forces cannot be used against a nuclear power. Thus the United States as well as the Soviet Union maintained unduly large forces both at home and abroad. Nuclear weapons negate both nuclear and conventional advantage.

Israel's military policy seems to fly in the face of deterrent logic. Its military budget has at times exceeded 20 percent of its GDP.[34] In fact Israel's policy bears deterrent logic out. So long as Israel continues to hold the Golan Heights and parts of the West Bank, it has to be prepared to fight for them. Since they by no means belong unambiguously to Israel, deterrent threats do not cover them. Because of America's large subsidies, economic constraints have not driven Israel to the territorial settlement that would shrink its borders sufficiently to make a deterrent policy credible. Global and regional forces, however, now do so. To compete internationally, Israel has to reduce its military expenditures. If a state's borders encompass only its vital interests, their protection does not require spending large sums on conventional forces.

The success of a deterrent strategy depends neither on the conventional capabilities of states nor on the extent of territory they hold. States can safely shrink their borders because defense in depth becomes irrelevant. The point can be put the other way around: With deterrent forces, arms races in their ultimate form—the fighting of offensive wars designed to increase national security—become pointless.

The Frequency and Intensity of War

The presence of nuclear weapons makes war less likely. One may nevertheless oppose the spread of nuclear weapons on the ground that they would make war, however unlikely, unbearably intense should it occur. Nuclear weapons have not been used in anger in a world in which more than one country has them. We have enjoyed half a century of nuclear peace, but we can never have a guarantee. We may be grateful for decades of nuclear peace and for the discouragement of conventional war among those who have nuclear weapons. Yet the fear is widespread that if they ever go off, we may all be dead. People as varied as the scholar Richard Smoke, the arms controller Paul Warnke, and the former defense secretary Harold Brown have all believed that if any nuclear weapons go off, many will. Although this seems the least likely of all the unlikely possibilities, it is not impossible. What makes it so unlikely is that, if a few warheads are fired, all of the countries involved will want to get out of the mess they are in.

McNamara asked himself what fractions of the Soviet Union's population and industry the United States should be able to destroy to deter it. This was the wrong question. States are not deterred because they expect to suffer a certain amount of damage but because they cannot know how much damage they will suffer. Near the dawn of the nuclear age, Bernard Brodie put the matter simply, "The prediction is more important than the fact."[35] Potential attacks are deterred by the knowledge that attacking the vital interests of a country having nuclear weapons may bring the attacker untold losses. As Patrick Morgan put it later, "To attempt to compute the cost of a nuclear war is to miss the point."[36]

States are deterred by the prospect of suffering severe damage and by their inability to do much to limit it. Deterrence works because nuclear weapons enable one state to punish another state severely without first defeating it. "Victory," in Thomas Schelling's words, "is no longer a prerequisite for hurting the enemy."[37] Countries armed only with conventional weapons can hope that their military forces will be able to limit the damage an attacker can do. Among countries armed with strategic nuclear forces, the hope of avoiding heavy damage depends mainly on the attacker's restraint and little on one's own efforts. Those who compared expected deaths through strategic exchanges of nuclear warheads with casualties suffered by the Soviet Union in World War II overlooked the fundamental difference between conventional and nuclear worlds.[38]

Deterrence rests on what countries *can* do to each other with strategic nuclear weapons. From this statement, one can easily leap to the wrong conclusion that deterrent strategies, if they have to be carried through, will produce a catastrophe. That countries are able to annihilate each other means neither that deterrence depends on their threatening to do so, nor that they will necessarily do so if deterrence fails. Because countries heavily armed with strategic nuclear weapons can carry war to its ultimate intensity, the control of force becomes the primary objective. If deterrence fails, leaders will have the strongest incentives to keep force under control and limit damage rather than launching genocidal attacks. If the Soviet Union had attacked Western Europe, NATO's objectives would have been to halt the attack and end the war. The United States had the ability to place thousands of warheads precisely on targets in the Soviet Union. Surely we would have struck military targets before striking industrial targets and industrial targets before striking cities. The intent to hit military targets first was sometimes confused with a war-fighting strategy, but it was not one. It would not have significantly reduced the Soviet Union's ability to hurt us. Whatever American military leaders thought, our strategy rested on the threat to punish. The threat, if it failed to deter, would have been followed not by spasms of violence but by punishment administered in ways that conveyed threats of more to come.

A war between the United States and the Soviet Union that got out of control would have been catastrophic. If they had set out to destroy each other, they would have greatly reduced the world's store of developed resources while killing millions outside of their own borders through fallout. Even while destroying themselves, states with few weapons would do less damage to others. As ever, the biggest international dangers come from the strongest states. Fearing the world's destruction, one may prefer a world of conventional great powers having a higher probability of fighting less-destructive wars to a world of nuclear great powers having a lower probability of fighting more-destructive wars. But that choice effectively disappeared with the production of atomic bombs by the United States during World War II.

Does the spread of nuclear weapons threaten to make wars more intense at regional levels, where wars of high intensity have been possible for many years? If weaker countries are unable to defend at lesser levels of violence, might they destroy themselves through resorting to nuclear weapons? Lesser nuclear states live in fear of this possibility. But this is not different from the fear under which the United States and the Soviet Union lived for years. Small nuclear states may experience a keen sense of desperation because of vulnerability to conventional as well as to nuclear attack, but, again, in desperate situations what all parties become most desperate to avoid is the use of strategic nuclear weapons. Still, however improbable the event, lesser states may one day fire some of their weapons. Are minor nuclear states more or less likely to do so than major ones? The answer to this question is vitally important because the existence of some states would be at stake even if the damage done were regionally confined.

For a number of reasons, deterrent strategies promise less damage than war-fighting strategies. First, deterrent strategies induce caution all around and thus reduce the incidence of war. Second, wars fought in the face of strategic nuclear weapons must be carefully limited because a country having them may retaliate if its vital interests are threatened. Third, prospective punishment need only be proportionate to an adversary's expected gains in war after those gains are discounted for the many uncertainties of war. Fourth, should deterrence fail, a few judiciously delivered warheads are likely to produce sobriety in the leaders of all of the countries involved and thus bring rapid de-escalation. Finally, war-fighting strategies offer no clear place to stop short of victory for some and defeat for others. Deterrent strategies do, and that place is where one country threatens another's vital interests. Deterrent strategies lower the probability that wars will begin. If wars start nevertheless, deterrent strategies lower the probability that they will be carried very far.

In a conventional world, to deter an attacker a status quo country must threaten a lot of force. It must do so to overcome doubts about the credibility of conventional threats and uncertainty about the effectiveness of conventional blows. In a nuclear world to deter one need threaten only a little force because so much more can easily be added. Limiting wars in a conventional world has proved difficult. In a nuclear world, *only* limited wars can be fought. In a conventional world, states are tempted to strike first to gain an initial advantage and set the course of the war. In a nuclear world, to strike first is pointless because no advantage can be gained against invulnerable forces. In a conventional world, combatants use their best, i.e. their most destructive, weapons. Although overlooked, this explains our use of atomic bombs in the Second World War. From Guadalcanal to Iwo Jima to Okinawa to the fire-bombing of Tokyo, America applied force on an ever-increasing scale. In the context of a conventional war, A-bombs looked simply like bigger and better weapons. The aim in a conventional war is to escalate to a higher level of force than your opponent can reach. In a nuclear world, no one can escalate to a level of force anywhere near the top without risking its own destruction. Deterrence in World War II worked only where combatants shared the ability to use a horrible weapon, poison gas. All of the major combatants were capable of using it. None did. On all of the above counts, nuclear weapons reverse the logic of war that operates in conventional worlds.

Nuclear weapons lessen the intensity as well as the frequency of war among their possessors. For fear of escalation, nuclear states do not want to fight long and hard over important interests—indeed, they do not want to fight at all. Minor nuclear states have even better reasons than major ones to accommodate one another and to avoid fighting. Worries about the intensity of war among nuclear states have to be viewed in this context and against a world in which conventional weapons have become ever costlier and more destructive.

CONCLUSION

The conclusion is in two parts. The first part applies the above analysis to the present. The second part uses it to peer into the future.

What Follows from My Analysis?

I have argued that the gradual spread of nuclear weapons is better than either no spread or rapid spread. We do not face happy choices. We may prefer that countries have conventional weapons only, do not run arms races, and do not fight.

Yet the alternative to nuclear weapons may be ruinous arms races for some countries with a high risk of their becoming engaged in devastating conventional wars.

Countries have to take care of their own security. If countries feel insecure and believe that nuclear weapons would make them more secure, America's policy of opposing the spread of nuclear weapons will not prevail. Any slight chance of bringing the spread of nuclear weapons to a halt exists only if the United States strenuously tries to achieve that end. To do so carries costs measured in terms of other interests. The strongest way for the United States to persuade other countries to forego nuclear weapons is to guarantee their security. How many states' security do we want to guarantee? Wisely, we are reluctant to make promises, but then we should not expect to decide how other countries provide for their security.

Some have feared that weakening opposition to the spread of nuclear weapons will lead numerous states to obtain them because it may seem that "everyone is doing it."[39] Why should we think that if we relax, numerous states will begin to make nuclear weapons? Both the United States and the Soviet Union were relaxed in the past, and those effects did not follow. The Soviet Union initially supported China's nuclear program. The United States helped both Britain and France to produce nuclear weapons. By 1968 the CIA had informed President Johnson of the existence of Israeli nuclear weapons, and in July of 1970, Richard Helms, director of the CIA, gave this information to the Senate Foreign Relations Committee. These and later disclosures were not followed by censure of Israel or by reductions of economic assistance.[40] And in September of 1980, the executive branch, against the will of the House of Representatives but with the approval of the Senate, continued to do nuclear business with India despite its explosion of a nuclear device and despite its unwillingness to sign the Nuclear Non-Proliferation Treaty.

Many more countries can make nuclear weapons than do. One can believe that American opposition to nuclear arming stays the deluge only by overlooking the complications of international life. Any state has to examine many conditions before deciding whether or not to develop nuclear weapons. Our opposition is only one factor and is not likely to be the decisive one. Many states feel fairly secure living with their neighbors. Why should they want nuclear weapons? Some countries, feeling threatened, have found security through their own strenuous efforts and through arrangements made with others. South Korea is an outstanding example. Many officials believe that South Korea would lose more in terms of American support if it acquired nuclear weapons than it would gain by having them.[41] Further, on occasion we might slow the spread of nuclear weapons by not opposing the nuclear weapons programs of some countries. When we opposed Pakistan's nuclear program, we were saying that we disapprove of countries developing nuclear weapons no matter what their neighbors do.

The gradual spread of nuclear weapons has not opened the nuclear floodgates. Nations attend to their security in the ways they think best. The fact that so many more countries can make nuclear weapons than do says more about the hesitation of countries to enter the nuclear military business than about the effectiveness of American nonproliferation policy. We should suit our policy to individual cases, sometimes bringing pressure against a country moving toward nuclear weapons capability and sometimes quietly acquiescing. No one policy is right in all cases. We should ask what the interests of other countries require before putting pressure on them. Some countries are likely to suffer more in cost and pain if they remain conventional states than if they become nuclear ones. The measured spread of nuclear weapons does not run against our interests and can increase the security of some states at a price they can afford to pay.

What Does the Nuclear Future Hold?

What will a world populated by a few more nuclear states look like? I have drawn a picture of such a world that accords with experience throughout the nuclear age. Those who dread a world with more nuclear states do little more than assert that more is worse and claim without substantiation that new nuclear states will be less responsible and less capable of self control than the old ones have been. They feel fears that many felt when they imagined how a nuclear China would behave. Such fears have proved unfounded as nuclear weapons have slowly spread. I have found many reasons for believing that with more nuclear states the world will have a promising future. I have reached this unusual conclusion for three main reasons.

First, international politics is a self-help system, and in such systems the principal parties determine their own fate, the fate of other parties, and the fate of the system. This will continue to be so.

Second, nuclear weaponry makes miscalculation difficult because it is hard not to be aware of how much damage a small number of warheads can do. Early in this century Norman Angell argued that war would not occur because it could not pay.[42] But conventional wars have brought political gains to some countries at the expense of others. Among nuclear countries, possible losses in war overwhelm possible gains. In the nuclear age Angell's dictum becomes persuasive. When the active use of force threatens to bring great losses, war becomes less likely. This proposition is widely accepted but insufficiently emphasized. Nuclear weapons reduced the chances of war between the United States and the Soviet Union and between the Soviet Union and China. One must expect them to have similar effects elsewhere. Where nuclear weapons threaten to make the cost of wars immense, who will dare to start them?

Third, new nuclear states will feel the constraints that present nuclear states have experienced. New nuclear states will be more concerned for their safety and more mindful of dangers than some of the old ones have been. Until recently, only the great and some of the major powers have had nuclear weapons. While nuclear weapons have spread slowly, conventional weapons have proliferated. Under these circumstances, wars have been fought not at the center but at the periphery of international politics. The likelihood of war decreases as deterrent and defensive capabilities increase. Nuclear weapons make wars hard to start. These statements hold for small as for big nuclear powers. Because they do, the gradual spread of nuclear weapons is more to be welcomed than feared.

Chapter 2

MORE WILL BE WORSE

Scott D. Sagan

Why should we worry about the spread of nuclear weapons? The answer is by no means obvious. After all, we have lived with nuclear deterrence for over half a century now. The two superpowers maintained a long peace throughout the Cold War, despite deep political hostilities, numerous crises, and a prolonged arms race. Why should we expect that the experience of future nuclear powers will be any different?

A prominent group of scholars has pointed to the apparent contradiction between a peaceful nuclear past and a fearful nuclear future and argue that the further spread of nuclear weapons may well be a stabilizing factor in international relations. In Chapter 1, Kenneth Waltz presents the strongest and most sustained set of arguments in support of this thesis.[1] It is important to note from the start, however, that Waltz is by no means alone in holding this position, as a number of other political scientists have jumped onto the pro-proliferation bandwagon. For example, Bruce Bueno de Mesquita and William Riker advocate the "selective" spread of nuclear weapons into areas where nonnuclear states face nuclear-armed adversaries since "the chance of bilateral conflict becoming nuclear . . . decreases to zero when all nations are nuclear armed."[2] John

This is a revised version of my article "The Perils of Proliferation: Organization Theory, Deterrence Theory, and the Spread of Nuclear Weapons," *International Security* 18, no. 4 (Spring 1994), pp. 66–107.

Mearsheimer also believes that "nuclear weapons are a superb deterrent" and argues that the world would be a safer place if Germany, Ukraine, and Japan became nuclear powers in the modern era.[3] Other scholars reach similar conclusions for different countries: Stephen Van Evera has advocated that Germany acquire a nuclear arsenal to deter Russia; Peter Lavoy predicted that nuclear weapons will prevent future wars between India and Pakistan; and both Martin van Creveld and Shai Feldman maintain that nuclear proliferation in the Middle East will stabilize the Arab-Israeli conflict.[4] This "proliferation optimist" position flows easily from the logic of rational deterrence theory: the possession of nuclear weapons by two powers can reduce the likelihood of war precisely because it makes the costs of war so great.

Such optimistic views of the effects of nuclear proliferation have not escaped criticism, of course, and a number of scholars have argued that nuclear deterrence may not be stable in specific regional settings.[5] What is missing in the debate so far, however, is an alternative theory of the consequences of nuclear proliferation; an alternative that is a broader conception of the effects of nuclear weapons proliferation on the likelihood of war. In this chapter, I present such an alternative, rooted in organization theory, which leads to a far more pessimistic assessment of the future prospects for peace.

There are two central arguments. First, I argue that professional military organizations—because of common biases, inflexible routines, and parochial interests—display organizational behaviors that are likely to lead to deterrence failures and deliberate or accidental war. Unlike the widespread psychological critique of rational deterrence theory—which maintains that some political leaders may lack the intelligence or emotional stability to make deterrence work[6]—this organizational critique argues that military organizations, unless professionally managed through a checks-and-balances system of strong civilian control, are unlikely to fulfill the operational requirements for stable nuclear deterrence.

Second, I argue that there are strong reasons to believe that future nuclear-armed states will lack the positive mechanisms of civilian control. Many current and emerging proliferators have either military-run governments or weak civilian-led governments in which the professional military has a strong and direct influence on policymaking. In such states, the biases, routines, and parochial interests of powerful military organizations, not the "objective" interests of the state, can determine state behavior. In addition, military organizations in many proliferators are "inward-looking," focusing primarily on issues of domestic stability and internal politics, rather than on external threats to national security. When such militaries are in power, senior officers' energies and interests necessarily shift away from professional concerns for the protection of national security; when civilians are in power, but are extremely fearful of military coups, defense policy is designed to protect their regime, not the nation's security, and officers are promoted according to their personal loyalty to current leaders, not their professional competence. In either case, such extensive military involvement in domestic politics, whether active or latent, means that the military's professional competence as a fighting force, and also as a manager of a deterrent force, will suffer.

What are the likely effects of the spread of nuclear weapons? My argument proceeds in three steps. First, I contrast the assumptions and logic of proliferation optimists to the assumptions and logic of a more pessimistic organizational-level approach to nuclear proliferation. Next, I compare the two theories' predictions about three major operational requirements of deterrence and, in each case, I present the existing empirical evidence concerning each requirement. Finally, at the end of the chapter, I present some lessons for international relations theory and United States nonproliferation policy.

RATIONAL DETERRENCE THEORY AND ORGANIZATION THEORY COMPARED

Rational Deterrence Theory

The influential writings of Kenneth Waltz are the most clear and confident expressions of faith in rational nuclear deterrence. "Nuclear weapons have been given a bad name," Waltz maintains. "Because catastrophic outcomes of nuclear exchanges are easy to imagine, leaders of states will shrink in horror from initiating them. With nuclear weapons, stability and peace rest on easy calculations of what one country can do to another. Anyone—political leader or man in the street—can see that catastrophe lurks if events spiral out of control and nuclear warheads begin to fly."[7] Given that the costs of nuclear war are so high, even a small risk of war can produce strong deterrence. Because "a nation will be deterred from attacking even if it believes that there is only a possibility that its adversary will retaliate," Waltz maintains that "the probability of major war among states having nuclear weapons approaches zero."[8] If this is true, then the spread of nuclear weapons should have very positive consequences: "The likelihood of war decreases as deterrent and defensive capabilities increase. Nuclear weapons make wars hard to start. These statements hold for small as for big nuclear powers. Because they do, the gradual spread of nuclear weapons is more to be welcomed than feared" (Ch. 1, p. 40).

Waltz writes with disdain about what he views as the ethnocentric views of psychological critics of deterrence: "Many Westerners write fearfully about a future in which Third World countries have nuclear weapons. They seem to view their people in the old imperial manner as 'lesser breeds without the law' (Ch. 1, p. 14). For nuclear deterrence to work, he argues, one does not need to assume that decision-makers in new nuclear states make intricate rational calculations about every policy decision: it is sufficient that statesmen are highly "sensitive to costs" (Ch. 1, p. 13), a requirement, Waltz elsewhere acknowledges, "which for convenience can be called an assumption of rationality."[9] When costs are so high, such sensitivity is easy and deterrence is therefore not difficult: "One need not become preoccupied with the characteristics of the state that is to be deterred or scrutinize its leaders," Waltz insists, since "in a nuclear world any state will be deterred by another state's second-strike forces."[10]

Within the rational deterrence framework, three major operational requirements for stable nuclear deterrence exist: (1) there must not be a preventive war during the transition period when one state has nuclear weapons and the other state is building, but has not yet achieved, a nuclear capability; (2) both states must develop, not just the ability to inflict some level of unacceptable damage to the other side, but also a sufficient degree of "second-strike" survivability so that its forces could retaliate if attacked first; and (3) the nuclear arsenals must not be prone to accidental or unauthorized use. Nuclear optimists believe that new nuclear powers will meet these requirements because it is in these states' obvious interests to do so. This is, as I will show, a very problematic belief.

An Organizational Perspective

The assumption that states behave in a basically rational manner is of course an assumption, not an empirically tested insight. Political scientists often assume high degrees of rationality, not because it is accurate, but because it is helpful: it provides a relatively simple way of making predictions, by linking perceived interests with expected behavior. The rational-actor view is clearly not the only one possible, however, and it is not the only set of assumptions that leads to useful predictions about nuclear proliferation.

An alternative set of assumptions views government leaders as intending to behave rationally, yet sees their beliefs, the options available to them, and the final implementation of their decisions as being influenced by powerful forces within the country. If this is the case, organization theory should be useful for the study of the consequences of proliferation. This is important, since such an organizational perspective challenges the central assumption that states behave in a self-interested, rational manner.

Two themes in organization theory focus attention on major impediments to pure rationality in organizational behavior. First, large organizations function within a severely "bounded," or limited, form of rationality: they have inherent limits on calculation and coordination and use simplifying mechanisms to understand and respond to uncertainty in the outside world.[11] Organizations, by necessity, develop routines to coordinate action among different units: standard operating procedures and organizational rules, not individually reasoned decisions, therefore govern behavior. Organizations commonly "satisfice": rather than searching for the policy that maximizes their utility, they often accept the first option that is minimally satisfying. Organizations are often myopic: instead of surveying the entire environment for information, organizational members have biased searches, focusing only on specific areas stemming from their past experience, recent training, and current responsibility. Organizations suffer from "goal displacement": they often become fixated on narrow operational measurements of goals and lose focus on their overall objectives. Organizational filters continually shape the beliefs and actions of individuals. As James March and Herbert Simon put it, "the world tends to be perceived by the organization members in terms of the particular concepts that are reflected in the organization's vocabulary. The particular categories it employs are reified, and become, for members of the organization, attributes of the world rather than mere conventions."[12]

Second, complex organizations commonly have multiple, conflicting goals, and the process by which objectives are chosen and pursued is intensely political.[13] From such a political perspective, actions that cut against the interests of the organization's leadership are often found to serve the narrow interests of some units within the organization. Organizations are not simply tools in the hands of higher-level authorities but are groups of self-interested and competitive subunits and actors. "Theory should see conflict as an inevitable part of organizational life stemming from organizational characteristics rather than from the characteristics of individuals," Charles Perrow has argued. For example, organizational divisions and responsibilities help explain why "sales and production [are] in conflict in all firms . . . or faculty and administration in colleges, doctors and nurses and administrators in hospitals, the treatment and custodial staffs in prisons."[14] This is also true in military organizations: weapon system operators often have different interests than their commanders, units in the field have different interests than the command headquarters, a particular service has different interests than the General Staff or the Joint Chiefs. And even when a professional military service or command acts in relatively rational ways to maximize its interests—protecting its power, size, autonomy or organizational essence—such actions do not necessarily reflect the organizational interests of the military as a whole, much less the national interests of the state. To the degree that such narrow organizational interests determine state behavior, a theory of "rational" state action is seriously weakened.

Although organization theory has been highly useful in a number of substantive areas of international relations—illuminating crisis behavior, alliance politics, weapons procurement, military doctrine and operations, and nuclear weapons safety[15]—it has not been used extensively to study the consequences of proliferation. This is unfortunate, since each of the three operational requirements for rational deterrence appear in a different light when viewed from an organizational perspective. What are professional military views about preventive war; could such views influence the probability of a nuclear attack during the transition period of an early arms race? What is the likelihood that professional militaries will develop and deploy survivable nuclear forces to maintain stable deterrence? What is the likely influence of the structures and biases of military organizations on the prevention of accidental and unauthorized uses of nuclear weapons in new proliferating states?

The next section presents predictions and empirical evidence concerning the three operational requirements for stable nuclear deterrence. In each section, I contrast the predictions made by nuclear optimists to the predictions deduced from an organizational approach and then present two kinds of evidence. The evidence from the United States case will be given first, both because there is more evidence available on American nuclear weapons operations and because the United States should be considered a tough test of my organizational approach since it is widely considered to have a highly professionalized military under a strong and institutionalized system of civilian control. If these problems are found to exist in the United States, therefore, they are likely to be even more pronounced in other nations. The currently available evidence about other nuclear states is then presented. Both kinds of evidence provide strong support for my pessimistic conclusion about the consequences of the spread of nuclear weapons.

PREVENTIVE WAR IN THE TRANSITION PERIOD

The first operational requirement of mutual nuclear deterrence between two powers concerns the transition period between a conventional world and a nuclear world: the first state to acquire weapons must not attack its rival, in a *preventive war*, in order to avoid the risk of a worse war later, after the second state has acquired a large nuclear arsenal.[16] There are two periods in a nuclear arms race, according to Waltz, during which a state might consider a preventive strike: when its rival is developing nuclear capability but has clearly not yet constructed a bomb, and when the rival is in a more advanced state of nuclear development and therefore might have a small number of weapons. Waltz maintains that a preventive strike might seem to make sense "during the first stage of nuclear development [since] a state could strike without fearing that the country it attacked would return a nuclear blow." Yet, he insists that such attacks are unlikely, because it would not be in a state's longer-term interests: "But would one country strike so hard as to destroy another country's potential for future nuclear development? If it did not, the country struck could resume its nuclear career. If the blow struck is less than devastating, one must be prepared either to repeat it or to occupy and control the country. To do either would be forbiddingly difficult" (Ch. 1, p. 18).

Later, once an adversary has developed "even a rudimentary nuclear capability," all rational incentives for preventive war are off, since "one's own severe punishment becomes possible" (Ch. 1, p. 19). A little uncertainty goes a long way in Waltz's world. If there is even a remote chance of nuclear retaliation, a rational decision maker will not launch a preventive war.

An organizational perspective, however, leads to a more pessimistic assessment of the likelihood of preventive nuclear wars, because it draws attention to military biases that could encourage such attacks. Waltz has dismissed this argument since he believes that military leaders are not more likely than civilians to recommend the use of military force during crises.[17] Although this may be true with respect to cases of military intervention in general, there are five strong reasons to expect that military officers are predisposed to view preventive war in particular in a much more favorable light than are civilian authorities.

First, military officers, because of self-selection into the profession and socialization afterwards, are more inclined than the rest of the population to see war as likely in the near term and inevitable in the long run.[18] The professional focus of attention on warfare makes military officers skeptical of nonmilitary alternatives to war, while civilian leaders often place stronger hopes on diplomatic and economic methods of long-term conflict resolution. Such beliefs make military officers particularly susceptible to "better now than later" logic. Second, officers are trained to focus on pure military logic, and are given strict operational goals to meet, when addressing security problems. "Victory" means defeating the enemy in a narrow military sense, but does not necessarily mean achieving broader political goals in war, which would include reducing the costs of war to acceptable levels. For military officers, diplomatic, moral, or domestic political costs of preventive war are also less likely to be influential than would be the case for civilian officials. Third, military officers display strong biases in favor of offensive doctrines and decisive operations.[19] Offensive doctrines enable military organizations to take the initiative, utilizing their standard plans under conditions they control, while forcing adversaries to react to their favored strategies. Decisive operations utilize the principle of mass, may reduce casualties, and are more likely to lead to a military decision rather than a political stalemate. Preventive war would clearly have these desired characteristics. Fourth, the military, like most organizations, tends to plan incrementally, leading it to focus on immediate plans for war and not on the subsequent problems of managing the postwar world. Fifth, military officers, like most members of large organizations, focus on their narrow job. Managing the postwar world is the politicians' job, not part of military officers' operational responsibility, and officers are therefore likely to be shortsighted, not examining the long-term political and diplomatic consequences of preventive war. In theory, these five related factors should often make military officers strong advocates of preventive war.

Evidence on Preventive War from the U.S. Case

What differences existed between U.S. civilian and military advice on the use of nuclear weapons during the early Cold War? During major crises, few disagreements emerged. For example, after the Chinese military intervention in the Korean War in late November 1950, both Truman's senior military and civilian advisors recommended against the use of the atomic bomb on the Korean peninsula.[20] If one focuses specifically on the issue of *preventive war*, however, strong differences between civilian and military opinions can be seen. During both the Truman and Eisenhower administrations, senior U.S. military officers seriously advocated preventive-war options and, in both cases, continued favoring such ideas well after civilian leaders ruled against them.

Although U.S. military officers were not alone in recommending preventive war during the Truman administration—as diverse a set of individuals as philosopher Bertrand Russell, mathematician John Von Neumann, and Navy Secretary Francis Matthews called for such a policy—within the government, military leaders were clearly the predominant and most persistent advocates.[21] The Joint Chiefs of Staff (JCS) were quite direct in their advocacy of preventive options, calling for the "readiness and determination to take prompt and effective military action abroad to *anticipate and prevent attack*," in their September 1945 top-secret report on postwar U.S. military policy: "When it becomes evident that forces of aggression are being arrayed against us by a potential enemy, we cannot afford, through any misguided and perilous idea of avoiding an aggressive attitude to permit the first blow to be struck against us."[22] Truman appears to have rejected the whole concept of preventive war rather quickly, however, largely on moral and domestic political grounds. "We do not believe in aggression or preventive war," he announced in a public broadcast in 1950. "Such a war is the weapon of dictators, not of free democratic countries like the United States."[23]

The issue was not thoroughly addressed at the highest levels, however, until April 1950, when NSC-68 (National Security Council Document 68) presented three key arguments against preventive nuclear war. First, intelligence estimates suggested that a U.S. atomic attack on the USSR "would not force or induce the Kremlin to capitulate and that the Kremlin would still be able to use the forces under its control to dominate most or all of Eurasia." Second, a preventive attack "would be repugnant to many Americans" and therefore difficult to justify at home. Third, U.S. allies, especially in Western Europe, would share such beliefs, hurting U.S. relations with them and making it "difficult after such a war to create satisfactory international order." The conclusion was clear: "These considerations are no less weighty because they are imponderable, and they rule out an attack unless it is demonstrably in the nature of a counter-attack to a blow which is on its way or about to be delivered."[24]

Senior military leaders were very cautious about discussing preventive nuclear strikes in public after that, with the exception of Major General Orvil Anderson, the commandant of the Air War College, whom Truman fired in September 1950 for advocating preventive nuclear war to the press.[25] Yet, in private, military support for preventive options remained high. Generals George Kenney, Curtis LeMay, Thomas Power, Nathan Twining, Thomas White, and Hoyt Vandenberg all privately expressed sympathy for preventive nuclear war and official air force doctrine manuals continued to support preventive-war ideas.[26]

More open discussions of preventive-war options reemerged at the highest levels of the U.S. government during the first two years of the Eisenhower administration. Throughout the new administration's reevaluation of U.S. security strategy, senior military officers again supported preventive options. The U.S. Air War College, for example, produced the extensive "Project Control" study in 1953 and 1954, which advocated preventive war if necessary.[27] This study called for taking direct control of Soviet airspace and threatening massive bombing unless the Kremlin agreed to an ultimatum to withdraw troops from Eastern Europe, dissolve the Cominform, and abandon the Sino-Soviet alliance. Project Control was greeted with enthusiasm when it was briefed to Chairman of the Joint Chiefs of Staff (JCS) Admiral Arthur Radford in July 1954, though State Department officials complained that such schemes were "simply another version of preventive war."[28] In addition, Eisenhower himself was briefed on a JCS Advanced Study Group report in mid-1954, which, according to a contemporary memorandum on the report, "pointed unmistakably to an advocacy of the US deliberately precipitating war with the USSR in the near future—that is before the USSR could achieve a large enough thermo-nuclear capability to be a real menace to the Continental US."[29]

The most extreme preventive-war arguments by a senior officer, however, can be found in General Twining's August 1953 memorandum to the JCS on "The Coming National Crisis," which would occur, he maintained, when the USSR developed sufficient nuclear forces so that "our military establishment would be unable to insure the survival of our nation":

> Prior to entering the second period of time [when the Soviet Union could destroy the U.S.] if our objectives have not been achieved by means short of general war, it will be necessary to adopt other measures. We must recognize this time of decision, or, we will continue blindly down a suicidal path and arrive at a situation in which we will have entrusted our survival to the whims of a small group of proven barbarians. If we believe it unsafe, unwise, or immoral to gamble that the enemy will tolerate our existence under this circumstance, we must be militarily prepared to support such decisions as might involve general war. [30]

The Joint Chiefs' final position was much more calm in tone, though it too displayed "better now than later" logic. While acknowledging that official U.S. policy prohibited preventive war, Admiral Radford told the National Security Council in November 1954 that "if we continue to pursue a policy of simply reacting to Communist initiatives, instead of a policy of forestalling Communist action, we cannot hope for anything but a showdown with Soviet Communists by 1959 or 1960," adding ominously that the JCS could "guarantee" a successful outcome in a nuclear war only if it occurred "prior to Soviet achievement of atomic plenty."[31]

Why did Eisenhower reject this line of thinking? Eisenhower clearly did not object to preventive war on moral grounds.[32] Eisenhower did question, however, whether war with the Russians was inevitable, given U.S. nuclear deterrent capabilities and his hope that the U.S. strategy of containment would eventually lead to an overthrow of the Soviet system from within. Moreover, his eventual rejection of preventive war appears to have been strongly influenced by his increasing belief that a preventive nuclear attack on the USSR would be too costly politically, *even if it succeeded* in narrow military terms. The political and human costs of maintaining control over a decimated Soviet society were especially appalling to Eisenhower. As he told a group of officers in June 1954:

> No matter how well prepared for war we may be, no matter how certain we are that within 24 hours we could destroy Kuibyshev and Moscow and Leningrad and Baku and all the other places that would allow the Soviets to carry on war, I want you to carry this question home with you: Gain such a victory, and what do you do with it? Here would be a great area from the Elbe to Vladivostok and down through Southeast Asia torn up and destroyed without government, without its communications, just an area of starvation and disaster. I ask you what would the civilized world do about it? I repeat there is no victory in any war except through our imaginations, through our dedication, and through our work to avoid it. [33]

Preventive War and New Nuclear States

This evidence presented here does not demonstrate that the United States almost launched a preventive war on the USSR in the early Cold War period. Nor do I mean to suggest that civilian leaders could never rationally choose to launch a preventive attack. This evidence does strongly suggest, however, that military officers have strong proclivities in favor of preventive war and that proliferation optimists are therefore wrong to assume that any leader of a state will automatically be deterred by an adversary's "rudimentary" arsenal, or even by a significantly larger one. Preventive nuclear attacks were clearly imagined, actively planned, and vigorously advocated by senior U.S. military leaders well beyond the initial development and deployment of nuclear weapons by the USSR.[34] Without Truman's and Eisenhower's broader mix of moral and political objections to preventive war, the narrow military logic in favor of such an option might have prevailed.[35]

This basic pattern—senior military officers favoring preventive war against new proliferators with civilian leaders being more skeptical—was repeated in a number of other cases as well. In the early 1960s, the U. S. government contemplated taking preventive action to destroy the nuclear program of the People's Republic of China. Senior State Department officials held the position that Beijing would remain a weak and cautious power, even after it developed its first nuclear weapons, and that any U.S. unprovoked military action against China would damage America's reputation abroad.[36] In contrast, the Joint Chiefs of Staff argued that "the attainment of a nuclear capability by Communist China will have a marked impact on the security posture of the United States and the Free World."[37] The JCS maintained that a conventional weapons strike on Chinese nuclear sites would be feasible but nevertheless also recommended that nuclear weapons be considered for such an attack.[38] The military position was eventually rejected. U.S. civilian authorities were not morally opposed to an unprovoked, preventive attack on the Chinese nuclear facilities. Indeed, officials in both the Kennedy and Johnson administrations approached the Russians, in the hope that Moscow would participate in or at a minimum acquiesce to an American strike against the Chinese. But when Moscow refused to cooperate, the U.S. government officials feared that the Soviets might retaliate in response to any attack on China, a key consideration in their decision not to use force to stop China from developing nuclear weapons.

A similar example occurred in the summer and fall of 1969, only this time the American and Soviet roles were reversed.[39] After Chinese forces along the disputed Ussuri River attacked Soviet troops in the summer of 1969, secret discussions were held in Moscow on whether to launch a preventive strike on Chinese nuclear forces. In this case as well, senior military leaders favored a preventive attack despite the existence of a small Chinese nuclear arsenal: Marshall Andrei Grechko recommended that Moscow initiate a major nuclear strike to "once and for all get rid of the Chinese threat."[40] The Soviet military

prepared for a possible strike by starting air force alert operations and conducting military exercises, including mock bombing runs against targets designed to resemble Chinese nuclear
facilities. The senior political authorities in the Politburo, however, did not approve the attack plan, at least in part because the
United States government alerted its nuclear forces, raising the
risks that it would strongly oppose such Soviet action.[41]

Whenever a new state is seen to be developing nuclear
weapons, it is likely that its rivals will consider preventive war
under this "better now than later" logic. My theory and the
evidence both suggest, however, that preventive war is more
likely to be chosen when military leaders, who minimize diplomatic considerations and believe war is inevitable in the long
term, have a significant degree of influence over the final decision. While there have not been, obviously, any nuclear preventive wars among the new proliferants, the probability of
such attacks will increase in the future since strict centralized
civilian control over military organizations is problematic in
some new and potential proliferant states.

Two proliferant states are especially problematic in this
regard. First, military biases in favor of preventive war could
be influential in Pakistan in the future if there is an emerging
imbalance in nuclear weapons and defensive systems with
India, and the Pakistani military feels that war now is better
than war later. This logic has prevailed in the past in Pakistan,
where the military has been in direct control of the government for more than half of the state's history. In the fall of
1962, senior military authorities unsuccessfully urged President Mohammed Ayub Khan, the leader of the military-
controlled government, to attack India while its army was tied
down in the conflict with China.[42] Three years later, in September 1965, the Ayub government did launch a preventive
war on India in an effort to conquer Kashmir before the anticipated Indian military build-up was completed.[43] Can we be
assured that similar military biases could not be influential in
future crises over Kashmir? (The problems in Pakistan are discussed further in Chapter 5).

A second case in point is Iran. The Iranian Islamic government reluctantly developed and then used chemical weapons in the 1980s in response to Iraq's use of chemical weapons against Iranian soldiers and revolutionary guards during the Iran-Iraq War.[44] Since that time, both the Iranian Army and the Islamic Revolutionary Guards have developed and practiced offensive doctrines for the use of chemical weapons, despite the more defensive or deterrent doctrine apparently espoused by the central government in Tehran. This pattern is disturbing for it suggests that if Iran is successful in its current quest to develop nuclear weapons, the leaders of the military or revolutionary guards in control of nuclear weapons may not be fully controlled by central authorities. The risks of a preventive war, caused by biased assessments of such Iranian leaders, cannot therefore be ruled out if Iran's acquisition of nuclear weapons forces its rivals such as Iraq or Saudi Arabia to institute their own nuclear weapons programs. (For additional discussion of Iran see Chapter 6.)

Other states with unstable civil-military relations could get nuclear weapons in the future. I cannot predict the exact strength of such preventive-war pressures or the timing of serious threats of war between all future nuclear states. Nevertheless, because civilians will not be in firm control in all future nuclear states, there are good reasons to fear that military biases in favor of preventive war will be more likely to prevail than was the case with the superpowers during the Cold War.

INTERESTS, ROUTINES, AND SURVIVABLE FORCES

The second operational requirement of deterrence is that new nuclear powers must build invulnerable second-strike nuclear forces. The United States and the former Soviet Union developed a large and diverse arsenal—long-range bombers, intercontinental ballistic missiles, cruise missiles, and submarine-launched missiles—and a complex network of satellite and radar warning systems, to decrease the risks of a successful first strike against their arsenals. Will new nuclear powers also construct invulnerable arsenals? How quickly?

Waltz addresses this issue with two related arguments. First, only a very small number of nuclear weapons are necessary for successful deterrence: since each nuclear warhead contains so much destructive power, "not much is required to deter" (Ch. 1, p. 22). Second, no rational nuclear power would permit all of its forces to be vulnerable to an enemy first strike. According to Waltz, "Nuclear forces are seldom delicate because no state wants delicate forces, and nuclear forces can easily be made sturdy. Nuclear warheads can be fairly small and light, and they are easy to hide and to move" (Ch. 1, p. 19). In short, Waltz is confident that any state will create the minimum deterrent of an invulnerable second-strike nuclear arsenal. "Because so much explosive power comes in such small packages, the invulnerability of a sufficient number of warheads is easy to achieve and the delivery of fairly large numbers of warheads impossible to thwart, both now and as far into the future as anyone can see."[45]

It is puzzling, however, for a theory that emphasizes the rationality of actors to note that both superpowers during the Cold War believed that they needed much larger forces than the minimum deterrence requirement. Waltz insists, however, that that belief was the result of "decades of fuzzy thinking" about nuclear deterrence: "The two principal powers in the system have long had second-strike forces, with neither able to launch a disarming strike against the other. That both nevertheless continue to pile weapon upon unneeded weapon is a puzzle whose solution can be found only within the United States and the Soviet Union."[46] Yet, if "fuzzy thinking" at the domestic level can cause a state to spend billions of dollars building more forces than are necessary for rational deterrence, couldn't similar "fuzzy thinking" at the organizational level of analysis also lead a state to build inadequate forces?

Why would professional militaries not develop invulnerable nuclear forces if left to their own devices? Five reasons emerge from the logic of organizational theory. First, military bureaucracies, like other organizations, are usually interested in having more resources: they want more weapons, more men in uniform, more of the budget pie. This could obviously lead to larger than necessary nuclear arsenals. Yet programs for making nuclear arsenals less vulnerable to attack (for example building concrete shelters or missile-carrying trains) are very expensive, and therefore *decrease* the resources available for the military hardware, the missiles or aircraft, that the organization values most highly. Military biases can therefore lead to more weapons but not necessarily more survivable weapons. Second, militaries, like other organizations, favor traditional ways of doing things and therefore maintain a strong sense of organizational "essence."[47] Since efforts to decrease the vulnerability of nuclear forces often require new missions and weapon systems—and, indeed, often new organizational units—one would expect that the existing organizations would be resistant. Third, if organizational plans for war and conceptions of deterrence do not require invulnerable forces, militaries will not have incentives to pursue building them. Thus, if military officers believe that they are likely to engage in preventive war, preemptive attacks, or even launch-on-warning options, then survivability measures may be perceived as simply unnecessary. Fourth, military organizations inevitably develop routines to coordinate actions among numerous individuals and subunits, and such routines are commonly inflexible and slow to change. Even if the technical requirements for invulnerability are met, however, poorly designed standard operating procedures and military routines can undermine a survivable military force. In particular, organizational routines of military forces can produce "signatures" to enemy intelligence agencies; these signatures can inadvertently reveal secret information and the location of otherwise "hidden" military units. Fifth, organizational learning tends to occur only after failures. Military organizations, like other organizations, have few incentives to review and adjust operations when they believe they are successful. Thus, if the first four problems create an undesirable

survivability problem with nuclear forces, military organizations are unlikely to fix the problem until after an attack has
revealed how vulnerable their forces really were.

Evidence from the Cold War

The history of U.S. and Soviet nuclear weapons programs
strongly supports these organizational arguments. The United
States eventually developed invulnerable second-strike forces,
but only after civilian authorities forced reluctant military organizations to deploy new weapons systems and change traditional operational practices. The influence of such factors can
be seen in the history of three major weapons developments:
the creation of a survivable basing system for strategic bombers in the United States; the development of the submarine-
launched ballistic missile (SLBM); and the construction of the
intercontinental-range ballistic missile (ICBM).

    The first case in point is the development of a survivable
basing system for Strategic Air Command (SAC) bombers in
the mid-1950s. SAC war plans at the time—based on routines
developed during World War II when the air force had not faced
threats of air strikes against their long-range bomber bases—
called for sending the nuclear retaliatory force to bases on the
periphery of the Soviet Union in crises.[48] These overseas bases,
however, became highly vulnerable to a surprise Soviet first
strike, and, making matters even worse, air force regulations
required SAC to concentrate the facilities at individual bases to
minimize the peacetime costs of utilities, pipelines, and roads.
When civilian analysts at the RAND Corporation pointed out
the ill-wisdom of such plans, narrow organizational interests
produced significant resistance to change. SAC's autonomy was
threatened: officers there feared that the RAND study would
lead to broader interference in SAC operations. Moreover, as
Bruce Smith put it, SAC officers feared that "the Air Force could
also be embarrassed before Congress" and that "the study
could undermine the confidence and morale of their units."[49]
The basing study led to radical changes in SAC operational

plans, including U.S. basing and in-flight refueling, only after independent civilian RAND analysts did a successful "end-run" around the system, bypassing layers of opposition in SAC and briefing senior air force leaders directly.[50]

The U.S. SLBM force has been the least vulnerable component of the strategic arsenal for over thirty years, yet it is important to note that this weapons system was developed against the wishes of the U.S. Navy leadership. The major impediment to development of the Polaris missile system was, as Harvey Sapolsky notes, "the Navy's indecisiveness about sponsoring a ballistic missile program."[51] Senior naval officers were concerned in the early 1950s that, given the Eisenhower administration's budget cuts, spending on missile programs would come at the expense of more traditional navy programs, and insisted that the Strategic Air Command should pay for sea-based missiles. Even navy submariners were unenthusiastic since "in their view, submarines were meant to sink ships with torpedoes, not to blast land targets with missiles."[52] The program's supporters within the navy eventually were forced to go to a group of civilian outsiders, the Killian Committee, to get endorsement of the program.[53] It is not clear whether or when a large-scale SLBM force would have been constructed without continued high-level civilian intervention.

Similar organizational resistance to innovation can be observed in the early history of the ICBM force. Why did the U.S. Air Force take so long to develop strategic missiles, eventually producing the perceived missile gap crisis? In his compelling study of the missile program, Edmund Beard concludes that "the United States could have developed an ICBM considerably earlier than it did but that such development was hindered by organizational structures and belief patterns that did not permit it."[54] Devotion to manned aircraft, and especially the manned bomber, led to a prolonged period of neglect for ICBM research and development funds. As late as 1956, General Curtis LeMay placed the ICBM as the air force's sixth-highest priority weapon, with four new aircraft and a cruise-missile program above it; and even within the air force's guided missile branch, air-to-air and air-to-surface missiles (which were to be used to help bombers penetrate to their targets) were given higher priority than intercontinental-range surface-to-surface missiles.[55] Again, civilian intervention was critical: not until the Killian Committee report recommended that ICBMs also be made a national priority, and civilian Pentagon officials threatened to create a separate agency to oversee the program, did the air force put adequate funds into ICBM development.[56]

Soviet nuclear history also contains three classic examples of how organizational routines and practices created serious vulnerabilities to what might otherwise have been their secure and survivable nuclear forces. First, the failure of the Soviet military to keep its 1962 missile deployment in Cuba secret, despite the strong desire for such secrecy by the Kremlin, was caused by construction crew routines that produced "signatures" leading American intelligence analysts to locate the "secret" missiles. The "Star of David" pattern of air defense missile battery placements and the easily recognized "slash marks" on missile pads, practices developed and seen in the USSR, gave away the secret Cuban operation to American intelligence officers.[57] Second, American photo-interpreters were also able to locate the "secret" ICBM silos of the Soviet Strategic Rocket Forces during the Cold War because the Soviet deployments had a discernable pattern. In each case, the Soviet military built triple security fences around the "secret" silo buildings and the distinctive wide radius curves in the entry roads, built to transport long missiles to the sites.[58] These routines made the missile deployments logistically easier and the nuclear warheads more secure from theft or sabotage; these routines also, however, made the Soviet missile silos more vulnerable to an American attack.

The third, and most dramatic, example of how a military organization's operational routines can produce serious strategic vulnerabilities concerns the U.S. secret penetration of the Soviet Navy's underwater communications system. Ballistic missile submarines (SSBNs) are widely considered to be the least vulnerable portion of a nuclear arsenal, providing a stabilizing, secure second-strike capability. In the early 1970s, however, the United States Navy initiated a secret intelligence operation against the Soviet SSBN fleet that enabled the U.S. to know the timing and locations of Soviet submarine patrols in the Pacific and to maintain a U.S. attack submarine trailing behind each Soviet SSBN. The organizational failures of the Russian military that led to this problem read more like the Keystone Cops than the KGB. The Soviets failed to encrypt many messages sent through an underwater communications cable in the Sea of Okhotsk to the missile submarine base at Petropavlovsk, figuring that such protected waters were safe from U.S. spying activities. To make matters worse, they gave away the location of the "secret" communications cable by posting a sign on the beach telling local fisherman "do not anchor, cable here." The crew of the *U.S.S. Halibut* thus easily located the line, tapped into the Soviet Navy's secret underwater communications, and received the operational plans and tactical patrol orders for the Russian SSBN fleet. It is important to note that the Soviet General Staff continued use of this vulnerable communication system, believing that their forces were secure unless proved otherwise, until an American spy revealed the secret operation to Moscow.[59]

Will New Nuclear Powers Build Survivable Forces?

This evidence demonstrates that there are strong organizational reasons to expect that professional militaries, if left on their own, may not construct invulnerable nuclear arsenals. Logic would therefore lead to a prediction that the development of a secure retaliatory force would be especially prolonged in time and imperfect in implementation in states in which civilian control over military organizations is problematic. Although these organizational impediments are likely to take somewhat different forms in different states, evidence does exist suggesting that parochial organizational interests and rigid routines have impeded the development of secure retaliatory forces in the developing world.

The influence of organizational biases on strategic weapons deployments can perhaps best be seen in the People's Republic of China. China tested its first nuclear weapon in 1964, yet it did not develop a confident and secure second-strike capability until the early 1980s, when initial deployments of ICBMs (1981), SLBMs (1982–83), and mobile and concealed intermediate-range ballistic missiles (IRBMs) were instituted (1980).[60] Why did China, which developed the atomic and hydrogen bombs very quickly, take so long to develop invulnerable missile-basing modes? The absence of perceived strategic threats is not a plausible answer, since the clashes along the Sino-Soviet border and the subsequent nuclear threats from Moscow occurred in 1969. Indeed, in 1970, U.S. intelligence agencies predicted that China would deploy ICBMs by 1975; and the failure to do so has been described as "a major enigma in the PRC's strategic weapons effort."[61]

While both technical problems and the political turmoil of the Cultural Revolution clearly played roles in the delayed development of Chinese strategic missiles, professional military biases also had an apparent impact in two specific areas. First, it is important to note that the military officers of Second Artillery Division, who controlled the operational missile forces in the 1970s, consistently argued for larger arsenals, but did not independently pursue the survivability measures needed for the existing land-based missiles. Only in 1975, after Mao Zedong approved a weapons institute report recommending that advanced deception measures be used to make China's medium-range ballistic missiles less vulnerable to Soviet attacks, were successful camouflage and cave-basing deployment methods developed.[62] As was the case in the United States, high-level intervention by civilian authorities was necessary to encourage operational innovation. Second, the strong bureaucratic power of traditional People's Liberation Army interests in the party and weapons institutes appears to have slowed the development of the Chinese navy's SLBM force. The SLBM and ICBM programs were started at the same time, but land-based systems were consistently given higher priority: the reverse engineering of SLBM missiles supplied by the Soviets was abandoned in 1961, while similar land-based missile programs continued; and in the late 1960s, the DF [ICBM] program was considered a "crash effort," while "the JL-1 [SLBM] designers did not feel an immediate or compelling urgency."[63] Thus, while China eventually developed a diverse set of survivable forces, it was a very vulnerable nuclear power for a longer period of time than can be explained by the rationalist assumptions of proliferation optimists.

Even if apparently invulnerable forces are built, however, their ability to withstand a first strike will be highly problematic if inappropriate organizational practices and operational routines are maintained. I will provide two examples. A useful illustration of how poorly designed organizational procedures and routines can produce "unnecessary" force vulnerabilities can be seen in Egyptian air force operations in June 1967. Given the balance between the Egyptian and Israeli air forces at the time (Egypt had over a 2-to-1 advantage in bombers, fighter-bombers, and interceptors),[64] Egyptian authorities had strong reasons to believe that their ability to retaliate against any Israeli air attack was secure. Indeed, President Nasser publicly emphasized that the Israeli "fear of the Egyptian air force and bombers" was a deterrent to war when he ordered that the Gulf of Aqaba be closed.[65] Two organizational routines of the Egyptian Air Force, however, created a severe vulnerability for what was "objectively" a sufficient retaliatory force. First, during the crisis, the air force lined up most of its aircraft wing-tip to wing-tip on the runways, making them easier to launch in a first strike, rather than dispersing them to reduce their vulnerability to an Israeli attack.[66] Second, the Egyptians always placed an interceptor force into defensive air patrol positions and held a "stand-to" alert at air bases at dawn, when they believed an Israeli strike was most likely. Both these operations routinely ended at 7:30 a.m., and, having observed these organizational practices, the Israelis attacked at 7:45 when the planes had landed for refueling and the pilots and crews were having breakfast.[67] What appeared to be an invulnerable force was thus virtually destroyed in the first hours of the war.

A second example concerns North Korea. If the North Korean government moves forward with its nuclear weapons program, in violation of international agreements, will it build a survivable deterrent force, successfully hiding the weapons from all potential adversaries? Possibly, but the fact that the North Korean government could not hide its secret nuclear weapons program from its adversaries does not bode well. Even in a highly secretive and centralized system, like the North Korean government, large organizations undertaking complex tasks will follow rules and develop routines that can create inadvertent vulnerabilities. How did the United States come to suspect that North Korea was developing nuclear weapons in violation of the Nuclear Non-Proliferation Treaty? Although the full details are shrouded in secrecy, it appears that inappropriate organizational routines were a critical factor. In the early 1990s, the North Korean leadership apparently sought to hide at the Yongbyon reactor facility nuclear-waste materials, evidence that could serve as a tip-off that they were in the process of developing nuclear weapons. The North Koreans, however, were trained by Soviet technical personnel and mimicked the designs of Soviet nuclear-waste storage facilities so closely that U.S. intelligence agencies could immediately identify the covert sites. According to David Albright, "these sites have a distinctive pattern of round and square holes in an above-ground concrete structure that holds liquid and solid waste."[68] This kind of organizational problem—building a covert site following a distinctive pattern developed while constructing earlier sites that were not hidden—is similar to the Soviet military mistakes in their missile deployment in Cuba. In the deadly cat-and-mouse game between nuclear forces and enemy intelligence agencies, such routinized behavior can inadvertently produce a high degree of military vulnerability.

From a purely rationalist perspective, the spread of nuclear weapons to very small powers might be worrisome since such states might not have the financial resources to procure hardened ICBMs or ballistic missile submarines nor sufficient territory to deploy mobile missiles. Awareness of organizational problems, however, leads to an even more pessimistic appraisal. Even if the economic resources and geographical conditions for survivable forces exist, a state may not develop a secure second-strike capability if organizational biases and inflexible routines of the professional military dominate its behavior.

ORGANIZATIONS, ACCIDENTS, AND PROLIFERATION

The final operational requirement for stable deterrence is that nuclear arsenals not be prone to accidental or unauthorized use. Waltz believes that any such dangers are temporary and can be easily fixed:

> All nuclear countries live through a time when their forces are crudely designed. All countries have so far been able to control them. Relations between the United States and the Soviet Union, and later among the United States, the Soviet Union, and China, were at their bitterest just when their nuclear forces were in early stages of development and were unbalanced, crude, and presumably hard to control. Why should we expect new nuclear states to experience greater difficulties than the ones old nuclear states were able to cope with? (Ch. 1, p. 20)

Waltz answers his own rhetorical question with a rationalist assumption. It is presumably in the interests of proliferating states to keep their forces under strict control; therefore, they will do so. As he puts it:

> We do not have to wonder whether they will take good care of their weapons. They have every incentive to do so. They will not want to risk retaliation because one or more of their warheads accidentally struck another country. (Ch. 1, p. 21)

What does organization theory say about the likelihood of nuclear weapons accidents? If organizations are highly rational, then they might be able to achieve extremely high reliability in managing hazardous technologies, avoiding serious accidents by following three basic strategies: construct highly redundant systems with numerous back-up safety devices; use trial-and-error learning to fix organizational problems after they emerge; and develop a "culture of reliability" through strong socialization and discipline of the organization's members.[69] If organizations are only "boundedly" rational and they contain political conflicts over goals and rewards, however, then a far more pessimistic appraisal is warranted. This approach raises doubts about whether any state can build a large nuclear arsenal that is completely "secure from accident," even if such strategies are followed.

Charles Perrow's *Normal Accidents* argues there are inherent limits to the degree to which any large organization can understand the technical systems it creates to manage hazardous technologies, such as nuclear power plants, petrochemical industries, advanced biotechnology, and oil tankers.[70] If organizations were omniscient, they could anticipate all potential failure modes in their systems and fix them ahead of time. Perrow argues, however, that boundedly rational organizations in the real world will inevitably have serious system accidents over time whenever they exhibit two structural characteristics: high *interactive complexity* (systems containing numerous interrelated, yet unplanned, interactions that are not readily comprehensible) and *tight coupling* (systems with highly time-dependent and invariant production sequences, with limited built-in slack).

My own book, *The Limits of Safety*, adds an explicitly political dimension to "normal accidents theory," combining with Perrow's structural arguments to produce even greater pessimism about the likelihood of organizational accidents. Conflicting objectives inevitably exist inside any large organization that manages hazardous technology: some top-level authorities may place a high priority on safety, but others may place a higher value on more parochial objectives, such as increasing production levels, enhancing the size of their subunit, or promoting their individual careers, which can lead to risky behaviors. Such a focus on the political manner in which conflicting goals are chosen and pursued is necessary to explain both why systems with such dangerous structural characteristics are constructed and why organizational learning about safety problems is often severely limited.[71]

Normal accidents theory suggests that each of the three basic strategies used to improve organizational safety is highly problematic. In some conditions, adding redundant back-up systems can be very counterproductive: redundancy makes the system both more complex and more opaque and therefore can create hidden catastrophic common-mode errors. Large organizations nevertheless often continue to add layers of redundancy upon redundancy to complex systems.[72] Why? Organizations often add redundancy not only when it is needed to improve reliability but also because they must appear to be doing something to solve problems after accidents occur. Unproductive redundancy is also sometimes constructed because such redundant systems serve the narrow interests of organizational subunits, when it enhances *their* size, resources, and autonomy. The politics of blame inside organizations also reduces trial-and-error learning from accidents because organizational leaders have great incentives to find operators at lower levels at fault: this absolves higher leaders from responsibility, and, moreover, it is usually cheaper to fire the operator than to change accident-prone procedures or structures. Knowing this, however, field-level operators have strong incentives not to report safety incidents whenever possible. Finally, from a normal accidents perspective, strong culture and socialization can have negative effects on organizational reliability since they encourage excessive concern about the organization's reputation, disdain for outsiders' and internal dissenters' opinions, and even organizational cover-ups.

The U.S. Nuclear Safety Experience

From the perspective of normal accidents theory, there are strong reasons to expect that the safety of modern nuclear arsenals is inherently limited: large-scale arsenals and command systems are highly complex, by necessity, and are tightly-coupled, by design, to ensure prompt retaliation under attack; the military organizations that manage them are inevitably politicized, with numerous conflicting interests existing between commands and the broader society and within the organizations themselves. How serious were the dangers of U.S. nuclear weapons accidents and even accidental war during the Cold War? The available evidence now demonstrates that there were many more near-accidents than previously recognized. Moreover, the U.S. military's reaction to these safety problems shows how only limited degrees of organizational learning took place.

New information on dangerous military operations during the October 1962 Cuban missile crisis demonstrates these points. At the start of the crisis, the Strategic Air Command secretly deployed nuclear warheads on nine of the ten test ICBMs in place at Vandenberg Air Force Base in California and then launched the tenth missile, on a prescheduled ICBM test, over the Pacific. No one within the responsible organizations thought through the risks that Soviet intelligence might learn of the nuclear weapons deployment and the alert at Vandenberg and then, in the tension of the crisis, might misinterpret a missile launch from that base. A second safety problem occurred at Malmstrom Air Force Base in Montana at the height of the crisis, when officers jerry-rigged their Minuteman missiles to give themselves the independent ability to launch missiles immediately. This was a serious violation of the Minuteman safety rules, but when an investigation took place after the crisis, the evidence was altered to prevent higher authorities from learning that officers had given themselves the ability to launch unauthorized missile attacks. A third incident occurred on October 28, when the North American Air Defense Command (NORAD) was informed that a nuclear-armed missile had been launched from Cuba and was about to hit Tampa, Florida. Only after the expected detonation failed to occur was it discovered that a radar operator had inserted a test tape simulating an attack from Cuba into the system, confusing control room officers who thought the simulation was a real attack.

Learning from these incidents was minimal: the relevant military procedures and routines were *not* altered after each of these incidents. In each case, the existence of serious safety problems was not reported to or was not recognized by higher authorities. Each one of the accident-prone nuclear operations was therefore repeated by U.S. military commands in October 1973, in the brief U.S. nuclear alert during the Arab-Israeli war.

More recently, on August 29, 2007, six AGM-129 ACM cruise missiles with W80-1 variable yield nuclear warheads were mistakenly loaded onto a B-52 heavy bomber at the Minot Air Force base and transported to Barksdale. Peacetimes prohibitions are placed on the transport of nuclear weapons by air, and the refueling or engine startup of planes with nuclear weapons onboard or nearby; in the Minot case, both transport and refueling/engine startup took place. Furthermore, the weapons transported did not have Fire Resistant Pits (FRPs), a feature that all modern U.S. nuclear weapons have for safety reasons. Pilots, unaware that nuclear weapons were on board, would follow normal procedures in case of accident or malfunction, not the policies for safely jettisoning nuclear weapons.

The *Report on the Unauthorized Movement of Nuclear Weapons* produced by the Defense Science Board Permanent Task Force on Nuclear Weapons Surety identified a number of problems leading to the accidental transport of these weapons across the U.S. Over time, military technicians became sloppy, procedures were rushed, and shortcuts became routinized. Requirements to identify nuclear-inert missiles with placards on multiple sides of the pylons and orange cones, for example, had at Minot been reduced to an 8x10 piece of paper placed somewhere on the pylon. Other verification measures, such as checking serial numbers, were simply not followed.[73]

Proliferation and Nuclear Weapons Safety

Waltz asked why we should expect new nuclear states to experience greater difficulties than did the old ones. The number of near-accidents with U.S. nuclear weapons during the Cold War suggests that there would be reason enough to worry about nuclear accidents in new nuclear states even if their safety difficulties were "only" as great as those experienced by old nuclear powers. Unfortunately, there are also five strong reasons to expect that new nuclear states will face even greater risks of nuclear accidents.

First, some emergent nuclear powers lack the organizational and financial resources to produce adequate mechanical safety devices and safe weapons design features. Although all countries may start with "crude nuclear arsenals," in Waltz's terms, the weapons of poorer states will likely be more crude, and will remain so for a longer period of time. Evidence supposing this prediction can be found in the case of the Iraqi nuclear weapons program, as United Nations' inspectors discovered soon after the 1991 Persian Gulf War:

> The inspectors found out one other thing about the Iraqi bomb [design]—it is highly unstable. The design calls for cramming so much weapon-grade uranium into the core, they say, that the bomb would inevitably be on the verge of going off— even while sitting on the workbench. "It could go off if a rifle bullet hit it," one inspector says, adding: "I wouldn't want to be around if it fell off the edge of this desk."[74]

Second, the "opaque" (or covert) nature of nuclear proliferation in the contemporary world exacerbates nuclear weapons safety problems. Fearing the international diplomatic consequences of a public crossing of the nuclear threshold, most new proliferants have developed weapons capabilities in a secret manner. Israel, India (until 1998), South Africa, Pakistan (until 1998), North Korea (until 2006), and Iran today fit this pattern. There are, however, both organizational and technical reasons to believe that this opaque path to nuclear weapons status is inherently less safe. Organizationally, the secrecy and tight compartmentalization of such programs suggests that there will not be thorough monitoring of safety efforts, and the lack of public debate about nuclear issues in such states increases the likelihood that narrow bureaucratic and military interests will not be challenged. (For example, even in the case of India—a very democratic state—the nuclear weapons complex is not thoroughly monitored and supervised by political leaders.)[75] Finally, an important technical constraint exacerbates the safety problem in such states: the inability to have full-scale nuclear weapons tests hinders the development of effective safety designs. For example, when the South African weapons engineers examined their first (untested) nuclear device, they considered it to be based on "an unqualified design that could not meet the rigid safety, security, and reliability specifications then under development."[76]

The third reason why new nuclear states will be accident prone is that their tight-coupling problem will be significantly worse at the beginning of this experience with nuclear weapons, since they are in closer proximity to their expected adversaries than were the United States and the Soviet Union. At the start of the Cold War, during the strategic bomber era, the superpowers had many hours to determine whether warnings were real or false; later, in the 1960s, they had approximately thirty minutes to react to reports of ICBM attacks; and only after many years of experience with nuclear arsenals did they have to face less than ten minutes of warning time, once missile submarines were deployed off the coasts in the 1970s. New and potential future nuclear rivals—Iran and Saudi Arabia, India and Pakistan, North and South Korea—will immediately have very small margins of error at the outset of nuclear rivalries, since they have contiguous borders with their adversaries. Moreover, the poorer of these states are likely to have less reliable warning systems trying to operate successfully in this more challenging environment.

Fourth, the risk of an accidental nuclear war will be particularly high if the leader of a government of a new nuclear power, fearing a "decapitation attack" (an attack against the central leadership) by an enemy, delegates the authority to use nuclear weapons to lower level commanders. Proliferation optimists argue that this will not happen because they assume that the leaders of new proliferators would never delegate authority for the use of nuclear weapons to subordinate officers due to fears of coups or insubordination. Although we lack detailed information about nuclear predelegation decisions within new nuclear states, the evidence concerning predelegation of biological and chemical weapons authority in Iraq during the Gulf War supports a more alarming view that predelegation is likely and that it can produce serious risks of accidental war due to responses to false warnings.

During the 1990–91 Gulf War, Saddam Hussein felt compelled by military necessity to predelegate authority to use twenty-five SCUD missiles (armed with warheads filled with botulinum toxin, anthrax, and aflatoxin) and fifty chemical warheads to senior commanders in Iraq's Special Security Organization (SSO). These officers were told to launch their chemical and biological weapons at Israel if they believed that Israel or the coalition forces had attacked Baghdad with nuclear weapons. The evidence that such an attack had occurred could have come through visual observation or because all communication links from Baghdad to the SSO missile unit were severed. Hussein underscored this strategy in a speech given to a group of U.S. senators in April 1990:

> [We] might be in Baghdad holding a meeting with the command when the atomic bomb falls on us. So to make the military order clear to air and missile base commanders, we have told them that if they do not receive an order from higher authority and a city is struck with an atomic bomb, they will point toward Israel any weapons capable of reaching it."[77]

Such a predelegation policy may be a reasonable response to the fear of a decapitation attack, but it inevitably raises the risks of accidental war. Two incidents from the 1991 Gulf War dramatically illustrate these dangers. First, on January 28, 1991, when the United States bombed a large ammunition bunker outside of Basra, the explosion was so large that both the Soviets (using their infrared satellite monitors) and the Israelis (who were receiving downlinks from the U.S. satellites) contacted Washington to ask if U.S. forces had just detonated a nuclear weapon.[78] Second, on February 7, 1991, when U.S. forces used a "Daisy Cutter" BLU-82 bomb, a British commando behind the lines reportedly saw the large explosion and announced on an open (unclassified) radio, "Sir, the blokes have just nuked Kuwait."[79] Given these occurrences during the Gulf War, it should not take too much imagination to think through similar scenarios in which the special security officers in charge of nuclear weapons might incorrectly believe that the conditions under which they were pre-delegated authority to use their weapons had in fact come into effect.

The fifth reason to anticipate a significant increase in the risks of accidental and unauthorized weapons detonations is that serious political and social unrest is likely in the future in a number of these nuclear states. Waltz, in contrast, insists that domestic instability in new nuclear powers will not cause serious problems:

> A nuclear state may be unstable or may become so. But what is hard to comprehend is why, in an internal struggle for power, the contenders would start using nuclear weapons. Who would they aim at? . . . One or another nuclear state will experience uncertainty of succession, fierce struggles for power, and instability of regime. Those who fear the worst have not shown how those events might lead to the use of nuclear weapons. (Ch. 1, p. 11)

This exclusive focus on *deliberate* uses of nuclear weapons is misleading, however, since severe domestic instability can produce *accidental* detonations under many plausible scenarios. If a civil war in a new nuclear state leads to a fire fight between rival military factions at a nuclear weapons base, the danger of an accidental detonation or spreading of plutonium increases.

If domestic unrest leads to severe economic hardships at military bases, disgruntled operators are more likely to engage in acts of sabotage that could inadvertently or deliberately produce accidents. An example of the type of dangerous incident one should anticipate in future nuclear states occurred in early 1992 at the Ignalina nuclear power plant in Lithuania, where a programmer reported that he had found a virus in the computer that ran the safety systems for the plant. Investigators later concluded, however, that he had placed the virus there himself in order to receive a pay bonus for improving safety.[80] Finally, domestic political unrest can increase the risk of nuclear weapons accidents by encouraging unsafe transportation, exercise, or testing operations. If warheads are moved out of unstable regions in haste (as occurred in the USSR in 1991) or if weapons tests are rushed to prevent rebellious military units from gaining access to the weapons (as occurred in Algeria in 1961),[81] safety is likely to be compromised. The most dramatic example of risky actions induced by domestic crises is Marshal Nie Rongzhen's October 1966 decision to launch a test missile eight hundred kilometers across China, with a live nuclear warhead onboard, in the middle of the Cultural Revolution. Nie was apparently fully aware of the risks involved in such an unprecedented test, but believed that the nuclear weapons program needed a dramatic and public sign of success as part of his "strategy of siding with the radicals to fend off radical penetration of the program."[82]

In short, while there have been no catastrophic nuclear weapons accidents in the new nuclear states yet, there are good reasons to anticipate that the probabilities will be high over time. Any serious nuclear weapons accident will have tragic consequences for the local community; and if an accidental detonation, false warning, or unauthorized use of a weapon leads to "mistaken retaliation" and accidental war, the consequences would be even more catastrophic. As long as would-be nuclear states choose not to cross the final threshold of "weaponization" by actually deploying fully assembled nuclear weapons and launchers, these safety problems will largely remain dormant. Once these states begin to deploy arsenals, however, such organizational safety problems are likely to emerge rapidly. The current positive safety record is therefore likely to be only the lull before the storm.

CONCLUSIONS: BRINGING ORGANIZATIONS BACK IN

The nuclear optimists' view that the spread of nuclear weapons will produce stable deterrence is based on a rationalist assumption that the behavior of new nuclear states will reflect their interest in avoiding nuclear war. New nuclear powers will avoid preventive nuclear wars, develop survivable nuclear arsenals, and prevent nuclear weapons accidents because it is in their obvious national interests to do so. I have argued, in contrast, that the actual behavior of new proliferators will be strongly influenced by military organizations within those states and that the common biases, rigid routines, and parochial interests of these military organizations will lead to deterrence failures and accidental uses of nuclear weapons despite national interests to the contrary. The concepts behind this more pessimistic vision of proliferation are well-grounded in the rich theoretical and empirical literature on complex organizations. My theory makes less heroic assumptions about the rationality of states. It provides useful insights into U.S. nuclear history during the Cold War, and it points to the checks-and-balances system of civilian control as a critical factor in creating the requirements of nuclear deterrence during the long peace. Although the jury of history is still out on the consequences of further nuclear proliferation, and will be for some time, the emerging evidence from the nuclear-proliferating world unfortunately supports this more pessimistic view.

Bringing Organizations Back into International Relations Theory

By assuming that all nuclear states will behave quite rationally and will therefore take all the necessary steps to fulfill the requirements of deterrence, Waltz and other nuclear proliferation optimists have confused prescriptions of what rational states *should* do with predictions of what real states *will* do. This is an error that the classical American realists rarely committed: Hans Morgenthau and George Kennan believed that states should follow the logic of balance-of-power politics, but their whole enterprise was animated by a fear that the United States would fail to do so.[83] This is also an error that Waltz avoided in *Theory of International Politics*, where he noted that "the theory requires no assumptions of rationality . . . the theory says simply that if some do relatively well, others will emulate them or fall by the wayside."[84]

Adding this element of natural selection to a theory of international relations puts less of a burden on the assumption of rationality. My approach is consistent with this vision. Many nuclear states may well behave sensibly, but some will not and will then "fall by the wayside." Falling by the wayside, however, means using their nuclear weapons in this case and thus has very serious implications for the whole international system.

"Realist theory by itself can handle some, but not all the problems that concern us," Waltz correctly noted in 1986. "Just as market theory at times requires a theory of the firm, so international-political theory at times needs a theory of the state."[85] Understanding the consequences of nuclear proliferation is precisely one case in point. To predict the nuclear future, we need to utilize ideas, building upon the theory of the firm, about how and when common organizational behaviors can constrain rational reactions to the nuclear revolution.

Bringing Organizations into Counter-Proliferation Policy

What are the policy implications of my organizational-level approach to nuclear proliferation? First, and most obviously, this approach suggests that the United States is quite correct to maintain an active nuclear nonproliferation policy. A world with more nuclear-armed states may be our fate; it should not be our goal. It is highly unfortunate, in this regard, that a growing number of defense analysts in new nuclear nations read the arguments of the U.S. nuclear optimists, most prominently the writings of Kenneth Waltz, and now cite that literature to legitimize the development of nuclear arsenals in their nations.[86] It is fortunate, however, that U.S. government officials have not been convinced of the merits of the optimists' views, and there is little evidence that U.S. policy is going to move away from its strong opposition to the further spread of nuclear weapons.

Second, a more effective approach to nuclear proliferation would add a larger dose of intellectual persuasion to our current policy efforts, which are aimed primarily at restricting the supply of materials and providing security guarantees to potential nuclear states. There are ongoing debates—often in secret, sometimes in the open—about the wisdom of developing nuclear weapons in many of these countries. To influence such debates, nonproliferation advocates need to develop better understandings of the perceptions and interests of the domestic organizational actors involved. Decision makers in potential nuclear powers do not need to be told that proliferation is not in the *United States'* interests. They need to be convinced that it is not in *their* interest. Civilian leaders, military leaders, and wider publics alike in these states need to be reminded that the development of nuclear weapons will make their states targets for preventive attacks by their potential adversaries, will not easily lead to survivable arsenals, and will raise the specter of accidental or unauthorized uses of nuclear weapons. Just as importantly, they also need to be persuaded that nuclear proliferation may not be in their narrow self-interest as civilian leaders seeking political power, as militaries seeking autonomy, and as citizens seeking safety.

Finally, an organizational approach offers a valuable, but pessimistic, perspective on efforts to manage proliferation if it occurs despite U.S. attempts to prevent it. At one level, an implication of an organizational perspective is that the United States should cooperate with new nuclear states—sharing knowledge of organizational "best practices," technology, and experience—to reduce the dangerous consequences of the spread of nuclear weapons. At a deeper level, however, the most disturbing lesson of this analysis is that, for organizational reasons, such cooperative efforts are not likely to succeed.

This is true with respect to all three of the requirements of deterrence. First, the most important step the United States could take to reduce the likelihood of military biases leading to preventive war in the new nuclear nations would be to encourage sustained civilian control of the military, with appropriate checks and balances, in those states. Such efforts are unlikely, however, to be completely effective. In some new nuclear states, strong military organizations are unlikely to give up their current positions of significant decision making power and influence. In some other nuclear states, unpopular civilian regimes will not create competent, professional military organizations, since they might serve as a threat to the regime's power. In either case, appropriate civil-military relations are problematic. Efforts to improve civil-military relations are therefore likely to be most effective precisely where they are least needed.

Second, to enhance survivability of new nuclear forces, the United States could also consider cooperating with new nuclear states—sharing information, operational practices, and advanced warning systems—to help them create invulnerable forces. This policy, however, is also unlikely to be widely implemented. Not only will U.S. policymakers fear that such cooperative efforts would signal that the United States is not really opposed to the further spread of nuclear weapons, but the leaders of new nuclear states, and especially the leaders of their military organizations, will also not want to discuss such sensitive issues in detail, fearing that it will expose their own nuclear vulnerabilities and organizational weaknesses to the United States.

Third, the large risk of unauthorized use or nuclear accidents in these countries suggests that the United States may want to share information on such subjects as security systems for storage sites, weapons-safety design improvements, and personnel reliability programs.[87] To the degree that the United States can share technology that only improves weapons safety and security, but does not enhance readiness to use the forces, such efforts would be helpful. A broad policy to make the weapons of new nuclear nations safer could be highly counter-productive, however, if it led them to believe that they could safely operate large nuclear arsenals on high states of alert.

Indeed, an organizational perspective on nuclear safety suggests that we need a paradigm shift in the way we think about managing proliferation. The United States should not try to make new nuclear nations become like the superpowers during the Cold War, with large arsenals ready to launch at a moment's notice for the sake of deterrence; instead, for the sake of safety, the United States and Russia should try to become more like some of the nascent nuclear states, maintaining very small nuclear capabilities, with weapons components separated and located apart from the delivery systems, and with civilian organizations controlling the warheads.

The United States and the Soviet Union survived the Cold War and did not use their massive nuclear-weapons arse-nals during the period's repeated crises. This should be a cause of celebration and wonder; it should not be an excuse for inac-tion with either arms control or nonproliferation policies. The superpowers' experience with nuclear weapons in the Cold War was like walking across thin ice. The fact that two states performed this feat one time should not lead us to think that other states can safely do it nor that Russia and America can continue walking along that dangerous path forever.

Chapter 3

WALTZ RESPONDS TO SAGAN

Kenneth N. Waltz

INTRODUCTION

"War is like love," the chaplain says in Bertolt Brecht's *Mother Courage*, "it always finds a way."[1] For more than half a century, *nuclear* war has not found a way. The old saying, "accidents will happen," is translated as Murphy's Law holding that anything that can go wrong will go wrong. Enough has gone wrong, and Scott Sagan has recorded many of the nuclear accidents that have, or have nearly, taken place. Yet none of them has caused anybody to blow anybody else up. In a speech given to American scientists in 1960, C. P. Snow said this: "We know, with the certainty of statistical truth, that if enough of these weapons are made—by enough different states—some of them are going to blow up. Through accident, or folly, or madness—but the motives don't matter. What does matter is the nature of the statistical fact." In 1960, statistical fact told Snow that within "at the most, ten years some of these bombs are going off."[2] Statistical fact now tells us that we are more than thirty years overdue. But the novelist and scientist overlooked the fact that there are no "statistical facts."

This is a revised version of my 2003 essay from the second edition of this book.

The long nuclear peace has to be explained, since divergence from historical experience is dramatic. Never in modern history, conventionally dated from 1648, have the great and major powers of the world enjoyed such a long period of peace. Scott Sagan emphasizes the problems and the conditions that conduce to pessimism. I emphasize the likely solutions and the conditions that conduce to optimism, bearing in mind that nothing in this world is certain.

Problems and Dangers

In section A, I consider a subject I neglected in Chapter 1: the possibility of terrorist bands gaining control of nuclear warheads. In sections B through F, I consider problems that supposedly grow as nuclear weapons spread slowly from country to country.

A. Terror

Before considering the likelihood of nuclear terror, I should put the menace of terrorism in perspective. John Deutch, a former director of intelligence, pointed out that in the twenty-five years ending in 1996, terrorism declined worldwide.[3] More recently, Larry Johnson, a former counterterrorism specialist in the State Department, pointed to its data showing that, worldwide, deaths from terrorism were down from 4,833 in the 1980s to 2,527 in the 1990s. Americans have thought of terror as something foreigners, especially Islamic fundamentalists, inflict on us. Yet if one subtracts Colombian terrorism directed against pipelines, Pakistani-Indian terrorism, and Israeli-Palestinian terrorism, not much terrorism was left. The State Department and the Central Intelligence Agency judged that only 153 of the terrorist incidents in the year 2000 were "significant," and only seventeen of these involved Americans. [4]

Then out of the blue on the morning of September 11, 2001, two hijacked planes struck and destroyed the towers of the World Trade Center in New York City, and another plane plunged into the Pentagon in northern Virginia. A fourth hijacked plane crashed south of Pittsburgh without finding its target. In one day, the number of deaths from terrorism exceeded the total of the previous decade. Government officials and many others labeled the attackers "cowardly terrorists" who murdered thousands of innocent men, women, and children. They were vicious terrorists all right, but hardly cowards. Cowards do not risk their lives in the planning and hijacking of airplanes and give their lives in carrying out their destructive acts. The terrorists in this and in some other instances have proved to be patient, clever, and ruthless.

In some parts of the world, low-level terrorism has been a constant worry. It has occasionally been punctuated by major acts of wanton destruction such as the 1988 explosion of an airliner over Lockerbie, Scotland, the 1995 bombing of the Federal Building in Oklahoma City, and the 1998 car bombings of American embassies in Nairobi and Dar es Salaam. September 11 makes high-level terrorism a more serious threat than ever before.

Distinguished by their objectives, terrorists fall into three categories.

1. Terrorists who threaten to use force to compel a particular performance. Palestinians threatening to strike Israeli targets if specified prisoners are not let free is one example. A more general example is the Palestinian terrorism mounted after peace talks broke down in the year 2000, terrorism apparently intended to make Israeli lives so perilous that they will shrink or abandon West Bank and Gaza settlements and offer better peace terms.

2. Terrorists who want to punish. Why on September 11, 2001, did the terrorists choose to kill so many? They see America as arrogant, themselves as humble; America as modern, themselves as traditional; America as secular, themselves as religious; America as global in reach, themselves as local; America as powerful, themselves as weak.

America supported Israel since its inception. America helped to overthrow the democratically elected government of Iran in 1953. America stations troops on Saudi Arabia's holy soil. In its being and by its acts, America, in the view of these terrorists, warrants punishment. Since its evil acts persist, terrorists must preserve their organization in order to continue to punish the infidel. Thus, Osama bin Laden, when threatened, took to the hills. The second type of terrorism spills into the third.

3. Terrorists who kill and destroy for the sake of doing so—nihilists, they used to be called, or millenarians, who expect to reap their rewards in another world. "Superterrorists" is the term now used. They would pull the temple down on all of us, themselves included. The damage they would do knows no limit.

All forms of terrorism arise from deep frustration and profound dissatisfaction with the world as it is. Terrorists do not play their deadly games to win in the short term. Their horizons are distant. Instead, they try to offer a voice to the unheard, to give a glimmer of hope to the forlorn, to force established societies to recognize alienated others, and ultimately to transcend given societies and establish their own.

Terrorists of the first type have objectives they hope to achieve, and the objectives limit the means used. For their purposes nuclear weapons are irrelevant. Palestinian nuclear weapons would, as Israeli nuclear weapons do, limit the extent of force that could be used in war, but not the extent of low-level force that could be used in peacetime.

For terrorists of the second type, objectives do not limit the means used. If they view the crimes as monstrous, the punishment the criminals deserve knows no limit. Osama bin Laden and his organization and sympathizers viewed the United States in this light. One read that bin Laden would have liked to have chemical, biological, and nuclear weapons at his command. The higher the level of force terrorists use, the greater the destructiveness of reprisals will be. Estimates are that fifty operatives participated in the acts of September 11, excluding those who financed and directed operations from afar. The greater the number of terrorists involved, the likelier they are to be detected before the event and to be identified, traced, and apprehended after it. The amount of destruction terrorists of the second type decide to inflict is limited less by ends and more by logistics. Their fear may not be of individual punishment but rather possible disruption of terrorist networks, which must be intricate for safety and extensive for effectiveness.

Terrorists live precarious lives. Nobody trusts them, not even those who finance, train, and hide them. If apprehended, they cannot count on the help of others. They have learned how to use conventional weapons to some effect, but nuclear weapons would thrust them into a world fraught with new dangers. Terrorists work in small groups. Secrecy is safety, yet to obtain and maintain nuclear weapons would require enlarging the terrorist band to include suppliers, transporters, technicians, and guardians. Inspiring devotion, instilling discipline, and ensuring secrecy become harder tasks to accomplish as numbers grow. Those who want to punish others have to preserve their organizations in order to continue to administer their perverted justice. Unfortunately they are very good at what they do. We know this from the long British experience with the Irish Republican Army, and from the Spanish experience with the Basque separatist group ETA.

Terrorists of the third type, the superterrorists, may not worry about the survival of their networks of saboteurs and assassins. They may gamble all in one spectacular destructive act. They are the ones who may try to get hold of nuclear materials and weapons. Deterrence does not work without targets. If terrorists who have political objectives threatened to use nuclear weapons, they would turn themselves into targets, and they would likely not accomplish their goals. Terrorists bent on destruction for its own sake cannot be deterred.

For terrorists who abandon tactics of disruption and harassment in favor of dealing in wholesale death and destruction, instruments other than nuclear weapons are more readily available. Poisons and germs are easier to get than nuclear weapons, and poisoning a city's water supply, though rather complicated, is more easily done than blowing a city up. Nevertheless, terrorists may seek to gain control of nuclear materials and use them to threaten or destroy. Yet, with shaky control of nuclear weapons materials in Russia and perhaps in Pakistan, and with the revelation in 1994 that the United States had lost track of some of its nuclear materials, one can hardly believe that nuclear weapons spreading to another country or two every now and then adds much to the chances that terrorists will be able to buy or steal nuclear materials. Plentiful sources are already available. Nuclear terror is a problem distinct from the spread of nuclear weapons to a few more countries.

Terrorists have done a fair bit of damage by using conventional weapons and have sometimes got their way by threatening to use them. Might terrorists not figure they can achieve more still by threatening to explode nuclear weapons on cities of countries they may wish to bend to their bidding?

Fear of nuclear terror arises from the assumption that if terrorists *can* get nuclear weapons they *will* get them, and then all hell will break loose. This is comparable to assuming that if weak states get nuclear weapons, they will use them for aggression. Both assumptions are false. Would the courses of action we fear, if followed, promise more gains than losses or more pains than profits? The answers are obvious. Terrorists have some hope of reaching their long-term goals through patient pressure and constant harassment. They cannot hope to do so by issuing unsustainable threats to wreak great destruction, threats they would not want to execute anyway.

B. Accidents

The more nuclear weapons there are, and the larger the number of countries that have them, the likelier it is that some will go off. That is C. P. Snow's reasoning, and it is the common wisdom. The United States has been lax in devising safety measures and has often found them difficult to apply. Until 1997, the American navy, unlike the Soviet navy, refused to use PALS (permissive action links), a system designed to prevent unauthorized firings. A former Minuteman missile launcher (Bruce Blair) and an M.I.T. physicist (Henry Kendall), wonder why even now we keep our ICBMs (intercontinental ballistic missiles) on hair-trigger alert.[5] The main hazards, they plausibly argue, are un-authorized firings and firings that result from a false warning. Keeping large numbers of strategic missiles ready to go in thirty minutes increases the danger. Hair-trigger forces are no longer needed, if they ever were, yet we continue to have them.[6]

When countries venture into the nuclear game, smallness of numbers works strongly against their accidentally firing nuclear weapons. Small countries fret about the damage they may suffer through retaliation if one or several of their war-heads go astray. They guard them with almost paranoiac zeal. Because countries, especially poor ones, can build sizable forces only over long periods of time, they have time to learn how to care for them.

Sagan is leery of the cognitive abilities of political leaders. Aren't we all? Yet some do better than others. Survival is an interesting test of learning ability. We continually worry about the leaders of "rogue" states —the likes of Qaddhafi, Saddam Hussein, Kim Il Sung, and Kim Jong Il. Yet these leaders survi-ved for many years, despite great internal and external dangers. Their cognitive skills, in the crabbed language of social scien-tists, were more impressive than those of, say, Jimmy Carter or the first George Bush. Given all of the advantages of presi-dential incumbency, Carter and Bush managed to stay in office for only four years. American politics is gentle compared to the politics of most of the countries that have recently joined, or are likely to join, the nuclear club. Are hardy political survivors in the Third World likely to run the greatest of all risks by drawing the wrath of the world down on them by accidentally or in anger exploding nuclear weapons they may have?

Some of the rulers of new and prospective nuclear states are thought to be ruthless, reckless, and war-prone. Ruthless, yes; war-prone, seldom; reckless, hardly. They do not, as many seem to believe, have fixed images of the world and unbend-ing aims within it. Instead, they have to adjust constantly to a shifting configuration of forces around them. Our images of leaders of Third World states vary remarkably little, yet their agility is remarkable.

America has long associated democracy with peace and authoritarianism with war, overlooking that weak authoritarian rulers often avoid war for fear of upsetting the balance of internal and external forces on which their power depends. Neither Italy nor Germany was able to persuade Franco's Spain to enter World War II. External pressures affect state behavior with a force that varies with conditions. Of all of the possible external forces, what could affect state behavior more strongly than nuclear weapons? Who cares about the "cognitive" abilities of leaders when nobody but an idiot can fail to comprehend their destructive force? What more is there to learn? How can leaders miscalculate? For a country to strike first without certainty of success, all of those who control a nation's nuclear weapons would have to go mad at the same time. Nuclear reality transcends political rhetoric. Did our own big words, or the Soviet Union's prattling about nuclear war-fighting, ever mean anything? Political, military, and academic hard-liners imagined conditions under which we would or should be willing to use nuclear weapons. None was of relevance. Nuclear weapons dominate strategy. Nothing can be done with them other than to use them for deterrence. The United States and the Soviet Union were both reluctant to accept the fact of deterrence. Weaker states find it easier to substitute deterrence for war-fighting, precisely because they are weak.

C. Civilian Control

The United States has a long tradition of civilian control of the military. Some present and prospective nuclear states lack both the tradition and the practice of civilian control. This worries Sagan more than it does me. The following three considerations reduce or eliminate the worries.

First, civilian control in the United States is not as sure as many believe it to be. A few examples illustrate the point.

President Harry S. Truman ordered that the defense budget for fiscal year 1950 not exceed $15 billion, of which $600 million was for stockpiling materials that might be needed in a prolonged war. Secretary of Defense James Forrestal appointed a board headed by retired General McNarney. The board came up with a military plan estimated to cost $23.6 billion. Forrestal thereupon ordered the Joint Chiefs of Staff to come up with a plan that he might be able to sell to the president, a plan that would cost about $17.5 billion. The Joint Chiefs refused, and Forrestal lacked the authority to bring them to heel.[7] With effective civilian control, military officers would have had to come up with a strategy within the budgetary limits set by the executive branch. They refused to do so.

President Dwight D. Eisenhower became more and more concerned in the later years of his presidency with the military's plans to fire hundreds or thousands of warheads at the Soviet Union if the occasion for retaliation should arise. He worried that force would be used in ways that would create an ungovernable postwar world.[8] Even with all of his military prestige, Eisenhower found control of the military difficult, if not impossible, to achieve.[9]

Early in John F. Kennedy's presidency, Secretary of Defense McNamara, Jerome Wiesner, and a few others asked themselves how many ICBMs we needed. They first came up with the number two hundred. Concerns about misfirings and force vulnerability led them to double the number. McNamara nevertheless asked Congress to authorize one thousand ICBMs, not four hundred. He did so for two main reasons. He and his advisors feared that the air force would weigh in with a request for three thousand. At the time, counterforce, aiming weapons at weapons, versus countervalue, aiming weapons at cities, was much debated. McNamara at first favored the former.[10] About one hundred Soviet cities were thought to be worth striking, in my view an absurdly high number. The air force, however, identified counterforce targets in the Soviet Union numbering in the thousands. Rather than ask Congress for the number he thought to be appropriate, McNamara asked for one thousand. Why? He thought that he could defend that number in congressional committee hearings against whatever the air force claimed that it needed. The second reason for McNamara's choosing the higher number is that President Kennedy wanted to conclude a test ban treaty with the Soviet Union. To get a treaty through the Senate would require the support, or at least the acquiescence, of the Joint Chiefs. As it is between states, so it is between civilian and military leaders—if allies are needed one has to do some things to please them.

These examples, among many I can think of, show that civilian control is not something that simply exists by constitutional and other laws. It has to be maintained through persistence and hard work, lest civilian control of the military give way to military control of the military. In the Kennedy and Johnson administrations, the Office of the Secretary of Defense firmly controlled the military until it became bogged down in trying to run the war in Vietnam. Prior to the Eisenhower administration's "New Look" defense policy, each of the services received about one-third of the defense budget. The "New Look" sharply skewed the distribution of dollars in favor of the air force: almost 50 percent of the budget for it, approximately 30 percent for the navy, and just over 20 percent for the army. One can tell when civilians are exercising control by the yelps of protest from military officers, sometimes followed by their resignations.[11] Under President Richard M. Nixon and Defense Secretary Melvin Laird, the budgetary division among the services quickly reverted to one-third, one-third, one-third, reflecting Laird's boast that under him the United States would have a budget made by the military. Later, when he was secretary of defense, Caspar Weinberger also let the services write their own tickets; a huge waste of dollars, with little gain in strength, was the country's reward.

Civilian control is won and maintained only by constant and politically costly effort. Some states accept military control of the military, but this simply puts them in the same position that the United States too often finds itself in.

Second, Sagan believes that civilian control of the military makes the world safer, and military control of the military makes the world more dangerous. I believe that either way the world is at peril. Historically, one notices that civilian leaders are sometimes, indeed fairly often, more reckless than military officers. In Chapter 1, I gave the Crimean War as an example. Military officers who saw the war coming called it an "impossible war." As the historian Alfred Vagts wrote, "The nonmilitary were warlike and the military were not."[12] Britain and France lacked the troops that would enable them to invade the Russian heartland. Luckily for them, the czar rejected the strategy that General Kutuzov had used to defeat Napoleon: retreat, draw the enemy into Russia's vast territory, and when supply lines lengthen and troops weary, turn upon them and drive them from the land. Because the czar sat shakily on his throne, he feared that retreat would be seen as defeat and he would be deposed. For political rather than military reasons, he sent his troops to the Crimea where British and French troops, disembarking at Black Sea ports, could meet them.

Like civilian leaders, military officers have interests they cherish. The belief is widespread that, when military responses to crises are feasible, military officers favor the use of force. The belief has often proved false. The common quality of military advice is caution, as a number of examples show. In the Moroccan crises of 1905 and 1911, military ministers and officers in France and Russia warned strongly against using force. American military leaders prior to World War II urged softer diplomacy and reduced economic pressure, fearing that stronger policies would goad Japan into a war they did not want at that time. Generals George Marshall and Omar Bradley opposed General Douglas MacArthur's policy of carrying the war in Korea across the Yalu River and into Manchuria. The Pentagon in 1958 opposed sending marines to Lebanon, a policy the State Department favored. American military leaders in 1983 opposed sending troops to Grenada quickly, perhaps because they wanted first to find it on the map, and in July of 1994, Pentagon officials opposed invading Haiti.[13] Even worse, we sometimes have military control of, or heavy influence over, civil government. General Colin Powell, then Chairman of the Joint Chiefs of Staff, oversaw the writing of Defense Secretary

Caspar Weinberger's 1984 speech setting forth six criteria to be met before using American forces abroad. The so-called Weinberger Doctrine proposed that we fight only wars that can be quickly and sweetly won. In doing so, he identified the military's interest with the national interest. Publicly, Powell offered his own opinions on foreign policy "in contravention," as military historian Richard H. Kohn put it, "to the tradition of American civil-military relations since the beginning of the republic." Kohn concludes, after giving a number of examples, that for some years now we have seen "the erosion of civilian control of the military."[14] In 1992, with the famous statement, "We do deserts, we don't do mountains," Powell stoutly opposed and seriously delayed military intervention in Bosnia.[15]

What is the point? Simply this: If the weakness or absence of civilian control of the military has not led America to use its plentiful nuclear weapons, we hardly have reason to think that new nuclear countries will misuse theirs because of an absence of civilian control.

Yet Sagan is right to emphasize that military officers have at times advocated preventive wars and preemptive strikes, although one must add that so have civilians. Ultimately, the military's concern is for national security. If civilian and military leaders think that their state is strong now but that an adversary may one day surpass it, then national leaders thump for preventive war. At times military officers have urged preventive war, and political leaders have opposed it. Such cases occur not because soldiers or civilians lust for blood, but because they worry about their nation's security. Most of Sagan's examples of America's preventive-war spirit come from the early Cold War years. We once had a monopoly of nuclear weapons followed by a wide superiority. Numerical superiority did not mean much, if anything, but unsurprisingly, military *and* civilian leaders thought it did. The idea of using a temporary military edge for one's advantage finds many precedents. We should remember, however, that preventive wars have been advocated many more times than they have been fought.

The situation that invites preventive-war thinking is this: State A initially believes itself to be in a superior position and fears that it may one day be surpassed by State B [see Figure 1]. The American–Soviet picture is shown in Figure 2. Americans should easily understand the mentality that prompts preventive-war thinking. We have fought enough of them. President Bush's 1990 war against Panama was a preventive one. Nobody thought that Panama posed either a short-term or a long-term threat to the United States. We were not fighting for an American vital interest. One cannot even say what threats to our national security we were trying to prevent. Soon thereafter, in 1991, we fought another preventive war, this one against Iraq. We could easily have deterred Iraq from invading any more countries, and the world did not need Iraq's or Kuwait's oil. Iraq and Kuwait together produced about 7 percent of the world's oil supply. What we feared was that Saddam Hussein would control the large oil *reserves* of Iraq and Kuwait combined, about 20 percent of the world's total. We feared how Saddam might use oil power not at the moment but in the future. Was it plausible to say that we needed to fight a country of fewer than 19 million people in order to control the future?

To say that a war should be fought preventively requires betting that the unknowable future will be a better one if an unnecessary war is fought now instead of waiting to see if it

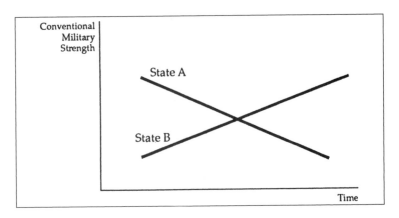

Figure 1

one day becomes necessary. "Unnecessary" means that the present threat to one's interest is not pressing. The reasoning goes this way: We do not need to fight now, but fighting now will be easy, and we'll win. Fighting later will be hard, and we may lose. To make a case for preventive war, one has to know that the balance of effective forces is roughly as the first figure shows, that the future development of forces is as depicted, and that in the end one side will fight the other. In a conventional world, the first two suppositions are suspect; in any world, the third one is as well. The second figure shows a different relation between two countries: one initially with some, or perhaps many, nuclear weapons; the other with none. If A (in this case, the United States) chooses to forego striking to prevent B (the Soviet Union) from making *any* nuclear weapons, then a later strike by A against B becomes risky even at an early stage of the competition.

Why preventive conventional wars are not often fought is an easily answered question. Why states shrink from striking to prevent other states from gaining nuclear capability in the first place may seem more puzzling. We could have strangled the Soviet nuclear baby in its crib, yet we have to wonder whether we and the world would be better off if we had done so. And would we and the world be better off now if the United States or the Soviet Union had destroyed China's budding nuclear capability in the early 1960s? One may even believe that if Israel had failed to destroy Iraq's nuclear facilities in 1981, the two countries would have soon settled into a stable, if unfriendly, relation of mutual deterrence, as others did before them.

To think that civilian leaders understand the problematic qualities of preventive-war arguments, and that military leaders do not, is wrong. Some do; some do not. The first President Bush did not. General Norman Schwarzkopf and I made the mistake of believing Bush when he said on August 7, 1990, that our response to Iraq's invasion of Kuwait would be defensive. Schwarzkopf defined his mission in accordance with what the president said: "Our mission is to deter attack, and if an attack comes, we are to defend." But on that fateful day, November 8, 1990, two days after congressional elections, Bush announced

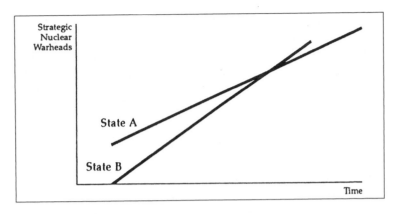

Figure 2

a decision that had been made earlier: namely, to increase America's deployment from a force of about 200,000 to a force of more than 500,000. He went from a force large enough to dissuade Saddam Hussein from further attacks to a force large enough to take the offensive. Once we moved to a force of more than half a million, which, with the additional forces of allies, made a total of more than 700,000 troops, it became hard to wait. Bush and then Secretary of Defense Richard Cheney led the way toward fighting a preventive war. Secretary of State James Baker followed with reluctance. The most reluctant of all—not surprisingly—were army and marine generals. Admirals and air force generals are often more willing to go because they believe they can win by dropping bombs and shooting weapons at distant targets. In late January of 1991, General Schwarzkopf said that "if the alternative to dying is sitting out in the sun for another summer, then that's not a bad alternative." Notice what a strong statement that was. He was not saying that we should wait a few more months but that we should be willing to sit in the desert sun for another summer. He was saying as clearly as he could, without flatly contradicting the president, that we did not need to go to war at all. We could have sat there and waited to see whether sanctions would work. If we had stuck with a much smaller force, we could have afforded to wait. Instead, our civilian leaders chose to fight.[16]

Third, Sagan believes that military leaders are more reckless and war-prone than civilian leaders are. I find this hard to believe. In the late 1930s, German generals knew that the balance of forces favored the British and French in aircraft, tanks, artillery, and manpower.[17] Their troops could have poured through the thin Siegfried Line when Germany took Austria or when it took the Sudetenland or when it took the rest of Czechoslovakia or when it invaded Poland. German generals understood this, and some of them stood against Hitler's policy. Hitler may have understood this too, but he acted on political insight rather than on military calculation, believing that France and Britain would not move. He was right, but only in the short run. Military organizations tend toward caution; civilian leaders sometimes do not.

Big and long wars work profound economic, social, political, and even cultural changes in the countries that fight them. The biggest change of all takes place in military organizations. World War II is a sufficient example. Regular military officers in the United States spent four years at West Point or Annapolis before earning commissions. Draftees, kids like me with no military background, could do four months of basic and advanced training, go to officer-candidate school for another four months, and become commissioned officers. World War II affected America's military services even more profoundly than it affected society at large.

The conservatism and restraint of soldiers and sailors is reinforced by the fact that they are not professionals. Instead, they are members of establishments. The difference is this: Professionals can hang their shingles anywhere. They can set their legal or medical practices up, work for any law firm or hospital, teach in any college or university that will have them. In contrast, members of an establishment have one legitimate employer, in this case, the military services. They may become free booters or seek non-military employment, but if they want to pursue the trade they trained for, they have to stick with the military organizations that prepared them for service. Members of an establishment develop unusually strong commitments to their organizations, making them less willing to place their group in a position of unnecessary danger.

Generals and admirals do not like to fight wars under unfamiliar conditions. The offensive use of nuclear weapons exponentially increases the uncertainties that abound on conventional battlefields. Nobody knows what a nuclear battlefield would look like, and nobody knows what would happen after a few nuclear shots were fired. *Uncertainty* about the course that a nuclear war might follow, along with *certainty* that destruction could be immense, strongly inhibits the use of nuclear weapons.

D. Second-Strike Forces

Can weak and poor states manage to deploy second-strike forces? The answer is "yes," quite easily. This answer contradicts Sagan's, and many others', belief that second-strike forces are difficult to build and deploy. Decades of American military worries feed this view. But as Bernard Brodie put it, if a "small nation could threaten the Soviet Union with only a single thermonuclear bomb, which, however, it could and would certainly deliver on Moscow," the Soviet Union would be deterred.[18] I would change that sentence by substituting "might" for "would" and by adding that the threat of a fission bomb or two would also do the trick. We now know that Britain, thinking as we did that the Soviet Union was hard to deter, pretended to have H-bombs when it had none.[19] Sagan believes that the American air force and navy had to be goaded into developing second-strike forces. He cites the Killian Report of 1955, written by civilians, as providing the push that caused the military to become concerned with the survivability of strategic weapons. In one sense, he is right. Our military services were more interested in their traditional missions and weapons than they were in nuclear deterrence. The navy's initial response to the Polaris program was to say that it was a national program, not a naval one. (Eisenhower wondered what the difference might be.) An unconventional naval officer, Hyman Rickover, drove the program through ahead of time and on budget. For this, the navy never forgave him. Congress had to add his name to the lists of officers to be promoted because the navy would not do so. Military organizations are renowned for their resistance to innovation.

Yet once a country has a small number of deliverable warheads of uncertain location, it has a second-strike force. Belatedly, some Americans and Russians realized this.[20] Former defense secretary Robert S. McNamara wrote in 1985 that the United States and the Soviet Union could get along with 2,000 warheads instead of the 50,000 they may then have had.[21] Talking at the University of California, Berkeley, in the spring of 1992, he dropped the number the United States might need to sixty. Herbert York, speaking at the Lawrence Livermore National Laboratory, which he once directed, guessed that one hundred strategic warheads would be about the right number.[22] It does not take much to deter.

The ease of deterrence raises the question of whether it was the Killian Report that pushed the military services to develop second-strike forces or whether we already had them. With more than a thousand warheads in America's arsenal and more than a hundred in the Soviet Union's hands, both had invulnerable forces. Who would dare to strike forces of that size when neither the United States nor the Soviet Union could be sure of destroying or disabling all of them? Remember that with nuclear weapons, if any part of a force is invulnerable, all of the force is invulnerable. Who will risk retaliation by the portion of a force that survives one's strike?[23] During the Cuban missile crisis, for example, the Tactical Air Command would promise only that it could destroy 90 percent of the missiles the Soviet Union had placed in Cuba. Retaliation by the remaining 10 percent was unacceptable to us. This was at the time when we thought the Soviet missiles in Cuba were backed up by only about seventy strategic warheads.[24]

Numbers are not very important. To have second-strike forces, states do not need large numbers of weapons. Small numbers do quite nicely. About one-half of the South Korean population lives in or near Seoul. North Korea can deter South Korea and the United States from invading if it can lead the South to believe that it has a few well-hidden and deliverable weapons. The requirements of second-strike deterrence have been widely and wildly exaggerated.

E. Uncertainty

Sagan thinks I put too much weight on the beneficial effects of uncertainty. Yet the effectiveness of nuclear deterrence rests on uncertainty. Because no one can be sure that a major conventional attack on a nuclear country's vital interests will not escalate to the nuclear level, it is deterred. Uncertainty about controlling escalation is at the heart of deterrence. If the United States had thought that Iraq might have had a few bombs, it would have had to manage the Iraq-Kuwait crisis differently, say, by employing only an embargo. Invasion might have prompted Iraq to dump a couple of warheads on Haifa and Tel Aviv. We would not have wanted to run the risk, and Israel surely would not have complained about our unwillingness to use force in a headlong attack. A big reason for America's resistance to the spread of nuclear weapons is that if weak countries have some they will cramp our style. Militarily punishing small countries for behavior we dislike would become much more perilous.

   Deterrence is also a considerable guarantee against accidents, since it causes countries to take good care of their weapons, and against anonymous use, since those firing the weapons can neither know that they will be undetected nor what form of punishment detection might bring. In life, uncertainties abound. In a conventional world, they more easily lead to war because less is at stake. Even so, it is difficult to think of wars that have started by accident even before nuclear weapons were invented. It is hard to believe that nuclear war may begin accidentally, when less frightening conventional wars have rarely done so.[25]

Fear of accidents works against their occurring. Again this is illustrated by the Cuban missile crisis. Accidents happened during the crisis, and unplanned events took place. An American U-2 strayed over Siberia, and one flew over Cuba. The American navy continued to play games, such as trying to force Soviet submarines to surface. In a crisis, rulers want to control all relevant actions, while knowing they cannot do so. Fear of losing control propelled Kennedy and Khrushchev to end the crisis quickly. In a conventional world, uncertainty may tempt a country to join battle. In a nuclear world, uncertainty has the opposite effect. What is not controllable is too dangerous to bear.

F. Missile Defenses and the Multiplication of Nuclear Weapons

Soon after taking office, the George W. Bush administration began preparing the public for new military policies by pronouncing that "the world is different now." Like the shaky notion that India and Pakistan are different from earlier nuclear states, the implications of the statement are seldom examined. That the world is different, and therefore military policies must be different too, is a mantra mumbled endlessly, without anyone saying what the differences are and what significance they have. The influential deputy national security adviser, Stephen J. Hadley, said that "we're talking about a whole new world."[26] Yes, the Cold War is over, and the new Russia is less menacing than the old Soviet Union. Yes, the number of nuclear states went up to twelve when the Soviet Union broke apart and then dropped to eight, with a few new ones in the offing.

Those who tout the importance of differences, however, fail to compare the supposedly new with what has remained the same. Obviously, it is not "a whole new world." Among the most important of the constants are nuclear weapons with their powerful deterrent effects. To justify the present Bush administration's attempt to revive old military policies, deterrence has to be played down and defense has to be played up. Although seldom put directly, the argument for trying to breathe life back into the Star Wars corpse is that although the strong can deter the strong as the United States and the Soviet Union did, and although the weak can deter the strong as we fear, the strong cannot deter the weak. This is not new thinking, as the present administration believes. It is old thinking tediously repeated. Secretary of Defense Rumsfeld, noting that in the Soviet Union the Politburo provided "some checks and balances," asks, "What checks and balances are there on Saddam Hussein or Kim Jong Il?"[27] Rumsfeld seemed to believe that, in the absence of internal restraints, rulers are free to use nuclear weapons and that rogues, too, might do so. One wonders what in Rumsfeld's view checked and balanced Mao Zedong. His question evokes the disproven belief that bad states cannot be deterred. Yet obviously the most effective check on them, as on others, is the military power of other states and ultimately the American nuclear deterrent.

The value of missile defenses was debated from the late 1950s onward. Earlier, as now, it was claimed that a fanatical, lightly armed nuclear state might try to blackmail its neighbors, or even attack the United States. In 1967, for example, Secretary of Defense McNamara argued for erecting defenses against China's nascent nuclear capability. He found it "conceivable" that, even though a Chinese nuclear attack on the United States or its allies would be "insane and suicidal," China might "miscalculate."[28] Obviously, it was conceivable— McNamara had just conceived of it. But for China then and for North Korea now, or for Iran or whomever, the conception is preposterous. Mao Zedong did not reign from 1949 to 1976 by pursuing insane foreign and military policies, nor did Kim Jong Il, Saddam Hussein, or other rulers of so-called rogue states.

Secretary Rumsfeld noticed that "the genie is out of the bottle. . . . People are going to have very powerful weapons. And they don't care about safety, they don't care about reliability, they don't care about making big volumes of these things. If they get them, they have power and they can alter behavior."[29] They surely are altering ours, and we have made much "bigger volumes of these things" than they ever will. Although rogues do some terrible things, if they behaved as Rumsfeld imagines, they would have awfully short careers. A secretary of defense ought to pay some attention to how other states, including bad states, behave militarily.

National missile defenses pose greater dangers to us and to others than the slow spread of nuclear weapons. The best thing about such defenses is that they won't work. The worst thing about them is that merely setting development and deployment in motion has damaging effects on us and on others.

The many reasons why defenses against nuclear weapons won't work have been rehearsed often enough. According to Rumsfeld, it does not matter if defenses do not work well. Deploying them will make would-be attackers uncertain about how many of their weapons will "slip past the shield," and uncertainty will deter them.[30] Our deterrent forces already make them tremble with fear at the thought of the destruction that might await the perpetrator of a nuclear attack. In Rumsfeld's view, that is not enough to deter, but the prospect of our shooting some things down would be. Presumably they are smart enough to calculate the problematic effects of our future defenses, but too dumb to understand the risks of launching attacks that risk their own destruction. In October of 1964, Khrushchev boasted that the Soviet Union had a new missile that could "hit a fly in the sky." That, of course, is not the problem. One would have to hit many flies in the sky after separating the flies from the fleas. Some warheads may get through, and the attacker and the attacked will both believe that.

Missile defenses would be the most complicated systems ever deployed, and they would have to work with near perfection in meeting their first realistic test—the test of enemy fire. No president will rely on such systems but will instead avoid actions that might provoke an attack. With or without defenses, the constraints on American actions are the same. The would-be attacker who doubts that some of its warheads will get through has three simple recourses. One is to multiply warheads. Since offensive nuclear weapons are much cheaper than defensive measures, that is easily done. To play nuclear defense is to play the mug's game, a game that cannot be won. McNamara, Khrushchev, Brezhnev, Caspar Weinberger, Putin, Sha Zukang, and many others have said that if "they" deploy defenses, "we" will increase the numbers of our warheads.[31] The second way to defeat defenses is by mounting decoys on missiles and spreading chaff to confuse the defense. The third way to thwart missile defenses is to avoid them. ICBMs are the least likely way a rogue state would choose to deliver warheads. Since they can easily be delivered in many other ways, why would rogues not choose the easier ones? An Indian commentator has even suggested delivery by oxcart. One can multiply the ways of placing warheads on targets. An especially bothersome way is delivery by cruise missiles. Dennis M. Gormley points out that the international commercial fleet has thousands of container ships, and American ports handle more than thirteen million containers yearly. Even bulky cruise missiles, such as Chinese Silkworms, fit into standard containers and can be fired at any port city in the world. Defending against cruise missiles is even more difficult than shooting ballistic missiles down.[32]

The threat of ballistic missile attacks by North Korea serves as an excuse, albeit a flimsy one, to build defenses that the administration hopes will be useful against China. When Secretary of State Colin Powell was briefed on the deal made by the Clinton administration to supply aid to North Korea in return for its easily verified promise not to develop and test medium- and long-range missiles, he called it "a splendid bargain."[33] His reaction less colorfully echoed George Schultz's earlier remark that trading Star Wars for reductions in the Soviet Union's nuclear arsenal would be like "giving them the sleeves off our vest."[34] The new George W. Bush administration nevertheless drew back from the arrangement that the Clinton administration had made.

If it is possible to be extremely moderate, Chinese nuclear programs have been that. A light American defense with about one hundred interceptors is expected to knock twenty-five warheads down. Impartial observers may not believe that the defenses will do that well, but China will assume that they may do even better, and it will arm itself accordingly. Where China leads, India and Pakistan will follow. The result, President Putin fears, may be "a hectic uncontrolled arms race on the borders of our country."[35] The only effective response to a nuclear threat, or to a conventional threat that one cannot meet, lies in the ability to retaliate. In the nuclear world, defense looks like offense; SDI, strategic defense initiative, should have been labeled SOI, strategic offense initiative. The shield makes the sword usable. Reagan understood the offensive implications of nuclear defenses, but played them down. With a lack of political sensibility that would be astonishing in other administrations, the present Bush administration plays them up. As Bush has said, "They seek weapons of mass destruction . . . to keep the United States and other responsible nations from helping allies and friends in strategic parts of the world."[36] In short, we want to be able to intervene militarily whenever and wherever we choose. Our nuclear defenses would presumably make that possible even against countries lightly armed with nuclear weapons.

The first effect of developing defenses is to cause other states to multiply the number of their nuclear weapons and to think of sneaky ways of delivering them. President Putin has said that if the Anti–Ballistic Missile (ABM) Treaty is abrogated, then other arms-control treaties of the past thirty years will be nullified. The 1993 treaty providing for the eventual elimination of missiles with multiple warheads was a proud achievement of the first Bush administration. It was confirmed in the Start II agreement ratified by Russia in the year 2000. The cheapest way for Russia to overcome fears that American defenses will diminish their deterrent, however, is to place more warheads on their land-based missiles, one of the most dangerous forms of nuclear weaponry. The new Bush administration surpasses Clinton's in foolishness. An official of Clinton's administration told Russian officials that if our potential defenses should make Russia uneasy, it could simply keep a thousand missiles on full alert.[37] To implement Bush's and

Rumsfeld's dreams of defense is more dangerous for us and the world than a small number of nuclear weapons in the hands of India and Pakistan, or North Korea or Iraq for that matter. Nuclear defenses destroy arms-control agreements. Agreements to control and reduce nuclear weapons are more useful than attempts to defend against them.

Some countries want us to be able to intervene militarily on their behalf; others do not. Given American nuclear and conventional dominance, what are the latter countries to do? Our dominance presses them to find ways of blocking our interventionist moves. As ever, dominance, coupled with immoderate behavior by one country, causes others to look for ways to protect their interests. China wants to incorporate Taiwan if only in loose form. Even if China has no intention of using force, and clearly it prefers not to, it believes that the prospect of American military protection of Taiwan removes the threat of force from China's set of diplomatic tools. Taiwan will have less reason to compromise. China reacts as one would expect it to. Acquiring Russian Oscar II class submarines, capable of disabling our aircraft carriers, is one response. Another is maintaining a minimal nuclear deterrent against the United States.

American intelligence reports that our defenses may prompt China to multiply its nuclear arsenal by ten and to place multiple warheads on its missiles.[38] The mere prospect of American missile defense promotes the vertical proliferation of nuclear weapons. It also encourages the horizontal spread of nuclear weapons from one country to another. Japan, already made uneasy by China's increasing economic and military capabilities, will become uneasier still as China acts to counter America's prospective defenses. Since the George W. Bush administration rendered the fabric of agreements that brought nuclear weapons under a modicum of control, and since we offer nothing to replace it, other countries try harder to take care of themselves. North Korea, Iran, and others believe that America can be held at bay only by deterrence. Iraq believed this too. Weapons of mass destruction are the only means by which they can hope to deter the United States. They cannot hope to do so by relying on conventional weapons. During the Cold War we used nuclear weapons to offset the Soviet Union's conventional strength. Other countries may now use nuclear weapons to offset ours. Les Aspin, when he was chairman of the house Armed Services Committee, put this thought in the following words: "A world without nuclear weapons would not be disadvantageous to the United States. In fact, a world without nuclear weapons would actually be better. Nuclear weapons are still the big equalizer, but now the United States is not the equalizer but the equalizee."[39]

Our conventional dominance spurs other countries to resort to unconventional means. To understand others' reactions we have to look to our own behavior. George W. Bush emphasized our readiness to consult other countries. In his lexicon, "consult" means that we explain our policies and then implement them whether other countries like them or not. "One reads about the world's desire for American leadership only in the United States," a British diplomat has observed. "Everywhere else one reads about American arrogance and unilateralism."[40] When we add to dominance and arrogance the unwillingness to ratify treaties made and the intention to renounce treaties ratified, we have a recipe for encouraging other states to go nuclear. The United States led the way in negotiating the Comprehensive Test Ban Treaty. One hundred and eighty-three countries had signed the treaty as of April 9, 2012, and one hundred and fifty-seven had ratified it. Yet administration officials now look for ways of escaping from the treaty's restrictions. Moreover, in recent years we have pursued ways of improving the design of warheads and enhancing their power by using such methods as computer simulations, methods in which our abilities far exceed those of others.[41] Why should we not welcome a treaty that so clearly serves our interests? We hope that other countries will reduce the number of their nuclear weapons while we build defenses and improve our weapons. If this fantasy were to become reality, America would be able to act on its whims whenever and wherever it chose to. Because other countries know this, our policies promote the spread of nuclear weapons both upwards and sideways.

Over a span of six decades, relations among nuclear countries have been peaceful beyond historical precedent. Nuclear pessimists have a simple explanation for this: We have been lucky. Kanti Bajpai believes that deterrence is "fragile and fraught" and in the long run unstable. Apparently, fifty-some years is not a long enough run to confirm the stability of nuclear deterrence. General George Lee Butler, commander of STRATCOM before his retirement in 1994, believes that "we escaped disaster by the grace of God."[42] God may, as Otto von Bismarck said, watch out for "fools, drunkards, and the United States."[43] Yet one wonders why He should favor the United States and just those other nations with nuclear weapons while showing little mercy for many others. If indeed the world has skirted nuclear disaster by sustained good luck or by God's grace, then it would be high time to take matters in our own hands. Those who credit the good-luck explanation sometimes propose remedies. Butler's is the abolition of nuclear weapons. Michael Mandelbaum's and Eliot Cohen's is preventive strikes at the nuclear facilities of would-be nuclear states.[44] Reagan's was, and Bush's is, nuclear defense.

Fortunately, all such remedies are fanciful. They would deny the peaceful benefits of nuclear weapons to those who need them. It is far more sensible to face the fact that nuclear weapons are here to stay, and that once in a long while they will spread to another country or two. We should ask how we can continue to reap the benefits of nuclear weapons while reducing the dangers inherent in them. Two obvious ways are by reducing the numbers in the absurdly large arsenals of the United States and Russia and by taking weapons off hair-trigger alert. Dropping defensive measures is a third way.

Even though in the nuclear business deterrence is cheap and easy while defense is costly and difficult, our thought seems to be that we can mount effective defenses because we have the money and the technology that others lack. When one side mounts defenses, however, others seek ways to defeat or outflank them. With conventional weapons, this may be difficult.

With nuclear weapons, it is easy. Nuclear defenses attempt to pose an absolute defense against an absolute weapon. The logic of nuclear defense is the logic of conventional warfare. Conventional war pits weapons against weapons. That is exactly what nuclear defenses would do, thereby recreating the instabilities that plague countries armed only with conventional weapons. We know the dangers of offensive/defensive races from centuries of experience with conventional weapons. The major mischief of American defensive efforts is not only that they may sharpen the efforts of a few countries to make their own nuclear weapons but also that they may recreate the contest between offense and defense with all its unfortunate consequences. Why should anyone want to replace stable deterrence with unstable defense?

How can we perpetuate peace without solving the problem of war? This is the question that states with nuclear weapons must constantly answer. Nuclear states continue to compete militarily. With each state tending to its interests as best it can, war is constantly possible. Although the possibility of war remains, nuclear weapons have drastically reduced the probability of its being fought by states having them. Wars that might bring nuclear weapons into play have become extraordinarily hard to start. Over the centuries, great powers have fought more wars and lesser states have fought fewer. The frequency of war has correlated less closely with the attributes of states than with their international standing. Yet, because of a profound change in military technology, waging war has more and more become the privilege of poor and weak states. Nuclear weapons have reversed the fates of strong and weak states. Never in modern history have great powers enjoyed a longer period of peace than we have known since the Second World War. One can scarcely believe that the presence of nuclear weapons does not greatly help to explain this happy condition.

CONCLUSION

In the conclusion I make three points. They reinforce what I have said earlier and add a little to it.

First, we can play King Canute if we wish to, but like him, we will be unable to hold the (nuclear) tides at bay. Nuclear weapons have spread slowly; conventional weapons have proliferated, and their destructiveness has grown alarmingly. Nuclear weapons are relatively cheap, and they work against the outbreak of major wars. For some countries, the alternative to nuclear weapons is to run ever-more expensive conventional arms races, with increased risk of fighting highly destructive wars.

Second, Sagan and others use the term "deterrence theory" or even "rational deterrence theory." Deterrence is not a theory. Instead, deterrent policies derive from structural theory, which emphasizes that the units of an international-political system must tend to their own security as best they can. The means available for doing so shape the policies of states and, when nuclear weapons become available, lead them to take deterrent stances even though they may still talk about the need to be able to defend and to fight for their nations' security. In applying theories, one considers salient conditions in the world, and nothing is more salient than nuclear weapons. Moreover, deterrence does not rest on rationality, whatever that term might mean. By a simple definition, one is rational if one is able to reason. A little reasoning leads to the conclusions that to fight nuclear wars is impossible and that to launch an offensive that might prompt nuclear retaliation is obvious folly.[45] To reach those conclusions, complicated calculations are not required, only a little common sense. Deterrence does not depend on rationality. It depends on fear. To create fear, nuclear weapons are the best possible means.

Third, new nuclear countries may, as Sagan says, lack safety devices for their weapons and may not have developed bureaucratic routines for controlling them. The smaller a force is, however, the more easily it can be guarded. States with large arsenals and faulty bureaucratic routines may accidentally fire warheads in large numbers. States with small arsenals cannot do so. Blair and Kendall estimated that a Soviet attack accidentally launched against us might have resulted in as many as three hundred warheads falling on the United States. In response, as many as five hundred of our warheads might then have been launched against the Soviet Union.[46] A policy of launch on warning makes no sense. If a country is struck, retaliation at leisure and calibration of one's response in an attempt to bring de-escalation is called for. Only big nuclear powers can implement the frightening practices we follow. Little ones cannot because they don't have the stuff.

As ever in international politics, the biggest dangers come from the biggest powers; the smallest from the smallest. We should be more fearful of old nuclear countries and less fearful of recent and prospective ones. Efforts should concentrate more on making large arsenals safe and less on keeping weak states from obtaining the small number of warheads they may understandably believe they need for security.

Chapter 4

SAGAN RESPONDS TO WALTZ

Scott D. Sagan

There are two basic kinds of errors that one can make in assessing nations other than one's own. The first error is rooted in ethnocentrism. This is a common mistake Americans make when looking at others: we too often assume that other nations are less competent, less intelligent, and less rational than the United States. Kenneth Waltz has performed an important service in this regard: his analysis of nuclear proliferation is a valuable corrective against such ethnocentrism and the blind spots it can create among both scholars and government officials. He is absolutely correct, in my view, to criticize a number of proliferation pessimists who argue, in effect, that the United States has been perfect in handling nuclear weapons (but others will not be), that the United States can control these awesome weapons forever (but no one else can), or that the United States has utterly unproblematic civil-military relations (but no one else does). Waltz's analysis should serve as a constant reminder of how dangerous it is in international affairs to assume, to put it crudely, that the United States is smart, but that other nuclear states are or will be stupid.

This is a revised version of my 2003 essay from the second edition of this book.

The second basic error, however, is the opposite: to assume that others are better than we are. This is, I believe, the central problem with Kenneth Waltz's arguments about the consequences of proliferation. He appears to now accept many of the arguments made by scholars who have studied the operational accidents and near-accidents, conflicts in civil-military relations, and other organizational problems experienced by the United States during the Cold War. Yet he maintains that other states will do better, will be smarter, will learn more quickly, will, in short, avoid the kinds of errors that we have suffered in the past. I believe, in contrast, that there are both strong theoretical reasons and empirical evidence to expect that new nuclear states will not avoid such problems. New nuclear powers may not make exactly the same mistakes as their predecessors; but they are likely to make their own serious errors, and some will be deadly.

The Roots of the Disagreement

What lies at the heart of our disagreement? Let me start by strongly emphasizing what we do *not* disagree about. First, we do not disagree about the awesome destructive power of nuclear weapons. These weapons are horrendous. They dwarf conventional and even chemical weapons in their destructive potential. A single nuclear weapon can virtually destroy a modern city, an unprecedented level of destruction packed into a single bomb. Second, we do not, for the most part, disagree on the normative question of how states *should* behave in response to the nuclear revolution. Nuclear states *should* be exceedingly cautious; they should place a high priority on nuclear weapons safety; they should build secure second-strike retaliatory forces for the sake of stable deterrence.[1]

What we disagree about is in some ways more fundamental. Waltz and I hold very different views about how best to explain and predict the behavior of states. While we may agree about how nuclear states should behave in an *ideal* world (if any nuclear world can be called ideal), we strongly disagree about how nuclear states actually do behave in the *real* world. Our different visions of international politics have led us to develop very different interpretations of our nuclear past and very different predictions of the nuclear future.

Waltz's optimism is fueled by a strong belief that the constraints of the international system, and the potential costs of any nuclear war, will produce similar, and essentially rational, decisions in all states. As he puts it, "Whatever the identity of rulers, and whatever the characteristics of their states, the national behaviors they produce are strongly conditioned by the world outside" (Ch. 5, p. 165). This assumption, that states will recognize and act in their "objective" interests, as determined by external forces, undergirds his entire argument. In contrast, my pessimism is fueled by the belief that the military and other government organizations play a very important intervening role between the interests of statesmen and the behavior of states. The information these organizations pass on, the plans and routines they develop, and the biases they hold continually shape the actions of states in very important ways.

Waltz stresses the unprecedented power of nuclear weapons and argues that "nobody but an idiot can fail to comprehend their destructive force[.] What more is there to learn?" (Ch. 3, p. 89). Unfortunately, there is a lot more to learn. States have to learn how to avoid accidents, how to prevent terrorists from stealing their weapons, how to build survivable forces, how to control their militaries, and how to limit escalation. All political leaders may well desire such reasonable things. Yet, between the desire and the deed lies the shadow of organizations. The difficult tasks of proper organizational design and management are not automatically achieved simply because senior statesmen understand the effects of nuclear weapons. And they certainly are not guaranteed to exist in every state that develops these horribly destructive weapons.

In this chapter, I will first respond to each of the six important issues that Waltz discusses in his spirited defense of "proliferation optimism": nuclear terrorism, accidents, civilian control and preventive war, building survivable second-strike forces, the effects of uncertainty, and national missile defense. I will then analyze future U.S. policy options with respect to nuclear nonproliferation. In the conclusion, I will offer some final observations about this debate and its importance to international relations theory and practice.

Terrorism and Nuclear Weapons

Before the World Trade Center and Pentagon attacks on September 11, 2001, many international security specialists claimed that terrorists were not interested in creating mass fatalities. Before the October 2001 anthrax attacks in Florida, Washington, and New York, many specialists also insisted that public fears that terrorists would use weapons of mass destruction were unwarranted. Brian Jenkin's 1975 aphorism—"Terrorists want a lot of people watching and a lot of people listening, but not a lot of people dead"—was widely quoted in the literature. This view of terrorists' motives, Jenkins argued, helped explain why "terrorists have not done some of the terribly damaging and terrifying things they could do, such as poisoning a city's water supply, spreading chemical or biological agents, or other things that could produce mass casualties."[2] As late as 1998, despite growing concerns after the 1995 Aum Shinrikyo gas attacks in the Tokyo subway, terrorism expert Ehud Sprinzak repeated that optimistic prediction, insisting that "the chances of a successful superterrorism attack are minimal" and arguing that public and governmental "obsession" with superterrorism was due to "sloppy thinking," government agencies' "vested interests" in increasing their budgets, and the "morbid fascination" of "suspense writers, publishers, television networks, and sensationalist journalists."[3]

After the events of September 11, 2001, no one doubts that terrorists might be interested in killing a lot of people. But two questions remain worth discussing in our effort to understand how serious the risk of nuclear terrorism is in the future. First, what kinds of terrorists are interested in seeing "a lot of people dead"? Second, what is the relationship, if any, between the spread of nuclear weapons to increased numbers of states and the danger that terrorist organizations will get and use nuclear weapons? Kenneth Waltz and I largely agree on the first question; but we are in strong disagreement on the second question.

Three general kinds of terrorist groups are the most likely ones to seek nuclear and radiological weapons: millenarian groups, who think the end of the world is just over the horizon; neo-Nazis and other racist hate groups, who seek to kill people because of their religious or racial identity; and Islamic Jihadi groups who believe that mass murder is both morally justified and effective in pursuing their political objective of creating radical Islamic governments in the Middle East.

The Aum Shinrikyo—which tried (unsuccessfully) to get nuclear weapons and which used biological weapons ineffectively before the 1995 Tokyo subway chemical weapons attack—is the best known example of a millenarian terrorist group.[4] Its leader, Shoko Asahara, claimed both that he had achieved enlightenment, like the Buddha, and that he was the Christian Messiah. He frequently told his followers that Armageddon would soon engulf the world and that only his followers would survive. Asahara's efforts to acquire biological agents (such as anthrax, botulinum, and the Ebola virus) and nuclear weapons appear to have been motivated by a belief that his use of such weapons might hasten the coming apocalypse. A radical Christian terrorist group in the United States—the Covenant, the Sword, and the Arm of the Lord (CSA)—held similar apocalyptic views in the mid-1980s. The CSA journal argued that communists, "witches and Satanic Jews," blacks, homosexuals, and Cuban refugees were forces of evil that must be destroyed, and CSA members tried to use cyanide to poison water supplies in major American cities. One of the CSA members best explained the logic of this kind of terrorism in an interview from prison:

> God wanted us to kill those people. The original timetable was up to God, but God could use us in creating Armageddon. That if we stepped out things might be hurried

along. You get tired of waiting for what you think God is planning.[5]

Terrorists in the second category—neo-Nazi and other racist organizations—have one similar characteristic: they believe they have a duty to use weapons of mass destruction. William Pierce, the head of the neo-Nazi organization National Alliance, wrote about right-wing extremists using nuclear weapons and biological weapons to take over the world in his fantasy novel *The Turner Diaries*. "We are in a war for the survival of our race," Pierce argues, "that ultimately we cannot win . . . except by killing our enemies."[6] Larry Harris, a member of both the National Alliance and the Aryan Nation organizations, succeeded in getting vials of bubonic plague bacteria in 1995 by ordering materials for research for a fake microbiology laboratory. Harris was caught when he called the company that sent the bacteria to complain that it had not yet arrived and then told an investigating official from the Center for Disease Control (CDC) that he needed plague bacteria to conduct biomedical research on how to counter the "imminent invasion from Iraq of super germ-carrying rats." After Harris's arrest, the CDC tightened up the rules for ordering toxins and infectious agents for research.[7] After Amber Cummings shot and killed her husband James G. Cummings in Belfast, Maine in February 2009, investigators discovered that he was a Neo-Nazi and at the time of his death he was planning to set off a dirty bomb during President Obama's inauguration. A leaked FBI Field Intelligence Report revealed a number of items that could be used to build a dirty bomb: four small jars of uranium; two jars of thorium; four one-gallon containers of 35% hydrogen peroxide; lithium metal; thermite; aluminum powder; beryllium; boron; black iron oxide; and magnesium ribbon. Literature on "dirty bombs," referencing cesium-137, strontium-90, and cobalt-60 were also found. Wife Amber Cummings stated that James would mix chemicals in the kitchen sink and often spoke of dirty bombs.[8]

Such terrorists may try to get nuclear weapons and it is difficult to see how a strategy of deterrence could succeed against individuals or groups who believe their duty or their God calls for mass murder. The threat to retaliate can have little deterrent effect on those for whom mass destruction is an objective, not a fear. The first line of defense must be to prevent such terrorist organizations from even getting close to acquiring nuclear weapons or nuclear materials.

The third category is Islamic Jihadi terrorists, like Osama bin Laden and the Al Qaida network, the perpetrators of the September 11 attacks. Before September 11, bin Laden was quite open in stating his desire for nuclear weapons. Indeed, after he declared a jihad (holy war) against the United States, he was asked about reports that he wanted nuclear weapons and replied that "to possess the weapons that could counter those of the infidels is a religious duty."[9] Waltz argues that such terrorists use mass murder of civilians because they want to punish the United States for what they see as an evil U.S. foreign policy. I think that is correct, and bin Laden said as much in his May 1998 warning that "we do not differentiate between those dressed in military uniforms and civilians":

> We must use such punishment to keep your evil away from Muslims, Muslim children, and women. American history does not distinguish between civilians and military, and not even women and children. They are the ones who used the bombs against Nagasaki. Can these bombs distinguish between infants and military? . . . We believe that the biggest thieves in the world and the terrorists are the Americans. The only way for us to fend off these assaults is to use similar means.[10]

Hatred and shame and a desire to punish Americans motivate such terrorist ravings. But I also fear that there is considerable method to bin Laden's madness. Immediately after the September 11 attacks, many observers wondered how bin Laden could think that he could get away with killing six thousand American citizens. How could such an attack serve his political purpose of overthrowing conservative Muslim regimes in the Middle East and destroying Israel, given that a massive U.S. military response was inevitable? The answer is that there is a kind of a strategic logic behind his use of mass murder, a logic that he also outlined in interviews. Two factors appear to be important: his belief that the U.S. public lacks the will to support a long war and his hope that large-scale U.S. intervention in the Middle East would destabilize the regimes that he seeks to overthrow.

In May 1998, bin Laden clearly expressed his views about the lack of U.S. willingness to fight long wars:

> We have seen in the last decade the decline of the American government and the weakness of the American soldier who is ready to wage Cold Wars and unprepared to fight long wars. This was proven in Beirut when the Marines fled after two explosions. It also proves they can run in less than 24 hours, and this was also repeated in Somalia. We are ready for all occasions. We rely on Allah.[11]

In addition, he argued that the Saudi government would eventually fall because of its support for the United States, just as the Shah's government fell in the Iranian revolution. U.S. military activities in the region could increase the likelihood of an uprising from the streets and mosques. "We predict that the Riyadh leader and those with him that stood with the Jews and the Christians . . . will disintegrate. They have left the Muslim nation." Bin Laden concluded that "the Muslims are moving toward liberating the Muslim worlds. Allah willing, we will win."[12]

In August 2004, the London Metropolitan Police arrested Dhiren Barot. Barot had been working with al-Qaeda to formulate a number of attacks against western targets, including targeting the IMF and World Bank buildings and the New York Stock Exchange. After a "scouting" operation in the U.S., Barot went to London and obtained falsified student identification cards to libraries at Brunel University and University College, London, to carry out research on chemical and radiological terrorist attacks.[13] Documents found in his possession—

"Final Presentation," "Hazards," and "Rough Presentation on the Gas Limos Project"—were shown to al-Qaeda leaders in Pakistan. "Final Presentation" examines the potential of using radiological dispersal devices in terrorist attacks, listing potentially available radioactive sources such as americium-241, cobalt-60, and californium-252.[14] In "Gas Limos Project" Barot recommends using up to 10,000 smoke detectors placed on explosive devices in a contained area to disperse americium-147, an idea he took from a report in the 2003 *World Almanac* that the explosion of 900 smoke detectors harmed 40 people. He writes: "the burning of 10,000 has the potential to affect around 500 people! (*Inshalla*)."[15]

Any terrorist leader with this strategic vision, whether it is bin Laden or a successor in the Al Qaida or a similar terrorist network, is not likely be deterred from using nuclear weapons or radiological weapons against the United States. U.S. threats to use conventional military forces to kill or capture such a terrorist may not be believed since such an effort could require a long and drawn out military campaign. It is also possible that nuclear weapons could be delivered in a covert manner (by a commercial airline or ship, by a cruise missile, or by truck). In such cases, deterrence would fail since the perpetrator would believe that there was no return address against which to retaliate. Finally, even if the perpetrator of such an attack was known, Jihadi terrorists might welcome U.S. threats to retaliate in kind, since the U.S. use of nuclear weapons could hasten the downfall of allied regimes in the Muslim world through protests in the mosques and riots in the streets.

Because deterrence will not work, the best way, by far, to prevent Jihadi terrorists from ever using nuclear weapons is to prevent them from ever possessing such weapons. This anti-terrorist imperative adds yet one more compelling reason why the spread of nuclear weapons to potential proliferant states is to be feared, not welcomed. The best way, by far, to prevent Islamic terrorists from possessing nuclear weapons is to prevent unstable states, especially unstable Islamic states, from possessing nuclear weapons.

Pakistan is clearly the most serious concern in the short run. Pakistani weapons lack the advanced Permissive Actions Link (PALs) locks that make it difficult for a terrorist or other unauthorized individual to use a stolen nuclear weapon. In June 2001, Pakistani officials also acknowledged that there were no specialized Pakistani teams trained on how to seize or dismantle a nuclear weapon if one was stolen. No dedicated personnel reliability program (PRP) was in place to ensure the psychological stability and reliability of the officers and guards of Pakistan's nuclear forces.[16] Instead, Pakistani soldiers and scientists with nuclear responsibilities were reviewed and approved for duty if they were not suspected of being Indian agents by the Inter Services Intelligence (ISI) agency.

It was clear after September 11, however, that this organizational arrangement was an inadequate answer to the vexing question of who would guard the guardians. After Pakistani president Musharraf decided to support the U.S. war against bin Laden and the Taliban regime, he forced a number of senior and junior officers of the ISI to leave office because of their ties to the Taliban (and to Al Qaida as well, in some cases) and placed a smaller number of nuclear scientists from the Pakistani program under house arrest.[17] This was certainly reassuring news, but it remains unknown how many secret Jihadi supporters still exist inside the shadows of Pakistan's military intelligence agencies. Nor do we know how close those shadows fall to nuclear weapons storage sites.

Prior to the September 11 attacks, the U.S. government had maintained that it would not assist new nuclear powers in making their arsenals more safe and secure for fear that this would signal other potential nuclear powers that the U.S. was not serious about its nonproliferation policy. The terrorist attacks forced a reevaluation of this policy and led to an emergency U.S. government effort to assist in providing increased security for Pakistani nuclear weapons and nuclear materials storage sites.[18] The fear among some policymakers in Islamabad also clearly increased. Despite the earlier assurances by the Pakistani Foreign Ministry that Pakistani "(nuclear) assets are

100 percent secure," Pakistani foreign minister Sattar quickly accepted at least some degree of U.S. technical assistance in nuclear security improvements in November 2001. When asked whether Pakistan would accept the new U.S. offer of assistance, Sattar answered, "Who would refuse?"[19] Although no details about the U.S. assistance program have been released by the U.S. government, press reports suggest that $100 million were spent by the U.S. on training and technology assistance for the Pakistani nuclear establishment.[20]

Kenneth Waltz and other proliferation optimists have assumed that the weapons of new nuclear states will remain in the hands of the central governments that built them. This assumption is not warranted. The risk of terrorist seizure of nuclear weapons or material is yet one more reason why we should fear nuclear proliferation. The spread of nuclear weapons to new states in the Islamic world will place tools of indiscriminate destruction closer and closer to the hands of terrorists, who will use them without fear of retaliation.

Accidents: Are They Likely?

Before the 1979 Three Mile Island accident, there was a widespread view among many specialists and much of the public that the risk of a reactor catastrophe was extremely low and that nuclear power had been rendered safe.[21] Before the 1985 space shuttle *Challenger* accident, NASA's confidence about space launch safety was so high that teachers and politicians were being permitted to join shuttle crews.[22] Throughout most of the Cold War, there was, I believe, a similar, significant underestimation of the risks of nuclear weapons accidents and even accidental nuclear war. Part of the reason for this underestimation was that we lacked adequate theories about the underlying political and organizational causes of accidents with hazardous technologies: only after Three Mile Island, Bhopal, and Chernobyl did social scientists enter the field in a significant way.[23] The other reason for this major underestimation, however, was more political in nature: there were strong reasons for the organizations that "control" nuclear weapons to insist that their safety record was unblemished. Even after serious accidents, such as when a nuclear bomber crashed in Greenland in 1968 or a nuclear missile blew up in Arkansas in 1980, the public was told that there were no serious risks involved. "Don't worry, be happy" was the message.

We now know better. Indeed, the history of the U.S. experience with nuclear weapons is being reevaluated in light of the number of nuclear accidents and near-accidents, false warning incidents, and other organizational snafus uncovered by scholars such as Bruce Blair, Paul Bracken, Peter Feaver, and myself. [24] Given this emerging evidence, even a hard-core neorealist like Waltz does not ignore the evidence that everything has not been perfectly safe inside the U.S. nuclear arsenal. He is certainly right to conclude now that, despite improvements made at the end of the Cold War, serious safety and security problems remain in the existing nuclear arsenals in the 1990s. Waltz is also correct, in my view, to argue that the United States maintains larger numbers of weapons at much higher states of readiness than are necessary in the post–Cold War world. Instead of concluding, however, that the fact that the richest and strongest nuclear powers have had serious problems maintaining nuclear safety suggests that others will also suffer accidents, Waltz concludes the opposite. New members of the nuclear club will have fewer safety problems than the experienced ones. Why?

Waltz outlines three arguments for why new states will not have accidents: the small size of their arsenals, their fear of retaliation, and the possibility of learning over time. Each of these points is highly debatable. Let me take them in turn.

First, it may be true that the smaller the number of weapons, the less likely an accident, other things being equal. Unfortunately, in real life, other things are rarely equal. What produces the likelihood of accidents is not just the size of an arsenal, but rather the technical characteristics of the weapons themselves and the organizational characteristics of the arsenal. On the technical side, the evidence presented in Chapter 2 provides strong reasons to worry about whether new nuclear states' weapons will be designed in a safe manner. The Pakistani and Indian experience shows that similar technical design problems can emerge and produce serious accidents with nuclear delivery systems and false warnings of attack from command-and-control and warning systems in new nuclear states. On the organizational side, the key issue concerns not the size, but the structure of any new state's arsenal. Is it complex and tightly-coupled? Here one needs to assess the command and control systems, the warning systems, and the launch doctrines of new nuclear states. States that develop complex arsenals and command systems, and operate their weapons on high-alert levels in order to permit rapid launches, will be more accident-prone than states that do not adopt such force structures.

Second, Waltz argues that new nuclear states will greatly fear retaliation, and will therefore make sure that their weapons are not used by accident or in an unauthorized manner. This is likely to be a leader's desire, but will it be the state's behavior? It is difficult to know, because strong contradictory pressures would exist in most new nuclear powers. On the one hand, strong incentives would certainly exist to keep such forces under very tight, centralized control. On the other hand, strong incentives would also exist to loosen such control in order to increase the likelihood that forces could retaliate after a first strike.[25]

Small arsenal size can have the opposite effect than what Waltz predicts. Fearing that an attack might destroy its forces, a small nuclear power will likely feel greater incentives to use increased missile alerts or unsafe aircraft operations (such as airborne alert), which inherently raise risks of accidents. Moreover, fearing a "decapitation" attack on its central leadership bunkers (as the United States tried to do to Iraq with conventional weapons in the Gulf War), the leader of a small nuclear power will feel incentives to delegate authority to alternative commanders in crises. Either policy increases the risks of accidents and unauthorized uses of nuclear weapons.

What is the evidence from new nuclear states? Good and bad news coexist here. On the positive side, some new nuclear nations—such as India, Pakistan, and North Korea—have thus far refrained from deploying alert weapons in peacetime, preferring to maintain "a bomb in the basement." This policy significantly reduces the risks of accidents and should be strongly encouraged, as I noted in Chapter 2. On the negative side, however, there are signs that new nuclear states are alerting their weapons in crises, using nuclear forces as signaling devices or preparing them for possible deliberate use in ways that also invariably raise the risks of accidental or unauthorized use. During the October 1973 Arab-Israeli war, for example, U.S. intelligence agencies picked up signals that Israel had started to placed its nuclear weapons on fighter-bomber aircraft, which were readied for immediate launch.[26] Similar though unconfirmed reports exist that Israel also placed nuclear-tipped Jericho missiles on a high state of alert readiness during the Persian Gulf War in January 1991.[27] Finally, the evidence that Pakistan initiated some form of nuclear-altering activity during the 1999 Kargil conflict and 2001 terrorism crisis suggests that South Asian nuclear powers respond to similar pressures to take dangerous operational steps with their nuclear arsenals in crises.

Third, Waltz argues that because new states, especially poor states, can "build sizable forces only over long periods of time, they have time to learn how to care for them" (Ch. 3, p. 88). This is true of some, but not of all new nuclear powers. Some, like the former republics of the USSR, were born nuclear, inheriting very large nuclear arsenals rather than slowly building their own small arsenals. Indeed, on its first day as an independent state, Ukraine possessed an estimated 4,000 nuclear weapons, Kazakhstan some 1,400 weapons, and Belarus around 800 weapons.[28] We are therefore especially fortunate that these powers gave up their nuclear status and returned their weapons to Russia. Moreover, even for other more traditional cases of slower proliferation, learning to operate forces safely is not likely to be an easy task. Some states may gain valuable information from older nuclear powers: the United States reportedly shared some design information with France, and China reportedly was involved in the design of the Pakistani bomb.[29] Other states, however, are left to cope on their own and will experience more serious problems, as occurred in the Iraqi and South African cases. Finally, organizational learning is not just a matter of time and experience; it is also a matter of sharing information and blame, and therefore, the structure of political power within the state is important. In states in which civil-military relations are problematic or where the military is in power, there are likely to be strong inhibitions against organizational learning since this would require that the military services accept the blame for any accidents or near-accidents that occur.

Civilian Control and Preventive War

Waltz is clearly much less concerned than I am about the possibility that new nuclear powers will be the victims of a preventive attack by their neighbors or other adversaries. There are two related disagreements here. First, Waltz and I differ on preventive war because we differ on how quickly and with what degree of confidence new states will develop *what potential attackers* see as survivable second-strike forces. Second, we disagree over whether civilian and military leaders are likely to differ in their attitudes toward the costs and benefits of preventive war once nuclear weapons are involved in the equation.

Waltz argues that preventive attacks are untenable because only a very small number of weapons are needed for deterrence. He therefore asserts that two or three weapons in North Korea will deter attacks and argues that the United States and the Soviet Union clearly had survivable second-strike forces in 1954, when the U.S. had some 1,500 weapons and the USSR had what the CIA estimated to be between 150 and 700 weapons. What matters for stable deterrence, of course, is *not* what Kenneth Waltz, or Scott Sagan, or any other scholar thinks is a sufficient retaliatory force. What matters is what an adversary state's decision makers think. Looking at the large arsenals that existed in 1954, Waltz asks, "Who would dare to strike forces of that size?" Well, quite a few people. As I noted in Chapter 2, many of the senior leaders of the U.S. military—Curtis LeMay, Orvil Anderson, Nathan Twining, Thomas Power, Thomas White, Hoyt Vandenberg, and Arthur Radford—advocated striking a preventive blow at the USSR during this period. Even as late as 1961, the chairman of the Joint Chiefs of Staff could tell President Kennedy that the United States would "prevail in [the] event of general nuclear war" with the USSR, even though the Soviet Union had what was then estimated to be an arsenal of approximately five hundred strategic nuclear weapons.[30]

The second disagreement is over whether civilians hold different views on the use of force. Waltz thinks that I worry too much about civilian control of the military in new nuclear states. (I agree with the general thrust of Waltz's first point in this section—that the United States has had problematic civil-military relations at times—yet I fail to see how this is comforting.) Waltz insists that military officers are not "more reckless and war-prone than civilian leaders" and presents a number of compelling examples. I agree in general, but not concerning the specific issue of *preventive war*.

Military officers certainly do tend to be highly conservative and cautious, as Waltz and I both note. Yet, that is precisely why they often have biases in favor of preventive war. Generals usually do not like war—"it spoils the army" one czarist officer said[31]—and often are highly opposed to military interventions; yet, if military officers believe that the use of force is necessary, they want to use it in as large and decisive a manner as possible. Here I would draw precisely the opposite lesson from the example that Waltz uses to show how conservative military planning works against preventive attacks. Waltz notes that the Tactical Air Command's senior commander, General Walter Sweeney, could not promise to destroy 100 percent of the nuclear missiles found in Cuba during the 1962 crisis, but rather only 90 percent. What Waltz does not note, however, is that Sweeney nevertheless told President Kennedy that "he was certain that the air strike would be 'successful.'"[32] Indeed, despite the inability to strike all the missiles, the Joint Chiefs of Staff strongly urged the Kennedy administration to attack the sites immediately in a preventive strike on October 20 (before the missiles were deemed operational), and then on October 27, after the Soviet missiles became operational, the Joint Chiefs of Staff again recommended that the United States attack the sites and then invade Cuba.[33] The military was conservative and cautious all right, but that did not lead to restraint.

Let me be very clear. Military officers are not more reckless or war-prone than are civilians. They often do, however, hold strong biases in favor of preventive war. The professional military, like members of any organization, have biases and blindspots. Military officers think that war is more likely in the long run than does the general population. Military officers, like members of other organizations, plan incrementally, which leads them to focus on achieving today's war aims, not on tomorrow's postwar problems. Like members of any organization, military officers focus on their narrow set of responsibilities, which limits their perspective and often produces very narrow definitions of success and victory.

In the final analysis, there is not too much that civilian authorities can do about these organizational level biases. Military organizations are boundedly rational because they are organizations. And ironically, military officers have limited perspectives in part because civilian leaders and publics want them to. Military professionals are trained to think in narrow ways: civilians do not want them to constrain their military advice because of political considerations, to contemplate the morals of their targeting plans, or to take the postwar world into deep consideration when planning attacks. Civilians want them to be professional soldiers, to make the most effective military plans possible, and to give stark and straightforward military advice. With respect to nuclear weapons, the result is that members of military organizations will more often advocate preventive war, will usually favor war-fighting doctrines, and will call for rapid escalation or none at all.

None of that should be particularly surprising or too disturbing. What is more disturbing is when such organizational biases are not successfully combatted by the checks and balances of strong civilian control. Bernard Brodie once wrote that "the civil hand must never relax, and must without one hint of apology hold the control that has always belonged to it by right."[34] Unfortunately, in this country, and especially in some new nuclear states with military-run or -controlled governments, that civil hand is not always in firm control.

Second-Strike Forces

Waltz and I clearly disagree on how easy it will be for new states to build secure second-strike forces. What is the basis of this disagreement? I think Waltz's confident position is again built on logic of interests rather than the logic of organizations and the evidence of history. Of course, states will have interests in building survivable forces. But will they do so or will they screw up?

The answer is clear to Waltz: weak and poor states can build secure second-strike forces "quite easily" (Ch. 3, p. 98) and "they guard them with almost paranoiac zeal" (Ch. 3, p. 88). In Chapter 2, I gave three recent counter-examples, showing how narrow organizational interests and poorly designed organizational routines can produce inadvertent and unnecessary vulnerabilities: first, the Chinese nuclear force was highly vulnerable in the mid-1970s, until Mao Zedong ordered that advanced deception plans be instituted; second, the Egyptian air force was destroyed in June 1967 because the Israelis noticed that all Egyptian air defense forces landed for refueling at the same time every morning; and third, in 1993, the North Korean construction of covert nuclear waste storage sites in a pattern identical to the sites found in Russia apparently helped the United States identify the location where the Koreans were hiding nuclear materials. In Chapter 5, I will also present several examples of how Pakistani organizational routines and poor communications secrecy revealed the nature of their "secret" military operations and their missile storage locations.

Here let me add that pre-nuclear history is filled with such examples of states zealously trying to guard valuable military assets, yet failing to do so. In 1941, the United States government desperately desired to protect the Pacific fleet at Pearl Harbor, because it was considered the central deterrent to war with Japan. The military alert plans of the army's antiaircraft units were so focused on preventing sabotage, however, that when they received the warning to expect "hostile action" at any moment on November 27, they locked up their ammunition in storage bunkers, rather than distributing it to the gunners. The guns were thus silent when the Japanese attacked on December 7.[35] Nine hours later, despite having received warning that Pearl Harbor had been attacked, the critical B-17 "Flying Fortress" force at Clark Air Field in the Philippines was destroyed on the runway, because the bombers had earlier been launched into the air for protection upon receiving a false warning of Japanese aircraft approaching the base, and were in the process of refueling on the ground when the real attack came.[36] In late 1943, the German high command sought with zeal to hide the location of their V-1 buzz-bomb bases from the British; the V-1 storage buildings at every base, however, had been constructed in a distinctive curved shape (to protect the weapons inside from a bomb blast at the door), which looked like a ski from the air, enabling British photo-reconnaissance analysts to find ninety-five of the ninety-six bases constructed by the Germans.[37] A final example of "normal" organizational incompetence producing a serious military vulnerability during World War II occurred in February 1942. After the British launched a successful commando raid on one of the few German radar sites that they had been able to spot through aerial reconnaissance, the German military issued orders that, henceforth, all radar sites were to be protected by circles of barbed wire. This of course showed up in future British aerial photographs, enabling the British to locate and bomb additional German radar facilities.[38] Modern military history would look very different indeed if every time a state tried to protect its most critical military forces with zeal, it did so successfully.

Perhaps new nuclear states will do better. But in light of the evidence of history, one should not be surprised if some states fail to develop secure second-strike forces despite all hopes to the contrary. Imperfect organizations provide an imperfect link between desires of political leaders and the outcomes of force postures. These organizations make predictable (but not always preventable) mistakes. To ignore such organizational difficulties leads to serious misunderstandings, for both scholars trying to analyze the nuclear revolution and for statesmen trying to cope with its dangerous implications.

Uncertainty and Escalation

Waltz places great emphasis on the benefits of uncertainty regarding nuclear deterrence. Given the horrendous costs of an all-out war, states *should* be exceedingly cautious if there is *any* chance of nuclear weapons being involved. Yet nuclear uncertainty is a two-edged sword: it cuts against any absolute assurance that nuclear weapons *will not* be used (this helps deterrence) and also cuts against any absolute assurance that nuclear weapons *will* be used (this hurts deterrence).

How far does the nuclear writ run? History suggests that while many states facing nuclear adversaries may well be cautious, some states have nevertheless launched attacks in the face of such uncertainty. In 1973, Egypt and Syria attacked Israel despite the fact that Israel had a small nuclear arsenal at the time. In 1982, Argentina invaded the British-owned Falkland Islands, despite the fact that Great Britain had hundreds of nuclear weapons. In January 1991, during the Persian Gulf war, Iraq launched barrage after barrage of SCUD missiles into the cities of Israel, despite Israel having an estimated one hundred nuclear weapons and long-range Jericho missiles in its possession.[39] After the invasion of Kuwait, Prime Minister Yitzhak Shamir declared that "anyone attempting an attack on

Israel will be bringing upon himself a great disaster."[40] How could Saddam Hussein have been *absolutely certain* that Israel would not retaliate with nuclear weapons? Governments take gambles, especially when they are in desperate straits. Nuclear weapons may well produce prudence, but it is a prudence that still leaves room for war.

CONCLUSIONS

So what is to be done? The difficult nonproliferation challenge in the future is *not* to ensure that the U.S. government and people are opposed to the further proliferation of nuclear weapons. Indeed, it is not difficult to understand why a large nuclear state, with the most powerful conventional forces in the world, would want to limit severely the spread of nuclear weapons to other states in the international system. The real challenge is to create a future in which the government leaders, the organizations under them, and the citizens of nonnuclear states around the globe believe that it is in their interests to remain nonnuclear states.

This is clearly no easy task. Yet, despite the emergence of many new nuclear states in the early 1990s, the South Asian nuclear tests in 1998, and the North Korean test in 2006, the recent history of nonproliferation efforts is not entirely bleak. Indeed, in the 1990s, there were also a number of very important positive developments. Civilian-run governments in Argentina and Brazil gave up the nuclear weapons programs started by earlier military governments, preferring to enter an agreement for a nuclear-free zone in the region rather than face the uncertainties of a nuclear arms race.[41] South Africa built and fully assembled seven atomic explosive devices in the late 1970s and early 1980s, but then voluntarily dismantled and destroyed them after F. W. de Klerk came to power and started the process of ending apartheid and South Africa's international isolation.[42] Three of the former republics of the Soviet Union—Belarus, Kazakhstan, and Ukraine—agreed, after prolonged international negotiations, to join the Nuclear Non-Proliferation Treaty and to return their weapons to Russia. In 1995 nuclear and nonnuclear members of the Non-Proliferation Treaty agreed to extend it in perpetuity.

None of these apparent success stories is guaranteed to last: treaties can be renounced, dismantlement discontinued, and weapons programs renewed. Yet such positive developments should be encouraged and reproduced elsewhere when possible. The United States plays a critical role in supporting these arms control regimens and must not shy away from leadership.

Ultimately, however, the key decisions will be made by the governments and peoples of new nuclear states and potential nuclear states, and not by the United States. Looking to the future, the goal of all states should not be a world of nuclear porcupines: every state sharply armed and vigorously trying to protect itself. Instead, the short-term goal should be radically smaller and safer arsenals in all existing nuclear states and the maintenance of nonnuclear status for other nations. The long-term goal should be the abolition or international control of nuclear weapons, once appropriate political and technical controls can be devised. I personally am not optimistic that I will ever see that goal achieved; but the difficulty of the task, and the distance we have to travel to achieve it, should not deter us from at least moving in the right direction.

BACK TO THEORY

Theories are lenses. They help us focus on specific parts of a complex reality and see the causal connections between those parts. Theories help us understand the world; they enable us to make sense of the past and predict the future. Waltz and I use a different lens—neorealist structural theory and organization theory—to look at the same world. This has led us to emphasize different aspects of nuclear history and to predict very different nuclear futures. Ultimately, the test of these different positions will be found in the experience of states that have acquired new nuclear weapons. I hope that Kenneth Waltz is right about the consequences of nuclear proliferation. I fear, however, that my more pessimistic predictions will eventually come true.

The awesome destructive power of nuclear weapons clearly increases the costs of war, and a statesman's awareness of this basic fact can be, in theory at least, a positive force for peace. But this cost-benefit logic of deterrence may not apply to many terrorists, who are more likely to get nuclear weapons if they spread to more countries in the Middle East. Even if terrorist access to weapons is prevented, these new states may become imperfect custodians of atomic power. Nuclear weapons are not controlled by states or statesmen; they are controlled by organizations. These organizations, like all complex organizations, will inevitably have biases and parochial interests, will by necessity develop routines and standardized procedures, and will occasionally make serious operational errors. These kinds of problems are likely to emerge, sometimes quietly and sometimes with a vengeance, in new nuclear nations. Nuclear weapons do not produce perfect nuclear organizations; they only make their inevitable mistakes more deadly. Because of the inherent limits of organizational reliability, the spread of nuclear weapons is more to be feared than welcomed.

Chapter 5

INDIAN AND PAKISTANI NUCLEAR WEAPONS: FOR BETTER OR WORSE?

Scott D. Sagan and Kenneth N. Waltz

In May 11 and 13, 1998, India tested five nuclear weapons. By the end of the month, Pakistan had followed suit, claiming to have detonated six nuclear devices—five to match New Delhi's tests and one in response to India's 1974 "peaceful nuclear explosive." With these tests, the governments in Islamabad and New Delhi loudly announced to the world, and to each other, that they held the capability to retaliate with nuclear weapons in response to major attack.

What has happened since May 1998? Has the spread of nuclear weapons to the region made India and Pakistan more or less secure? What is the likely future of a nuclear South Asia? Readers of this book will not be surprised to learn that we hold different views on these issues. In this chapter, we will first present a brief history of the conflict between India and Pakistan. Sagan then offers his pessimistic perspective on the risks of nuclear war in South Asia, and Waltz follows with

This is a revised version of the 2003 chapter from the second edition of this book. An earlier version of Sagan's section was published as "The Perils of Proliferation in South Asia." *Asian Survey* 61, no. 6 (November–December 2001), pp. 1064–86.

a more optimistic assessment. Readers will decide for themselves which one of us provides the stronger logic and evidence to support his argument.

INDIA, PAKISTAN, AND THE KASHMIR CONFLICT

India and Pakistan were born into conflict, and the disputed territory of Kashmir has been a political and military battleground for over fifty years. The British partitioned their "Jewel in the Crown" in 1947, granting independence to a Muslim Pakistan and a secular, but predominantly Hindu, India. Kashmir—the largest of the semi-autonomous princely states within British India—was 80 percent Muslim in population. Its maharajah, however, was Hindu. London expected Kashmir to become part of Pakistan, given its geographic and religious characteristics. When the Hindu maharajah in Kashmir failed to choose sides, Muslim rebels from the British colonial army, aided by Pakistani troops dressed as guerrilla forces and Pathan tribesmen from Pakistan, attacked the Kashmiri state militia and marched on the state capital, Srinagar. The maharajah, having fled to India, quickly announced that Kashmir should become part of India. Indian military units immediately flew into Kashmir to defend the territory. This brief conflict set the pattern of future clashes between India and Pakistan.

Conservative estimates of the number of civilians killed in the communal violence that accompanied the partition of India range from two hundred thousand to five hundred thousand. The 1947–48 war, in which from three thousand to eight thousand soldiers were killed, ended in stalemate. A bipartite Pakistani state was created that embodied the Muslim majority territories (except for Kashmir) on both sides of India: East Pakistan and West Pakistan were one state separated by the vast expanse of northern India. Pakistani forces held significant portions of the northern sector of Kashmir, and Pakistan created "Azad Kashmir" (Free Kashmir) in territory it held. A "line of control" was established separating the armed forces of

India and Pakistan. The Indian government has never accepted the United Nations mandate calling for a plebiscite to determine the fate of Kashmir. In India's view, a plebiscite would set a dangerous precedent, stimulating demands for independence by other Indian states. Pakistan, in turn, has never accepted Indian control over Kashmir. Every Pakistani government, whether civilian or military, has insisted that the Kashmiri population wants to join its Muslim neighbor and should be allowed to do so.

Since the cease-fire in 1948, tensions between India and Pakistan have led to numerous military clashes. In the spring and summer of 1965, Pakistani armed forces attacked Indian territory in both Gujarat (in southwest India) and across the line of control into Kashmir, leading to a two-month war in which an estimated four to five thousand soldiers were killed.[1] In 1971, Indian armed forces dismembered the Pakistani state, countering attacks from Pakistan in the west and crossing into East Pakistan to help rebel forces there declare the independent state of Bangladesh. Estimates of the military fatalities in that war range from six thousand to twelve thousand. In 1984, Indian forces took control of a Pakistani army post on the disputed Siachen glacier at the dizzying heights of over twenty thousand feet. The ensuing conflict—which has been described as "two bald men fighting over a comb"—has continued since 1984, with the loss of an estimated one thousand Indian and Pakistani soldiers.[2] In Kashmir, occasional artillery duels across the line of control and infiltration of guerrilla forces continued throughout the 1990s, with estimates of up to fifty thousand civilian and military fatalities.

This bloody history shows that South Asia is a tinderbox filled with tension and danger. The region thus provides an important test of the ideas we developed in the first two chapters of this book. What the spread of nuclear weapons will do to this strife-torn region is one of today's most urgent questions.

FOR THE WORSE:
TILL DEATH DO US PART

Scott D. Sagan

The emerging nuclear history of India and Pakistan strongly supports the pessimistic predictions of organizational theorists. Chapter 2 showed how military organizational behavior has led to serious problems in meeting all three requirements for stable nuclear deterrence—prevention of preventive war during periods of transition when one side has a temporary advantage, the development of survivable second-strike forces, and avoidance of accidental nuclear war—and argued that similar problems will emerge in new nuclear states. In this chapter, I will demonstrate that these problems have, in fact, now appeared in India and Pakistan.

It should be acknowledged from the start that there are important differences between the nuclear relationship emerging between India and Pakistan and the Cold War system that developed over time between the United States and the Soviet Union. While the differences are clear, however, the significance of these differences is not. For example, the nuclear arsenals in South Asia are, and are likely to remain, much smaller and less sophisticated than were the U.S. and Soviet arsenals. This should make each arsenal both more vulnerable to a counterforce attack (an attack on the adversary's own nuclear forces) and less capable of mounting counter-force attacks, and thus the net effect is uncertain. There are also important differences in civil-military relations in the two cases, but these differences, too, are both stabilizing and potentially destabilizing. The Soviets and the Americans both eventually developed an "assertive" command system with tight high-level civilian control over their nuclear weapons.[3] Also India has an extreme system of assertive civilian control of the military, with (at least until recently) very little direct military influence on any aspect of nuclear weapons policy. Pakistan, however, is at the other end of the spectrum, with the military in complete control of the nuclear arsenal, and with only marginal influence from civilian political leaders, even during the periods when there was a civilian-led government in Islamabad. There are, finally, important differences in mutual understanding, proximity, and hostility. India and Pakistan share a common colonial and pre-colonial history, have some common cultural roots, and share a common border; they also have engaged in four wars against each other, and are involved in a violent fifty-year dispute about the status of Kashmir. In contrast, the Americans and Soviets were on opposite sides of the globe and viewed each other as mysterious, often unpredictable adversaries. The Cold War superpowers were involved in a deep-seated ideological rivalry, but held no disputed territory between them and had no enduring history of armed violence against each other.

There is also, however, a crucially important similarity between the nuclear conditions that existed in Cold War and those that exist in South Asia today. In both cases, the parochial interests and routine behaviors of the organizations that manage nuclear weapons limit the stability of nuclear deterrence. The newest nuclear powers will not make exactly the same mistakes with nuclear weapons as did their superpower predecessors. They are, however, also unlikely to meet with complete success in the difficult effort to control these weapons and maintain nuclear peace.

The Problem of Preventive War

Pakistan has been under direct military rule for almost half of its existence, and some analysts have argued that the organizational biases of its military leaders had strong effects on strategic decisions concerning the initiation and conduct of the 1965 and 1971 wars with India.[4] In contrast, India has a sustained tradition of strict civilian control over the military since its independence. These patterns of civil-military relations influence nuclear weapons doctrine and operations. In India, the military has traditionally not been involved in decisions

concerning nuclear testing, design, or even command and control. In Pakistan, the military largely runs the nuclear weapons
program; even during the periods in which civilian prime
ministers have held the reins of government, they have neither
been told the full details of the nuclear weapons program nor
been given direct control over the operational arsenal.[5]

An organizational theory lens suggests that it is very
fortunate that it was India, not Pakistan, that was the first to
develop nuclear weapons in South Asia. Military rule in Islamabad (and military influence during periods of civilian rule)
certainly has played an important role in Pakistani decision
making concerning the use of force (see the discussion of the
Kargil conflict below). But the Pakistani military did not possess nuclear weapons before India tested in 1974, and thus was
not in a position to argue that preventive war now was better
than war later after India developed a rudimentary arsenal.

The preventive war problem in South Asia is a complex
one, however, and new evidence suggests that military influence in India produced serious risks of preventive war in the
1980s, despite strong institutionalized civilian control. The
government of Prime Minister Indira Gandhi considered, but
then rejected, plans to attack Pakistan's Kahuta nuclear facility
in the early 1980s, a preventive attack plan that was recommended by senior Indian military leaders.[6] Yet, as occurred in
the United States, the preferences of senior officers did not suddenly change when civilian leaders ruled against preventive
war. Instead, the beliefs went underground, only to resurface
later in a potentially more dangerous form.

These beliefs emerged from the shadows during the 1986–
87 "Brasstacks" crisis.[7] This serious crisis began in late 1986
when the Indian military initiated a massive military exercise
in Rajasthan, involving an estimated 250,000 troops and 1,500
tanks, including the issuance of live ammunition to troops and
concluding with a simulated "counter-offensive" attack, including Indian Air Force strikes, into Pakistan. The Pakistani military, fearing that the exercise might turn into a large-scale
attack, alerted military forces and conducted exercises along

the border, which led to Indian military countermovements closer to the border and an operational Indian Air Force alert. The resulting crisis produced a flurry of diplomatic activity and was resolved only after direct intervention by the highest political authorities.[8]

The traditional explanation for the Brasstacks crisis has been that it was an accidental crisis, caused by Pakistan's misinterpretation of an inadvertently provocative Indian Army exercise. For example, Devin Hagerty's detailed examination of "New Delhi's intentions in conducting Brasstacks" concludes that "India's conduct of 'normal' exercises rang alarm bells in Pakistan; subsequently, the logic of the security dilemma structured both sides' behavior, with each interpreting the other's defensive moves as preparations for offensive action."[9] A stronger explanation, however, unpacks "New Delhi's intentions" to look at what different Indian decision makers in the capital wanted to do before and during the crisis.

The key is to understand the preventive-war thinking of the then-Indian chief of the Army Staff, General Krishna-swami Sundarji. Sundarji apparently believed that India's security would be greatly eroded by Pakistani development of a usable nuclear arsenal and thus deliberately designed the Brasstacks exercise in hopes of provoking a Pakistani military response. He hoped that this would then provide India with an excuse to implement existing contingency plans to go on the offensive against Pakistan and to take out its nuclear program in a preventive strike.[10] According to the memoirs of Lieutenant General P. N. Hoon, the commander in chief of the Western Army during Brasstacks:

> Brasstacks was no military exercise. It was a plan to build up a situation for a fourth war with Pakistan. And what is even more shocking is that the Prime Minister, Mr. Rajiv Gandhi, was not aware of these plans for war. [11]

The preventive war motivation behind Sundarji's plans helps to explain why the Indian military did not provide full notification of the exercise to the Pakistanis and then failed to use the special hotline to explain their operations when information was requested by Pakistan during the crisis.[12] A final piece of evidence confirms that Sundarji advocated a preventive strike against Pakistan during the crisis. Considerations of an attack on Pakistani nuclear facilities went all the way up to the most senior decision makers in New Delhi in January 1987:

> [Prime Minister] Rajiv [Gandhi] now considered the possibility that Pakistan might initiate war with India. In a meeting with a handful of senior bureaucrats and General Sundarji, he contemplated beating Pakistan to the draw by launching a preemptive attack on the Army Reserve South. This would have included automatically an attack on Pakistan's nuclear facilities to remove the potential for a Pakistani nuclear riposte to India's attack. Relevant government agencies were not asked to contribute analysis or views to the discussion. Sundarji argued that India's cities could be protected from a Pakistani counterattack (perhaps a nuclear one), but, upon being probed, could not say how. One important advisor from the Ministry of Defense argued eloquently that "India and Pakistan have already fought their last war, and there is too much to lose in contemplating another one." This view ultimately prevailed. [13]

The Kargil Conflict and Future Problems

Optimists cannot accept that the Brasstacks crisis may have been a deliberate attempt to spark a preventive attack, but they might be reassured by the final outcome, as senior political leaders stepped in to stop further escalation. The power of nuclear deterrence to prevent war in South Asia, optimists insist, has been demonstrated in repeated crises: the Indian preventive attack discussions in 1984; the Brasstacks crisis; and the 1990 Kashmir crisis. "There is no more ironclad law in international relations theory than this," Devin Hagerty's detailed study concludes, "nuclear states do not fight wars with each other." [14]

    In the spring and summer of 1999, however, one year after the exchange of nuclear tests, India and Pakistan did fight a war in the mountains along the line of control separating the portions of Kashmir controlled by each country, near the Indian town of Kargil. The conflict began in May, when the Indian intelligence services discovered what appeared to be Pakistani regular forces lodged in mountain redoubts on the Indian side of the line of control. For almost two months, Indian Army units attacked the Pakistani forces and Indian Air Force jets bombed their bases high in the Himalayan peaks. Although the Indian forces carefully stayed on their side of the line of control in Kashmir, Indian prime minister Atal Bihari Vajpayee informed the U.S. government that he might have to order attacks into Pakistan. U.S. spy satellites revealed that Indian tanks and heavy artillery were being prepared for a counter-offensive in Rajasthan.[15] The fighting ended in July, when Pakistani prime minister Nawaz Sharif flew to Washington and, after receiving "political cover" in the form of a statement that President Bill Clinton would "take a personal interest" in resolving the Kashmir problem, pledged to withdraw forces to the Pakistani side of the line of control.[16] Over one thousand Indian and Pakistani soldiers died in the conflict, and Sharif's decision to pull out was one of the major causes of the coup that overthrew his regime in October 1999.

The 1999 Kargil conflict is disturbing not only because it demonstrates that nuclear-armed states can fight wars, but also because the organizational biases of the Pakistani military were a major cause of the conflict. Moreover, such biases continue to exist and could play a role in starting crises in the future. This increases the dangers of both a preventive and preemptive strike if war is considered inevitable, as well as the risk of a deliberate, but limited, use of nuclear weapons on the battlefield.

Three puzzling aspects of the Kargil conflict are understandable from an organizational perspective. First, in late 1998, the Pakistani military planned the Kargil operation, paying much more attention, as organization theory would predict, to the tactical effects of the surprise military maneuver than to the broader strategic consequences. Ignoring the likely international reaction and the predictable domestic consequences of the military incursion in India, however, proved to be a significant factor in the ultimate failure of the Kargil operation.

Second, the Pakistani Army also started the operation with the apparent belief—following the logic of what has been called the "stability/instability paradox"—that a "stable nuclear balance" between India and Pakistan permitted more offensive actions to take place with impunity in Kashmir.[17] It is important to note that this belief was more strongly held by senior military officers than by civilian leaders. For example, at the height of the fighting near Kargil, Pakistani Army leaders stated that "there is almost a red alert situation," but they nevertheless insisted "there is no chance of the Kargil conflict leading to a full-fledged war between the two sides."[18] Although Prime Minister Nawaz Sharif apparently approved the plan to move forces across the line of control, it is not clear that he was fully briefed on the nature, scope, or potential consequences of the operation.[19] The prime minister's statement that he was "trying to avoid nuclear war" and his suggestion that he feared "that India was getting ready to launch a full-scale military operation against Pakistan" provide a clear contrast to the confident military assessment that there was virtually no risk of an Indian counterattack or escalation to nuclear war.[20]

Third, the Pakistani government's interpretation of the Kargil crisis, at least in public, is that Nawaz Sharif lost courage and backed down unnecessarily. This view is not widely shared by Pakistani scholars and journalists, but such a "stab in the back" thesis does serve the parochial self-interests of the Pakistani army, which does not want to acknowledge its errors or those of the current Musharraf regime. The New Delhi government's interpretation, however, is that the Indian threats that military escalation—a counterattack across the international border—would be ordered, if necessary, forced Pakistan to retreat. These different "lessons learned" could produce ominous outcomes in future crises: each side believes that the Kargil conflict proved that if its government displays resolve and threatens to escalate to new levels of violence, the other side will exhibit restraint and back away from the brink.

Future military crises between India and Pakistan are likely to be nuclear crises. Proliferation optimists are not concerned about this likelihood, however, since they argue that the danger of preventive war, if it ever existed at all, has been eliminated by the development of deliverable nuclear weapons in both countries after May 1998. The problem of preventive war during periods of transition in South Asia is only of historical interest now, optimists would insist.

I am not convinced by this argument for two basic reasons. First, there is an arms race looming on the horizon in South Asia. The Indian government gave strong support to the Bush administration's plans to develop missile defense technology and continued to express interest in eventually procuring or developing its own missile defense capability. I believe that the Indian nuclear program is strongly influenced by the fact that hawkish nuclear policies are popular among Indian voters and thus serve the domestic political interests of Indian politicians. China is likely to respond to the U.S. decision to build national missile defenses by increasing the size and readiness of its own missile force. This will in turn encourage the Indian government to increase its own missile deployments and develop defense technology.

These deployments in India, however, will threaten the smaller nuclear deterrent forces in Pakistan, and this would inevitably reopen the window of opportunity for preventive war considerations. Military biases, under the preventive war logic of "better now than later," could encourage precipitous action in either country if the government had even a fleeting moment of superiority in this new kind of arms race.

The second reason to be pessimistic is that, in serious crises, attacks might be initiated based on the belief that an enemy's use of nuclear weapons is imminent and unavoidable. While it is clear that the existence of nuclear weapons in South Asia made both governments cautious in their use of conventional military force in 1999, it is also clear that Indian leaders were prepared to escalate the conflict if necessary. Pakistani political authorities, however, made nuclear threats during the crisis, suggesting that nuclear weapons would be used precisely under such conditions.[21] Moreover, according to U.S. officials, the Pakistani military, apparently without the Prime Minister's knowledge, took initial steps to alert its nuclear forces during the Kargil conflict.[22]

This dangerous alerting pattern was repeated in the South Asian crises that occurred after the September 11, 2001, terrorist attacks in the United States and the December 13, 2001, terrorist attack on the Parliament in New Delhi. In both cases, the Pakistani government feared that its nuclear forces would be attacked and therefore took alert measures to disperse the nuclear weapons and missiles to new locations away from their storage sites.[23] Pakistani fears that attacks on their nuclear arsenal were being planned may not have been entirely fanciful.

After the September 11 Pentagon and World Trade Center attacks, President Bush warned Islamabad that Pakistan would either side with the United States in the new war against terrorism or else be treated as a terrorist state. The development of military plans for U.S. commando raids against the Pakistani nuclear weapons sites was soon widely reported.[24] President Musharraf defused the crisis by deciding to abandon support for the Taliban regime in Afghanistan and to provide logistical and intelligence support for the U.S. war there.

After the December 13 terrorist attack against the Indian Parliament, the Indian government sent massive military forces to the Pakistani border and threatened to attack unless Musharraf cracked down on the radical Islamic groups that supported terrorist operations in Kashmir and New Delhi. Before Musharraf could respond, General S. Padmanabhan, the Indian Army chief, issued a bellicose statement announcing that the military buildup "was not an exercise": "A lot of viable options (beginning from a strike on the camps to a full conventional war) are available. We can do it. . . . If we go to war, jolly good."[25]

Senior Indian political authorities criticized the Army chief for making the statement, and diplomats in New Delhi speculated that General Padmanabhan had deliberately made it more difficult for the Pakistanis to back down in this crisis, thus increasing the likelihood of war.[26] Again, President Musharraf defused the crisis, at least temporarily, by initiating a crackdown on Islamic Jihadi groups promoting terrorism in Kashmir and the rest of India.

What lessons should be drawn from these dangerous crises? Optimists will look at only the final result and assume that it was inevitable: Deterrence and coercion worked, as serious threats were issued, the Pakistani president compromised, and no war occurred. At a deeper level, however, two more ominous lessons should be learned. First, President Musharraf's decision to back down was by no means inevitable, and he was subject to significant criticism from Islamic parties and some military circles for his conciliatory stance. Other Pakistani leaders could have gone the other way in 2002, and future Pakistani leaders might be less willing to make compromises with India in future crises. Second, the Pakistani fear that a preventive or preemptive strike against its nuclear arsenal was imminent forced it to take very dangerous military alerting steps in both crises. Taking nuclear weapons and missiles out of their more secure storage locations and deploying them into the field may make the forces less vulnerable to an enemy attack, but it makes the weapons more vulnerable to theft or internal attacks by terrorist organizations. Given the number of Al Qaida members and supporters in Pakistan, this hidden terrorist problem may well have been the most serious nuclear danger of the crises. In short, the crises of 2001 and 2002 demonstrate that nuclear weapons in South Asia may well produce a modicum of restraint, but also momentous dangers.

In future crises in South Asia, the likelihood of either a preventive or preemptive attack will be strongly influenced by a complex mixture of perceptions of the adversary's intent, estimates about its future offensive and defensive capabilities, and estimates of the vulnerability of its current nuclear arsenal. Organizational biases could encourage worst-case assumptions about the adversary's intent and pessimistic beliefs about the prospects for successful strategic deterrence over the long term. Unfortunately, as will be seen below, inherent organizational characteristics can also produce vulnerabilities to an enemy strike.

Survivability of Nuclear Forces in South Asia

The fear of retaliation is central to successful deterrence, and the second requirement for stability with nuclear weapons is therefore the development of secure, second-strike forces. Unfortunately, there are strong reasons to be concerned about the ability of the Indian and Pakistani military to maintain survivable forces. Two problems can already be seen to have reduced (at least temporarily) the survivability of nuclear forces in Pakistan. First, there is evidence that the Pakistani military, as was the case in the Cold War examples cited earlier, deployed its missile forces, following standard operating procedures, in ways that produce signatures giving away their deployment locations. Indian intelligence officers, for example, identified the locations of planned Pakistani deployments of M-11 missiles by spotting the placement of "secret" defense communication terminals nearby.[27] A second, and even more dramatic, example follows a Cold War precedent quite closely. Just as the road engineers in the Soviet Union inadvertently gave away the location of their ICBMs because construction crews built roads with wide-radius turns next to the missile silos, Pakistani road construction crews have inadvertently signaled the location of the "secret" M-11 missiles by placing wide-radius roads and roundabouts outside newly constructed garages at the Sargodha military base.[28]

Finally, analysts should also not ignore the possibility that Indian or Pakistani intelligence agencies could intercept messages revealing the "secret" locations of otherwise survivable military forces, an absolutely critical issue with small or opaque nuclear arsenals. The history of the 1971 war, for example, demonstrates that both states' intelligence agencies were able to intercept critical classified messages sent by and to the other side: for example, the Pakistanis learned immediately when the Indian Army commander issued operational orders to prepare for military intervention against East Pakistan; and before the war, Indian intelligence agencies acquired a copy of a critical message from Beijing to Rawalpindi informing the Pakistanis that China would not intervene militarily in any Pakistani-Indian war.[29] Perhaps most dramatically, on December 12, 1971 the Indians intercepted a radio message scheduling a meeting of high-level Pakistani officials at Government House in Dacca, which led to an air attack on the building in the middle of the meeting.[30]

The Kargil conflict provides newer evidence of the difficulty of keeping knowledge about "secret" operations away from one's adversary. Throughout the conflict, the Pakistani government insisted that the forces fighting on the Indian side of the line of control were "mujahideen," indigenous Islamic freedom fighters. This cover was exposed, however, when some of the "mujahideen" failed to leave their Pakistani military identification cards at their base in Pakistan and wrote about General Musharraf's involvement in the operation's planning process in a captured diary.[31] Indian intelligence organizations also intercepted a critical secret telephone conversation between General Musharraf and one of his senior military officers, which revealed the Pakistani Army's central involvement in the Kargil intrusion.[32] These are the kinds of organizational snafus that compromise highly secret operations—including "secret" nuclear weapons locations—in the future.

Normal Accidents and Unauthorized Use in Nuclear South Asia

Will the Indian and Pakistani nuclear arsenals be more safe and secure than were the U.S. and Soviet arsenals during the Cold War? It is clear that the emerging South Asian nuclear deterrence system is both smaller and less complex today than was the case in the United States or Soviet Union at the height of the Cold War. It is also clear, however, that the South Asian nuclear relationship is inherently more tightly coupled, because of geographical proximity. With inadequate warning systems in place and with weapons with short flight times emerging in the region, the time-lines for decision making are highly compressed and the danger that one accident could lead to another and then lead to a catastrophic accidental war is high and growing. The proximity of New Delhi and Islamabad to their potential adversary's border poses particular concerns about rapid "decapitation" attacks on national capitals. Moreover, there are legitimate concerns about social stability and support for terrorists inside Pakistan, problems that could compromise nuclear weapons safety and security.

Proliferation optimists will cite the small sizes of India and Pakistan's nuclear arsenals as a reason to be less worried about these problems. Yet the key from a normal accidents perspective is not the numbers, but rather the structure of the arsenal. Here there is both good and bad news. The good news is that under normal peacetime conditions, neither the Indians nor the Pakistanis regularly deploy nuclear forces mated with delivery systems in the field. The bad news, however, is that Pakistan has started to alert its nuclear weapons in crises; it did so in 1999 during the Kargil crisis and then again in September and December of 2001, in response to fears of Indian (and maybe U.S.) military action after the terrorist attacks in New York, Washington, and New Delhi.[33] Here what could be called the vulnerability/invulnerability paradox comes into play. When nuclear weapons are de-mated from delivery vehicles and locked inside a guarded facility, they are more secure from theft or seizure, but more vulnerable to an enemy strike; when nuclear weapons are taken out of the base, mated with road-mobile missiles, and dispersed into the countryside, they are less vulnerable to a first strike, but more vulnerable to theft.

From an organizational perspective, it is not surprising to find evidence of serious accidents emerging in the Indian nuclear and missile programs. The first example is disturbing, but predictable. On January 4, 2001, Indian defense secretary Yogendra Narain led a special inspection of the Milan missile production facility in Hyderabad. The Milan missile—a short-range (two kilometer) missile normally armed with a large conventional warhead—had failed in test launches and during the Kargil war, and Narain was to discuss the matter with the plant's managers and technical personnel. For reasons that remain unclear, the electrical circuitry was not disconnected and the live conventional warhead was not capped on the missile displayed for the visiting dignitary from New Delhi. When the plant manager accidentally touched the start button, the missile launched, flew through the body of one official, killing him instantly, and then nose-dived into the ground, catching on fire and injuring five other workers. The defense secretary was shocked, but unharmed. The official killed was the quality control officer for the Milan-missile program.[34]

The false warning incident that occurred just prior to the Pakistani nuclear tests in May 1998 is a second case demonstrating the dangers of accidental war in South Asia. During the crucial days just prior to Prime Minister Sharif's decision to order the tests of Pakistani nuclear weapons, senior military intelligence officers informed him that the Indian and Israeli air forces were about to launch a preventive strike on the test site.[35] The incident is shrouded in mystery, and the cause of this warning message is not clear. Although it is certainly possible that Pakistani intelligence officers simply misidentified aircraft in the region, a more likely explanation is that Inter-Service Intelligence (ISI) officials did not believe there was any threat of an imminent Indian-Israeli attack in 1998, but deliberately concocted (or exaggerated) the warning of a preventive strike to force the prime minister, who was wavering under U.S. pressure, to test the weapons immediately.[36] It is not clear which of these is the more worrisome interpretation of the incident: false warnings could be catastrophic in a crisis whether they are deliberate provocations by rogue intelligence officers, or genuinely believed, but inaccurate, reports of imminent or actual attack.

It is important to note that the possibility of a false warning producing an accidental nuclear war in South Asia remains a genuine concern. India added caveats to its traditional no-first-use doctrine in 2003, including statements that it might respond to Pakistani chemical weapons use with nuclear retaliation. Either government could misidentify an accidental nuclear detonation occurring during transport and alert activities at one of their own military bases as the start of a counterforce attack by the other state. Pakistani officials should be particularly sensitive to this possibility because of the 1988 Ojheri incident, in which a massive conventional munitions explosion at a secret ammunition dump near Rawalpindi caused fears among some decision makers that an Indian attack had begun.[37] The possibility of this kind of accident producing a false warning of an attack cannot, however, be ruled out in India, either, as long as the government plans to alert forces or mate nuclear weapons to delivery vehicles during crises.

In addition, there should be serious concern about whether both countries can maintain centralized control over their nuclear weapons. Although government policy in this regard is, for obvious reasons, kept classified, it is clear that Pakistan in particular is at serious risk to insider threats. In 1995, the Pakistani Army arrested forty officers implicated in a coup plot led by Maj. Gen. Zahirul Islam Abbasi, who had alleged links to Islamic fundamentalist groups.[38] Another case came to light in June 2011, when Brig. Gen. Ali Khan was arrested in Pakistan on charges of suspected ties to Islamic fundamentalists.[39]

Effective Personnel Reliability Programs (PRP) are necessary in Pakistan to address the insider threat. We lack evidence about the record inside the Pakistani Strategic Plans Division, but certainly the record inside the Pakistani personal security organizations does not engender confidence. In January 2011, Punjab Governor Salman Taseer was assassinated by one of his own bodyguards, who later told police that he had murdered the governor for his opposition to Pakistan's blasphemy law.[40] Two assassination attempts in 2003 against President Pervez Musharraf also involved insiders, and in these cases the security guards were not "lone wolves" but were tied to jihadist terror organizations.[41]

Finally, there is evidence that neither the Indian nor the Pakistani military has focused sufficiently on the danger that a missile test launch during a crisis could be misperceived as the start of a nuclear attack. There was an agreement, as part of the Lahore accords in January 1999, to provide advance notification of missile tests, but even such an agreement is not a fool-proof solution, as the Russians discovered in January 1995 when a bureaucratic snafu in Moscow led to a failure to pass on advance notification of a Norwegian weather rocket launch, that resulted in serious false warning of a missile attack.[42] Moreover, both the Pakistanis and the Indians appear to be planning to use their missile test facilities for actual nuclear weapons launches in war. In India, Wheeler Island is reportedly being used like Vandenberg air force base, a test site in peacetime and crises, and a launch site in war.[43] During Kargil, according to the Indian Army chief of staff, nuclear alert activities were also detected at "some of Pakistan's launch areas—some of the areas where they carried out tests earlier of one of their missiles."[44]

Beyond Denial

Nuclear South Asia will be a dangerous place, not because of ill will or irrationality among government leaders, nor because of any unique cultural inhibitions against strategic thinking in both countries. India and Pakistan face a dangerous nuclear future because they have become like other nuclear powers. Their leaders seek security through nuclear deterrence, but imperfect humans inside imperfect organizations control their nuclear weapons. If my theories are right, these organizations will someday fail to produce secure nuclear deterrence. Unfortunately, the evidence from these first years of South Asia's nuclear history suggests that the pessimistic predictions of organization theory are likely to come true, even though I cannot predict the precise pathway by which deterrence will break down.

The organizational perspective suggests that there are more similarities than differences between nuclear powers in the way they manage, or at least try to manage, nuclear weapons operations. There is, however, one important structural difference between the new nuclear powers and their Cold War predecessors. Just as each new child is born into a different family, each new nuclear power is born into a different nuclear system in which nuclear states influence each other's behavior. Some observers believe that the possibility that other nuclear powers—such as the United States or China—can intervene in future crises in South Asia may be a major constraint on undesired escalation. I fear the opposite: the possibility of intervention may encourage the governments of India and Pakistan to engage in risky behavior, initiating crises or making limited uses of force, precisely because they anticipate (correctly or incorrectly) that other nuclear powers may bail them out diplomatically if the going gets rough.

The possibility that other nuclear states might be able to influence nuclear behavior in South Asia does, however, lead to one final optimistic note. There are many potential unilateral steps and bilateral agreements that could be instituted to reduce the risk of nuclear war between India and Pakistan, and the U.S. government can play a useful role in helping to facilitate such agreements. Many, though not all, of the problems identified in this article can be reduced if nuclear weapons in both countries are maintained in a de-alerted state, with warheads removed from delivery vehicles. U.S. assistance could be helpful in providing the arms verification technology that could permit such de-alerting (or non-alerting in this case) to take place within a cooperative framework. The United States could also be helpful in providing intelligence and warning information, on a case-by-case basis, in peacetime or in crises to reduce the danger of false alarms. Finally, increased security of storage sites and safer management of nuclear weapons operations can be encouraged by sharing better security devices for storage sites and discussing organizational "best practices."

There will be no progress on any of these issues, however, unless Indians, Pakistanis, and Americans stop denying that serious problems exist. A basic awareness of nuclear command and control problems exists in New Delhi and Islamabad, but unfortunately Indian and Pakistani leaders too often trivialize them. The United States, in turn, refused to assist the Indians and Pakistanis in developing improved safety and security for their nuclear weapons until after the terrorist attacks on September 11, 2001. Washington officials argued before the September 11 attacks that any assistance in this area would "reward" Islamabad and New Delhi for testing, and signal to other potential nuclear weapon–states that the United States was not serious about its nonproliferation goals. The September 11 attacks led the U.S. government to switch its position, and Pakistani officials accepted assistance with their nuclear weapons security. According to David Sanger of *The New York Times*, approximately $100 million was spent on an American nuclear cooperation program, which included roughly two hundred Pakistanis receiving training about security best practices and security equipment being transferred directly to the Pakistani military.[45] It is crucial that such efforts to improve nuclear security continue regardless of the ups and downs of U.S.-Pakistani relations. Cooperative nuclear security efforts could also be usefully extended to India.

Update

Much has happened in South Asia over the past decade, but the basic set of nuclear dangers and its fundamental causes remain the same. I see no reason to think that, despite the growing internal security crisis inside Pakistan, the military will stop seeing India as its primary enemy. The Pakistani military continues to see support for terrorist attacks in Kashmir and elsewhere in India as a useful way to keep Indian forces tied down in Kashmir and to weaken the Indian state. Maintaining a crisis atmosphere between the two South Asian states, not incidentally, also ensures that the Pakistani military maintains its traditional position of power and privilege. And I fear that Pakistani civilian authorities, even when they disagree with military priorities or operational decisions, will never be able to assert control.

Following the seminal ideas of Thomas Schelling, Neil Joeck has nicely compared India and Pakistan in different crises to two teenagers engaged in a "game of chicken": they are driving their cars toward each other on a collision course and the first to swerve loses.[46] The analogy is a good one but needs to be altered to fully capture the dangers here. The Pakistani car is being driven poorly, by more than one individual: one driver is putting his foot on the gas pedal, the other is stamping down on the brakes, and both are pulling on the steering wheel trying to move it in different directions.

Adding nuclear weapons into this volatile situation has not been helpful. It has led the Pakistani military to believe it can more safely engage in low-level violence against India. Knowing this, Indian officials have started to create new conventional options, under a doctrine called Cold Start, to enable the Indian army and air force to launch conventional strikes into Pakistan more rapidly in future crises. The Pakistanis have responded by claiming that they may be forced to use a limited number of nuclear weapons early on Pakistani soil, if necessary, to thwart an Indian invasion. The Indians have responded, however, by stating that any Pakistani use of a nuclear weapon, even on Pakistani soil, would result in a full-scale punitive nuclear response by India. India claims that the Pakistanis are bluffing and will be deterred. The Pakistanis claim that India is bluffing and will be deterred. This is hardly a recipe for nuclear stability.[47]

Nuclear weapons will remain in Pakistan and India for the foreseeable future, and the conflict over Kashmir will continue to smolder, threatening to erupt into a wider and more dangerous war. The deep political problems between the two South Asian nuclear states may someday be resolved, and the U.S. government should encourage progress toward that end. In the meantime, the U.S. government should do whatever it can to reduce the risk that India and Pakistan will use nuclear weapons against each other.

FOR BETTER: NUCLEAR WEAPONS PRESERVE AN IMPERFECT PEACE

Kenneth N. Waltz

The American government and most American journalists look on the blossoming of nuclear forces in South Asia as an ominous event, different in implication and effect from all the similar events that we worried about throughout the Cold War. A 1998 *New York Times* headline, for example, proclaimed that "India's Arms Race Isn't Safe Like the Cold War."[48] Few thought the American-Soviet arms race safe at the time, and for good reasons few Indians and Pakistanis expect an arms race now. Most of the alarmist predictions about the fate of the subcontinent display forgetfulness about the past and confusion over the effects of nuclear weapons. In the same *New York Times* article, Joseph Cirincione, president of the Ploughshares Fund, reports that Pentagon war games between Pakistan and India always end with a nuclear exchange. Has everyone in that building forgotten that deterrence works precisely because nuclear states fear that conventional military engagements may escalate to the nuclear level, and therefore they draw back from the brink? Admiral David E. Jeremiah, once vice-chairman of the Joint Chiefs of Staff, laments the cultural mindset that leads Americans to believe that "everybody thinks like us," and a cofounder of the Henry L. Stimson Center, Michael Krepon, worries that because of the Pressler Amendment, which cut off aid to nations developing nuclear weapons, Pakistani officers have not had the benefit of attending our military schools.[49] One's reaction to both statements may well be "thank goodness."

The Brookings Institution totaled up the cost of American nuclear weapons over the decades and arrived at the figure of 5.5 trillion dollars. Strobe Talbott, when he was deputy secretary of state, implied that military competition between

Pakistan and India will cause them to spend on a proportion-ate scale. When asked why we should not provide India and Pakistan with advice about, and equipment for, safe deter-rence, he retorted that "if they locked themselves into the men-tality of MAD (Mutual Assured Destruction), they will then be tempted into—like us—a considerable escalation of the arms race."[50] Yet nuclear states need race only to the second-strike level, which is easy to achieve and maintain.

Indian and Pakistani leaders have learned from our folly. A minimal deterrent deters as well as a maximal one. Homi Jehangar Bhabha, father of the Indian bomb, called this "abso-lute deterrence." K. Subrahmanyam, a foremost strategist, emphasizes that Indians have learned that to build large forces is wasteful and foolish. An arsenal of about sixty weapons, he believes, will deter either Pakistan or China; and Pakistan might need, say, twenty to deter India.[51] Some have claimed that no nuclear country has been satisfied with having only a minimum deterrent.[52] Yet China, with even today only about twenty ICBMs, has been content with small numbers; and India and Pakistan would follow its example were it not for the disrup-tive effects of American missile defenses on the strategic arms balance in Asia, discussed below. Political as well as economic constraints on both countries ensure this. Talbott has discerned "a global trend away from reliance on nuclear weapons."[53] The United States does rely less on nuclear weapons now because it is the world's dominant conventional power, spending as much on its armed forces in the year 2000 as the next eight big spend-ers combined. Partly for that reason, some other countries rely more on their nuclear weapons—Russia, for example, with its conventional forces in shambles. Countries that once counted on one of the two great powers for military assistance are now concerned to provide security for themselves. Pakistan, India, Iraq, Japan, and North Korea are all examples.

India tested its "peaceful bomb" in 1974. Its next tests came twenty-four years later. The United States complained loudly both times. Yet the United States tested nuclear weap-ons many times yearly for many years on end—more than a thousand above and below ground, which is more tests than all other countries combined. America's initial reason was that it anticipated a mortal threat from the Soviet Union and, later, that it actually faced such a threat. America's nonproliferation policy denies that such reasoning can legitimate other countries' entering the tight circle of nuclear powers. Nevertheless, the reasoning the United States applied to itself applies to India and to Pakistan as well. Does anyone believe that testing nuclear warheads is something that, in their place, we would not have done?

The question raised by India's and Pakistan's nuclear tests is not whether they should have been conducted, but whether their security requires them becoming nuclear powers. Some countries need nuclear weapons; some do not. Brazil and Argentina set themselves on course to become nuclear states. Both decided to abandon the effort, because each realized that neither posed a threat to the other. South Africa became a nuclear state and then, finding no commensurate threat, reversed its policy.

Pakistan obviously needs nuclear weapons. When asked why nuclear weapons are so popular in Pakistan, former prime minister Benazir Bhutto answered, "It's our history. A history of three wars with a larger neighbor. India is five times larger than we are. Their military strength is five times larger. In 1971, our country was disintegrated. So the security issue for Pakistan is an issue of survival." From the other side, Shankar Bajpai, former Indian ambassador to Pakistan, China, and the United States, has said that "Pakistan's quest for a nuclear capability stems from its fear of its larger neighbor, removing that fear should open up immense possibilities"—possibilities for a less worried and more relaxed life. Shamshad Ahmad, Pakistan's foreign secretary, has echoed their thoughts: "In South Asia nuclear deterrence may . . . usher in an era of durable peace between Pakistan and India, providing the requisite incentives for resolving all outstanding issues, especially Jammu and Kashmir."[54] In recent years, some Indians and Pakistanis have begun to talk about a peaceful accommodation, and according to a *New York Times* reporter, "just about every-body" in Kashmir "cites the two countries' possession of nuclear weapons as a factor pushing towards peace."[55]

In the 1980s, after the Soviet occupation of Afghanistan, the United States, knowing of Pakistan's nuclear progress, nevertheless continued to supply Pakistan with sophisticated conventional weapons. The United States did not care much about Pakistan's nuclear progress as long as Soviet worries dominated American policy. Once the Soviet Union went into steep decline and then disappeared, America dropped Pakistan, with a speed that surprised not only Pakistan but India as well, only to pick it up again when Afghanistan became a problem in American foreign policy. For Pakistan to compete conventionally with India was economically impossible. Nuclear weapons linked to a sensible strategy are a low-cost way of leveling the playing field. Understandably, Pakistan felt itself pressed to follow the nuclear course.

Can India be seen in a similar light? With its superior conventional forces, it needed no nuclear weapons to protect itself against a Pakistan that lacked them, but what about China? Americans think of India as the dominant power in South Asia. India feels differently. India is part of a hostile world. With a Muslim minority of about 150 million, it adjoins Muslim Pakistan, and beyond lies a Muslim world becoming more fundamentalist and more hostile. To the north is an increasingly nationalist, steadily more powerful, and potentially unstable China. The United States has reinforced India's worries about a Chinese-Pakistani-American axis, notably when America "tilted" toward Pakistan in the 1971 war with India. In the middle of the war, Henry Kissinger told Mao Zedong, "We want to keep the pressure on India both militarily and politically," adding that if China "took measures to protect its security, the U.S. would oppose efforts of others to interfere."[56] In a show of support for Pakistan, the American navy moved the aircraft carrier *Enterprise* into the Indian Ocean. To this day, India considers this an attempt to hold them in nuclear awe. They call it blackmail.[57]

India also continues to believe that America favors China over India. A professor at Jawaharlal Nehru University found nuclear cooperation between Beijing and Islamabad "unprecedented in the history of international relations."[58] And an Indian minister of defense wondered, as many Indians do, "why India and Pakistan should be seen as blowing each other up when nuclear weapons in the hands of the United States and China are seen as stabilizing factors."[59] That the United States seems to trust China as an old nuclear power, and not India as a new one, is a cause of bitter resentment.

The decision to make nuclear weapons was a momentous one for India. The tests of May 1998 were overwhelmingly popular with the public at large, but the decision emerged over decades, with much opposition along the way. Even today, Indians who view nuclear deterrence as a difficult and demanding task believe that India will be unable to develop and deploy a nuclear force sufficient for the deterrence of China. In their view, the main effect of India's developing nuclear capabilities was to cause Pakistan to develop its own. India is therefore worse off with nuclear weapons than it would have been without them. The Indian view that carried the day rests on the contrary argument, developed in Chapter 1—namely, that it does not take much to deter.

Is it farfetched for India to worry about a Chinese threat to its security? Any country has trouble seeing the world as others do. Let's try. If the United States shared a two-thousand mile border with a country that was more populous, more prosperous, more heavily armed, and in possession of nuclear weapons, we would react militarily and, judging from our response to the Soviet Union, more vigorously than India has done. What *is* farfetched is for the United States to worry about a Chinese threat to its security and then wonder why India does too.

Kanti Bajpai, a professor at Nehru University, strongly opposes India's nuclear armament. He doubts that India's nuclear deterrence would dissuade China from seizing Arunachal Pradesh in the northeast or Pakistan from seizing Kashmir in the northwest. This is comparable to the worry, dreamt up in the 1960s, about a "Hamburg grab." Some American military commentators worried that the Soviet Union might suddenly seize Hamburg, which jutted into East Germany, and then in effect ask, "Is NATO's fighting to regain Hamburg worth risking a nuclear conflagration?" Similarly, Kanti Bajpai imagines "a quick grabbing thrust into the two states, backed by nuclear weapons, in the hope of presenting India with a fait accompli."[60] Such worries are as fanciful as American worries were in the Cold War. The invader would have to assemble troops near the border. India would then alert its forces, including nuclear ones. With the potential crisis easily foreseeable, why would China or Pakistan run such risks?

One answer to the question is that Pakistan did move troops across the line of control into Kashmir and fight for a time at a fairly high level in the engagement known as Kargil. Joseph Cirincione voices widespread fears when, with the Kashmir conflict in mind, he says, "Just assemble all the risk factors and multiply it out. . . . This is the most dangerous and unstable military situation in the world."[61] His pronouncement repeats the tired old error of inferring from the conventional past what the nuclear future holds, a mistake made almost every time another country gets nuclear weapons. With nuclear weapons added, conventionally dangerous and unstable situations become safer and more stable ones. Nuclear weapons produce what Joseph Nye calls the "crystal ball" effect—everyone knows that if force gets out of hand, all the parties involved in a conflict face catastrophe.[62] With conventional weapons, the crystal ball is clouded. With nuclear weapons, it is perfectly clear.

What reasons do we have to believe that India's and Pakistan's crystal balls are clouded? Well, again, Kargil. Some observers worry that Pakistan may believe that it can safely raise the level of conventional violence since nuclear weapons limit the extent of India's response. But, of course, they also limit the size and scope of Pakistan's attack, since Pakistan knows it could face nuclear retaliation. The same reasoning applies to India. It's the same old story: in the presence of nuclear weapons, a country can achieve a significant victory only by risking devastating retaliation.

Sagan calls Kargil the fourth Indian-Pakistani war because it fits the social science definition holding that a military encounter is a war if it produces more than one thousand battle-related deaths. If Kargil is called a war, then the definition of war requires revision; and now that both countries have nuclear weapons the fifth "war" will be no worse than the so-called fourth one. The late Pakistani chief of the army staff, General Mirza Aslam Beg, remarked that India and Pakistan can no longer fight even a conventional war over Kashmir, and his counterpart, the chief of the Indian army staff, General Krishnaswami Sundarji, concurred.[63] Kargil showed once again that deterrence does not firmly protect disputed areas but does limit the extent of the violence. Indian rear admiral Raja Menon put the larger point simply: "The Kargil crisis demonstrated that the subcontinental nuclear threshold probably lies territorially in the heartland of both countries, and not on the Kashmir cease-fire line."[64]

The obvious conclusion to draw from Kargil is that the presence of nuclear weapons prevented escalation from major skirmish to full-scale war. This contrasts starkly with the bloody 1965 war, in which both parties were armed only with conventional weapons.

Another question is whether India and Pakistan can firmly control and safely deploy nuclear forces sufficient to deter. Because I have already said enough about the ease of deterrence, I shall concentrate on questions of safety and control. Sagan claims that "the emerging nuclear history of India and Pakistan strongly supports the pessimistic predictions of organizational theorists" (Ch. 5, p. 138). Yet the evidence, accumulated over five decades, shows that nuclear states fight with nuclear states only at low levels, that accidents seldom occur, and that when they do they never have bad effects. If nuclear pessimists were right, nuclear deterrence would have failed again and again. Nuclear pessimists deal with the potential causes of catastrophe; optimists, with the effects the causes do *not* produce. Since the evidence fails to support the predictions of pessimists, one wonders why the spread of nuclear weapons to South Asia should have bad rather than good effects. What differences in the situation of India and Pakistan may cause their fates to depart from the nuclear norm? If they and their situations are different, then the happy history of the nuclear past does not forecast their futures. American commentators dwell on the differences between the United States and the Soviet Union earlier and India and Pakistan today. Among the seeming differences, these are given prominence: differences in the states involved, differences in their histories of conflict, and differences in the distance between the competing parties. I consider them in turn.

Does Deterrence Depend on Who Is Deterring Whom?

For decades we believed that we were trying to deter two monstrous countries—one an "evil empire" and the other a totalitarian country ruled by a megalomaniac. Now we learn that deterrence worked in the past because the United States, the Soviet Union, and China were settled and sensible societies. Karl Kaiser, of the Research Institute of the German Society for Foreign Affairs, and Arthur G. Rubinoff, of the University of Toronto, for example, argue that the success of deterrence depends on its context, that is, on who the countries are and on how they relate to each other. In Kaiser's view, "the stability of nuclear deterrence between East and West rest[ed] on a multitude of military and political factors which in other regions are either totally missing or are only partially present." In Rubinoff's view, it is foolish to compare the American-Soviet conflict with South Asia, where the dynamics are "reminiscent of the outbreak of the First World War." Reminiscence flickers, however, since no one then had nuclear weapons. With a Hindu chauvinist in power in New Delhi and an Islamic party governing India, Rubinoff finds "no resemblance to the deterrent situation that characterized the U.S.-Soviet conflict."[65] That statement may once have applied to India and Pakistan, but only until they armed themselves with nuclear weapons. The history of the Cold War shows that what matters is not the character of the countries that have nuclear weapons but the fact that they have them. Differences among nuclear countries abound, but for keeping the peace what difference have they made?

Whatever the identity of rulers, and whatever the characteristics of their states, the national behaviors they produce are strongly conditioned by the world outside. With conventional weapons, a defensive country has to ask itself how much power it must harness to its policy in order to dissuade an aggressive state from striking. Countries willing to run high risks are hard to dissuade. The characteristics of governments and the temperaments of leaders have to be carefully weighed. With nuclear weapons, any state will be deterred by another state's second-strike forces; one need not be preoccupied with the qualities of the state that is to be deterred or scrutinize its leaders. In a nuclear world, any state—whether ruled by a Stalin, a Mao Zedong, a Saddam Hussein, or a Kim Jong Il—will be deterred by the knowledge that aggressive actions may lead to its own destruction.

Does Deterrence Depend on the Deterrers' Recent History?

India and Pakistan have fought three wars in little more than fifty years, and Kashmir is a bone in the throat of Pakistan. In contrast, America and Russia have never fought a war against each other. Yet some other nuclear countries look more like India and Pakistan, and nuclear weapons have kept the peace between them. Russia and China have suffered numerous military invasions by one another over the centuries. In the 1960s, when both had nuclear weapons, skirmishes broke out from time to time along the Siberian frontier, and the fighting was on a fairly large scale. The bitterness of the antagonists rivaled that between India and Pakistan, fueled by ethnic resentments and ideological differences.

Clashes between nuclear countries over peripheral areas are hardly the exception. Of today's nine nuclear countries, six have fought their neighbors in the past half century: Russia, China, Israel, Pakistan, India, and North Korea. Those who believe that the South Asian situation is without parallel often ignore the Middle East. The parallel is not exact, but it is instructive. The Middle East is unrivalled for long-standing conflict, irreconcilable disputes, feelings of distrust and hatred, and recurrent wars. In 1973, two nonnuclear Arab countries, Egypt and Syria, attacked Israel and fought what by anyone's definition was a war. Limited in extent by one side's nuclear weapons, it nonetheless did not spiral out of control.[66]

Does Deterrence Depend on Distance?

Proximity is a constantly emphasized difference between the relations of India and Pakistan and that of the United States and the Soviet Union. America and Russia are separated by vast distances; Pakistan and India live cheek by jowl. They continually rub against each other in irritating and dangerous ways. George Perkovich had this in mind when he expressed his fear that "Somebody blows up something big and India says, 'That's it, and takes out targets. Then you're on your way. Who's going to back down?'"[67] Much the same fears in much the same words were expressed during the Cold War. The two antagonists might "go to the brink"; one would slip over the edge, and once the exchange of warheads began neither side would be willing to stop it by giving in to the other. In actuality, however, backing down in times of crisis proved not to be such a big problem. Never do two countries share a common interest more completely than when they are locked in death's embrace. Each may want something else as well, but both want most of all to get out of the dire situation they are in. During the Kargil fighting, India went to "Readiness State 3," which means that warheads were prepared for placement on delivery vehicles, and Pakistan apparently took similar steps. These were seen as rash and dangerous moves, but what does one expect? The United States and the Soviet Union alerted their forces a number of times. Doing so is a way of saying, "This is getting serious, and we both had better calm down." Despite the pessimism engendered by the history of South Asia, Indian-Pakistani wars have been, as wars go, quite restrained. As Admiral Menon has written, "Any analysis of the three wars fought often refers to the rather gentlemanly manner in which they were fought with care taken to avoid civilian casualties."[68] Pakistan's 1999 thrust into Kashmir may have been rash, yet as Menon has rightly said, "Subsequent Pakistani attempts to signal an unwillingness to escalate were mature and sober."[69] And in the Kargil campaign, India never sent its troops across the line of control.

History tells us only what we want to know. A pair of *New York Times* journalists contrasts then with now by claiming that, except in Cuba, "the Americans and Soviets took care not to place their troops in direct military confrontation."[70] What, then, were NATO and Warsaw Treaty Organization troops doing in the middle of Europe, where confrontation was a constant and serious business?

Proximity does make warning time short. Missiles can fly between Islamabad and New Delhi in less than five minutes. Yet nuclear countries in the past have often been close militarily if not geographically. Cuba is only ninety miles from American shores, and that is proximity enough. The United States flew planes at the Soviet Union's borders and across them, believing its radars would not spot them. American bravado continues. In April 2001, an American surveillance plane was struck by a Chinese plane over waters near China. Close surveillance is provocative even if international legalities are nicely observed. As President Dwight D. Eisenhower said when an American plane went down thirty-two miles from the Chinese coast in August 1956, "If planes were flying 20 to 50 miles from our shores, we would be very likely to shoot them down if they came in closer, whether through error or not."[71]

Operation Brasstacks was an all-service Indian operation staged in 1987. As Sagan says, it is widely believed that General Sundarji intended it to be a prelude to a war in which India would destroy Pakistan's nuclear facilities. Sundarji may have thought that even if Pakistan had a few bombs, India would be able to destroy them on the ground. In retrospect, Brasstacks looks more like a typical instance of Indian failure to coordinate policies among the Prime Minister's Office, the External Affairs Ministry, the Defense Ministry, and the military services.

Brasstacks is not something new in the nuclear annals. It pales in comparison to provocative acts by the United States and the Soviet Union. In 1983, for example, Able Archer—a recurrent NATO military exercise—was more extensive than ever before. It was held at a time of extraordinary tension. The Soviets believed that surprise was the key to American war plans. During the exercise, the simulated alert of NATO nuclear forces was thought by the Soviets to be a real one. American Pershing II missiles were to be deployed in Europe soon. The Soviets believed that some of them, with their fifty-kiloton payload, fifty-meter accuracy, and ten-minute delivery time to Moscow, had already arrived.[72] Early in the Reagan administration, Defense Secretary Caspar Weinberger and other officials proclaimed that it was our aim to be able to fight, sustain, and win a nuclear war. With some reason, Soviet leaders believed it was about to begin.

Vast distances lie between the United States and Russia. What difference do these distances make when American troops and missiles are stationed in Europe and Northeast Asia? Those who believe that the Indian-Pakistani confrontation is without precedent have either little knowledge of Cold War history or oddly defective memories.

Proximity shortens the time between launch and landing. With little warning time, quick decisions would seem to be required. However, acting on early warnings of incoming missiles that may turn out to be false could be fatal to both sides. The notion that deterrence demands the threat of swift retaliation was ingrained in American and Russian thinking, and it remains so today, with both forces still on hair-trigger alert. Yet deterrence of a would-be attacker does not depend on the belief that retaliation will be prompt, but only on the belief that the attacked may in due course retaliate. As K. Subrahmanyam has put it, "The strike back need not be highly time-critical."[73] A small force may be a vulnerable force, but smaller is worse than bigger only if the attacker believes he can destroy *all* of the force before *any* of it can be launched.

Students of organizations rightly worry about complex and tightly coupled systems because they are susceptible to damaging accidents. They wrongly believe that conflicting nuclear states should be thought of as a tightly coupled system. Fortunately, nuclear weapons loosen the coupling of states by lessening the effects of proximity and by cutting through the complexities of conventional confrontations. Organizational theorists fail to distinguish between the technical complexities of nuclear-weapons systems and the simplicity of the situations they create.

Sagan points out that the survival of Indian and Pakistani forces cannot be guaranteed. But neither can their complete destruction, and that is what matters. Oddly, many pessimists believe that countries with small and technologically limited nuclear forces may be able to accomplish the difficult feat of making a successful first strike but not the easy one of making their own nuclear force appear to be invulnerable. They over-look a basic nuclear truth: If some part of a force is invulnerable, all of the force is invulnerable. Destroying even a major portion of a nuclear force does no good because of the damage a small number of surviving warheads can do. Conventional weapons put a premium striking first to gain the initial advantage and set the course of the war. Nuclear weapons eliminate this premium. The initial advantage is insignificant if the cost of gaining it is half a dozen cities.

More important than the size of arsenals, the sophistication of command and control, the proximity of competitors, and the history of their relations, are the sensibilities of leaders. Fortunately, nuclear weapons make leaders behave sensibly even though under other circumstances they might be brash and reckless.

The South Asian situation, said so often to be without precedent, finds precedents galore. Rather than assuming that the present differs significantly from the past, we should emphasize the similarities and learn from them. Fortunately, India and Pakistan have learned from their nuclear predecessors. Nuclear maturity for some countries comes at an early age. During the George W. Bush administration, the United States, however, seemed to be entering its second childhood.

Sagan believes that future Indian-Pakistani crises may be nuclear. Once countries have nuclear weapons any confrontation that merits the term "crisis" is a nuclear one. With conventional weapons, crises tend toward instability. Because of the perceived, or misperceived, advantage of striking first, war may be the outcome. Nuclear weapons make crises stable, which is an important reason for believing that India and Pakistan are better off with than without them.

Yet because nuclear weapons limit escalation, they may tempt countries to fight small wars. Glenn Snyder long ago identified the strategic stability/tactical instability paradox. Benefits carry costs in the nuclear business just as they do in other endeavors. The possibility of fighting at low levels is not a bad price to pay for the impossibility of fighting at high levels. This impossibility becomes obvious, since in the presence of nuclear weapons no one can score major gains, and all can lose catastrophically.

Sagan carries Snyder's logic a step further by arguing that Pakistan and India may nevertheless fight to a higher level of violence, believing that if one side or the other begins to lose control, a third party will step in to prevent the use of nuclear weapons. The idea is a hangover from Cold War days when the United States and the Soviet Union thought they had compelling reasons to intervene in other countries' conflicts. The end of the Cold War reduced the incentives for such intervention. As K. Subrahmanyam has said, "In a world dominated by the Cold War, there was a certain predictability that any Chinese nuclear threat to India would be countervailed by one or the other super power or both. In the aftermath of the Cold War that predictability has disappeared."[74] Intervention by a third party during low-level fighting would still be possible, but neither side could count on it.

Kanti Bajpai spotted another consequence of nuclear weapons that may be harmful: they may drive the antagonists apart by removing the need to agree. Since deterrence works, Bajpai wonders why countries would try to settle their differences. India and Pakistan, however, did not reach agreement on Kashmir or on other issues when neither had nuclear weapons; now both sides have at least an incentive to discuss their problems.

Crises on the subcontinent recur, and when they do, voices of despair predict a conventional clash ending in nuclear blasts. On December 13, 2001, five gunmen attacked the Indian Parliament. Fourteen people died, including the gunmen. India, blaming Pakistani terrorists, mounted its largest mobilization in the past thirty years and massed troops and equipment along the India-Pakistan border. As in the crisis of 1990, the United States deployed its diplomats, this time dispatching Secretary of State Colin Powell to calm the contestants. Tempers on both sides flared, bombast filled the air, and an American commentator pointed out once again that all of the American military's war games show that a conventional Indian-Pakistani war will end in a nuclear conflagration.[75] Both India and Pakistan claimed that they could fight conventionally in the face of nuclear weapons. What reason do we have to believe that military and civilian leaders on either side fail to understand the dangers of fighting a conventional war against a nuclear neighbor? The statements of Pakistan's leader, General Musharraf, were mainly conciliatory. Indian military leaders emphasized that any military engagements would have to be limited to such targets as guerrilla training camps and military facilities used by extremists. As an astute analyst put it, "India's way of looking at this is that we're not threatening Pakistan's core interests, so they would have no incentive to launch their weapons."[76] Indian leaders made it clear that they intended to pressure Pakistan to control military intrusions by irregular forces. Pakistan made it clear that its pressure for a Kashmiri settlement would be unremitting. Except to alarmist observers, mainly American, neither side looked as though it would cross or even approach the nuclear threshold. The proposition that nuclear weapons limit the extent of fighting and ultimately preserve peace again found vindication.

Update

Since I wrote this chapter in 2003, there have been a number of important developments in India and Pakistan. These include India's new "Cold Start" conventional doctrine, the Mumbai terrorist attacks of 2008, and revelations about the A. Q. Khan network. These developments are important to note, but none of them change my assessment that a nuclear subcontinent will be more stable than the nonnuclear India and Pakistan of the past.

In 2004, India developed a new conventional military doctrine known as "Cold Start." The Cold Start doctrine was adopted to reduce India's mobilization time and increase its options for fighting a limited conventional war. Scholars of South Asian security have suggested that Cold Start may be destabilizing, but I do not agree.[77] It is highly unlikely that this more offensive posture could beget an escalation to nuclear war.

Despite India's revised conventional posture, the presumption that India or Pakistan will fight a serious conventional war in the face of nuclear weapons is simply false. Both countries know that a serious conventional conflict risks a resort to nuclear weapons. Given that neither India nor Pakistan can know whether its opponent will resort to nuclear use, either inadvertently or on purpose, both are disincentivized from beginning a conventional conflict at all as the anticipated result is simply disastrous. Even the small possibility of nuclear use by either side will continue to be enough to deter a nonnuclear war on the subcontinent. Cold Start, or any other doctrine, cannot change that fact.

In 2008, the terrorist group Lakshar-e-Taiba launched a series of attacks on Mumbai, killing 163 people. These events were truly lamentable. But I do not agree with those who suggest that Pakistan's nuclear shield made these attacks possible.[78] Scores of horrible acts have occurred in Indo-Pakistani history, and while this one was on a large scale, it does not necessarily represent a new chapter of violence on the subcontinent. Moreover, India's restrained response following the attacks suggests that nuclear weapons do indeed have the stabilizing effects I have suggested here.[79]

Following atrocities on this scale, one might have expected India to respond to Pakistan more decisively. After all, these attacks were apparently planned in Pakistan and likely had the support of its intelligence agency, the ISI.[80] But despite the new Cold Start posture, India did not retaliate conventionally against Pakistan in 2008. It did not even attack LeT-training camps in retribution. India's response focused mostly on beefing up its own counterterror efforts.[81] This suggests that Indian officials understood that a conventional war with Pakistan could escalate too easily and with disastrous results. Thus, they chose a more cautious course. It is my hope that we will not continue to see brutal terrorist acts against civilians in the future. But it is certain that the presence of nuclear weapons means we will continue to see prudence where the use of force is concerned.

Finally, in 2003 it was revealed that A. Q. Khan, the former head of Pakistan's uranium enrichment program, had been operating a black market nuclear network that sold sensitive materials including centrifuges and weapons designs to countries like Iran, North Korea, and Libya. Reports in 2011 suggested that Syria might also have been a customer.[82] I cannot and will not suggest that black market nuclear trading is unproblematic. Indeed, there will likely be others who follow in Khan's footsteps. But I strongly believe this is a problem that we can manage through vigilant surveillance and intelligence.

The United States, Britain, and Germany all engaged in active efforts to thwart the Khan network. They disrupted financing to his research lab, interdicted illicit cargo, and ultimately forced Khan to confess publicly. While they did not stop Khan's mischievous activities, these efforts certainly helped to contain them.

Further, Khan's home country recognized that his dealings were problematic. Even rickety states like Pakistan realize that they cannot tolerate non-state actors who challenge their authority in destabilizing ways. The Pakistani government knew that the A. Q. Khan network put them at peril. President Pervez Musharraf forced Khan into retirement well before the black market network was revealed, and Pakistan agreed to try him and place him under house arrest.[83] One would have liked to see a much more robust effort at state intervention in Khan's dealings, but the basic point is clear—state sponsorship of illicit nuclear activities is very risky business.

Finally, we must ask ourselves how much Khan's illegal dealings really altered our nuclear future. I do not deny the significance of Khan's assistance to unsavory states. Trading in centrifuges and weapons designs is no small matter. But Iran and North Korea had nuclear programs that began decades before they ever interacted with Khan. His black market materials may have sped along their weapons pursuits, but it is hard to believe that his assistance was crucial to either program. Terrorism and black market dealings are not to be taken lightly, but they are also a far cry from the wars India and Pakistan have fought in the past.

Are India and Pakistan worse or better off now that they have nuclear weapons? Are their futures dimmer or brighter? I will surprise no one by saying "brighter." I have looked in vain for important differences between the plight of India and Pakistan and that of other nuclear countries. Nuclear weapons put all countries that possess them in the same boat. South Asia is said to be the "acid test" for deterrence optimists. So far, nuclear deterrence has passed all of the many tests it has faced.

Chapter 6

IRAQ, NORTH KOREA, AND IRAN

Scott D. Sagan and Kenneth N. Waltz

with Mira Rapp-Hooper

In his January 2002 State of the Union address to Congress, President George W. Bush announced that Iraq, North Korea, and Iran formed a dangerous "Axis of Evil" that threatened the United States and other nations around the globe. Of particular concern was a set of U.S. intelligence estimates stating that Iraq, North Korea, and Iran likely possessed chemical and biological weapons and that all three were believed to have started nuclear weapons development programs. Bush outlined why he believed the emerging threat was unacceptable:

> States like these, and their terrorist allies, constitute an axis of evil, arming to threaten the peace of the world. By seeking weapons of mass destruction, these regimes pose a grave and growing danger. They could provide these arms to terrorists, giving them the means to match their hatred. They could attack our allies or attempt to blackmail the United States. In any of these cases, the price of indifference would be catastrophic.[1]

The nuclear landscape has changed significantly in all three states in the decade since Bush made his Axis of Evil pronouncement. One of the three states—Iraq—was invaded and occupied by the United States in 2003. A second—North Korea—developed and then tested nuclear weapons in 2006 and 2009. The third—Iran—produced significant amounts of enriched uranium, was accused of violating its Nuclear Non-Proliferation treaty (NPT) commitments not to seek nuclear weapons, and was then repeatedly subject to ever stronger sanctions by the United Nations Security Council.

Readers of this book will not be surprised to learn that we hold very different views about these developments. In this chapter, we will first present a brief history of nuclear proliferation and nonproliferation activities in Iraq, North Korea, and Iran. After this background, Waltz then presents his arguments for why the acquisition of nuclear weapons by Saddam Hussein's Iraq would not have been as dangerous as the Bush administration believed in 2003; why North Korea's development of a small number of nuclear weapons has deterred, not provoked, aggression on the Korean peninsula; and why Iran, if it succeeds in getting nuclear weapons, will not pose a significant risk to its neighbors or the United States. Sagan then presents his views on why a nuclear-armed Iraq would have been a severe threat to regional and global security, why North Korean possession of nuclear weapons has led to novel proliferation problems, and why a nuclear-armed Iran in the future would be exceedingly dangerous.

The October 2002 U.S. National Intelligence Estimate declared that Saddam Hussein had started to reconstitute the Iraqi nuclear weapons development program which had been discovered and destroyed after the 1991 Gulf War and had likely maintained some of the chemical weapons capability that Iraq had used in the 1980s in the war against Iran.[2] Secretary of State Colin Powell presented the evidence to support these claims to the UN Security Council in February 2003 but was not able to persuade many of the members (including the veto-wielding French and Russians) to support military intervention against Iraq. The Bush administration nevertheless ordered the attack of Iraq in late March 2003 and quickly defeated Saddam Hussein's army, including the elite Republican Guard divisions protecting Baghdad. Although the president announced "Mission Accomplished" to great fanfare soon after the fall of Baghdad, the administration was quickly confronted with two nasty surprises. First, their own post-invasion investigation quickly revealed that Saddam Hussein had not reconstituted his efforts to acquire nuclear weapons after United Nations weapons inspectors were withdrawn from Iraq in December 1998. Second, instead of the paradise of post-Saddam peace predicted by some Bush administration officials, Iraq quickly descended into a complex and bloody civil war between Sunni insurgents, Shia militias, Al Qaida in Iraq, and Iraqi government forces—with U.S. occupying forces caught in the crosshairs. As of April 2012, 4,488 U.S. troops and over 106,000 Iraqi civilians are believed to have lost their lives in the resulting cycles of violence.[3]

The history of the North Korean nuclear weapons program is quite different. In 1993, International Atomic Energy Agency (IAEA) inspectors caught the North Koreans violating their NPT commitments by first covertly removing nuclear fuel rods containing plutonium from the Yongbyon reactor and then denying they had done so. The crisis escalated when Pyongyang kicked out the IAEA inspectors and announced that it would withdraw from the treaty—which is within its legal right—in ninety days. Facing both economic sanctions and threats of U.S. air strikes on the reactor complex, the Kim Il Sung regime backed down and the Clinton administration successfully negotiated the 1994 "Agreed Framework" compromise, under which the North Koreans stopped running their Yongbyon reactor and permitted the IAEA to safeguard the remaining fuel rods at the site in exchange for American promises to build a set of light water, more proliferation-resistant, reactors.

The incoming Bush administration was deeply skeptical of the utility of the Agreed Framework, however, and not only labeled North Korea as a member of the Axis of Evil but in the fall of 2002 accused Pyongyang of cheating again on its agreement, this time by secretly starting a uranium enrichment program based on centrifuges received from Pakistan. In response to these accusations and growing hostility with Washington, the North Koreans again kicked out the IAEA inspectors, withdrew from the NPT in 2003, removed the spent fuel rods from their storage ponds, and began to separate the plutonium to make materials for nuclear weapons. Pointedly referring to the events in the Middle East, spokesmen for the regime in Pyongyang proclaimed that they would not be another Iraq:

> Only the physical deterrent force, tremendous military deterrent force powerful enough to decisively beat back an attack supported by any ultra-modern weapons, can avert a war and protect the security of the country and the nation. This is a lesson drawn from the Iraqi war.

> The U.S is seriously mistaken if it thinks that the DPRK will accept the demand for disarming while watching one of the three countries the U.S. listed as part of an "axis of evil" already subject to the barbarous military attack.[4]

In October 2006, the North Koreans conducted their first nuclear weapons test; in May 2009 they repeated the process, this time with more technical success. It was now clear that despite treaty commitments, U.N. sanctions, and military threats, the North Koreans had successfully built a small number of nuclear weapons.[5]

The Islamic Republic of Iran has taken a different tack in its quest for nuclear weapons. Article IV of the NPT delegates to nonnuclear state members of the treaty the "inalienable right" of the peaceful use of nuclear energy, and the Iranian government has repeatedly insisted that its nuclear activities are all part of a national nuclear energy program. The existence of a large-scale uranium enrichment plant at Natanz was first disclosed by Iranian dissidents in August 2002 and confirmed when IAEA inspectors were later permitted to monitor the facility in 2003.[6] Suspicions were aroused, not only because Tehran had failed to inform the IAEA of the construction of the facility ahead of time, but also because Iran had covertly received centrifuge technology from the Pakistani A. Q. Khan network, and evidence of weapons-related experiments was also soon found by both IAEA inspectors and American intelligence agencies.

The Bush administration made no secret of its goal of "regime change" in the Middle East after the Axis of Evil speech; when asked by a reporter what lesson Tehran should learn from the 2003 fall of Baghdad, a senior Bush administration official said "take a number"—in other words, you are next in line.[7]

It initially appeared as if the invasion of Iraq and the accusations of covert military-related nuclear activities had encouraged Iran to stop such activities and limit its nuclear program to producing low-enriched uranium at Natanz. The crisis again escalated during the Obama administration as Iran was discovered to have started construction of a second covert enrichment facility near Qom. Tehran then started to enrich the uranium from Natanz to higher levels, shortening the time it would take to make weapons-grade materials, and the IAEA again reported in March 2011 that it could not confirm Iran's compliance with its NPT commitments. In November 2011, the IAEA went one step further and issued a report declaring that they now had credible information indicating that "Iran has carried out . . . activities that are relevant to the development of a nuclear explosive device."[8]

Throughout this period, Tehran has continued to defy UN Security Council demands to end its enriched uranium production and as of the time of this writing, in April 2012, Iran is estimated to have a 5,451kg stockpile of low-enriched uranium, which is in theory enough to make one to four nuclear weapons, if Iran withdrew from the NPT and further enriched the uranium to weapons-grade levels.[9] Both the Obama administration in Washington and the Netanyahu government in Israel have reportedly developed and analyzed airstrike options for attacking Iranian nuclear facilities and both have, as of the time of this writing, decided not to initiate military action, reportedly on the grounds that Iran still might be deterred or prevented from breaking out of the NPT by other means and that a military attack would only delay, but not completely destroy, the Iranian nuclear program.

How dangerous are these developments? We disagree with each other about the likely effects of these recent and potential cases of nuclear proliferation and therefore on how best to address these problems. Waltz will first discuss the Iraq, North Korea, and Iran cases, arguing that nuclear weapons possession by these states should not have been feared in the past and should not be feared in the future. Sagan will then argue the opposite case.

THE REASONS NOT TO WORRY

Kenneth N. Waltz with Mira Rapp-Hooper

Over the course of the past decade, Iraq, North Korea, and Iran have been placed in the international spotlight as nascent nuclear rogues to be feared by all. It is hardly surprising that these three states have exhibited bellicose behavior of late. President Bush's 2002 decision to term all three countries the "Axis of Evil" all but assured roguish reactions from Iraq, North Korea, and Iran. And his subsequent endorsement of the use of preventive force guaranteed that these countries would attempt to deter the United States however possible. Because states in international politics are like units, it should not surprise us that all three of these countries responded similarly. Given the security environment in which each of these states was placed, this behavior should be expected. That Iran or North Korea would step up its nuclear efforts following Bush's Axis of Evil speech is hardly surprising. What is surprising, however, is that leaders around the world seem to believe that these new nuclear programs present insurmountable international challenges.

Some scholars argue that domestic politics is the best lens through which to view states' nuclear decisions. Sagan favors an organizational perspective on these issues. But these considerations are minor in comparison to the influence that the basic structure of international politics has on states, including on their nuclear decisions. Examining the cases of Iraq, Iran, and North Korea from a systemic perspective clarifies why each of these states wanted to acquire nuclear weapons. A systemic perspective also elucidates why these nuclear aspirants *do not* present novel challenges. Contrary to those who argue that nuclear weapons in the hands of "rogue" states present new dangers, I suggest that a nuclear North Korea or a nuclear Iran will exhibit behavior much like a nuclear China or Soviet Union during the Cold War.

Like all of those states that have come before them, these countries can only use nuclear weapons for deterrence. They will become less, and not more, violent once they possess nuclear weapons. Iran and North Korea will lack incentives to transfer nuclear materials and weapons to terrorists, and they will have great incentives to control their stockpiles. And if they do attempt to export sensitive technology, then the world's major powers can manage this problem. Iraq, Iran, and North Korea's interests in nuclear weapons stem from serious security concerns. This has been true of every nuclear aspirant since 1945. And just as for every other state, these weapons can do no more than deter. We should not fear, and could live comfortably with, a nuclear North Korea and a nuclear Iran; we could have done the same for Iraq.

Iraq

On September 26, 2002, thirty-three international relations scholars took out an ad in *The New York Times*. In the announcement, we argued that a war with Iraq was *not* in America's national interest. Among the points we made was this one: "Even if Saddam Hussein acquired nuclear weapons, he could not use them without suffering massive U.S. or Israeli retaliation."[10] Additionally, we recommended vigilant containment of Iraq, arguing that Saddam was not preparing to attack America or its allies at that time. Nearly a decade later, I am as committed to the content of this message as ever: the United States should not have invaded Iraq in 2003. Vital U.S. interests were not at stake; the United States and her allies were not in immediate danger. Saddam Hussein could never have used nuclear weapons even if he had acquired them.

The 2002 National Security Strategy of the United States called for the preemptive use of force against "rogue" countries attempting to acquire nuclear weapons.[11] This was not, however, a doctrine of preemption but one of prevention— Saddam Hussein was not prepared to attack anyone in the near future. In fact, it is hard to argue that 2003 Iraq posed much of a threat to the United States at all. Iraq was economically feeble, with a Gross Domestic Product of only $20 billion dollars.[12] Compare this to a U.S. defense budget of nearly $400 billion.[13] Saddam's military and infrastructure in general was much weaker than it had been before the 1991 Gulf War. The prevalent belief that Saddam was a pressing threat to the United States was based on the idea that he was trying to acquire nuclear weapons. The invasion of Iraq of course proved this untrue—Iraq had *not* restarted its nuclear program. But even if the Bush administration's worst fears had been substantiated, the use of preventive force would have been irresponsible and unnecessary. A nuclear-armed Iraq still would not have constituted an imminent threat.

Three arguments were used in 2003 to justify an invasion to disarm Saddam. First, there was a fear that Saddam Hussein might actually use nuclear weapons. Second, some argued that he might have transferred those weapons to non-state actors. Third, there was the possibility that Iraq would have been unable to control a nuclear arsenal had it had one. All three of these contingencies were highly unlikely. A nuclear-armed Iraq would not have posed a serious threat to the United States and did not warrant an invasion or a decade-long war.

First, consider the idea that Saddam Hussein might have acquired and used nuclear weapons himself. There is no question that Saddam Hussein was a brutal tyrant, known for mistreating his own people and causing trouble internationally. But deterrence would have applied to him just as it does to any other ruler. As with most dictators, Saddam's primary goal was regime survival. Holding on to power for thirty-four years is no small task and can only be achieved by a leader who is very sensitive to the costs of his actions, both internally and internationally. Had Saddam used a nuclear weapon against Israel or another regional power, there is no question that he would have suffered a swift and devastating retaliatory response. This would hardly have been advisable for a ruler whose lifelong goal was to maintain his tenuous grip on power. While Iraq may not have hesitated to launch SCUD missiles at Israel during the first Gulf War, nuclear weapons are a far different animal, and their use would necessarily warrant an overwhelming response. Saddam would have known this and would not have used nuclear weapons.

The Bush administration liked to cite the fact that Saddam had used chemical weapons on his own people to suggest that he would also be inclined toward nuclear use. While Saddam's treatment of the Kurds was, without question, brutal and lamentable, this parallel is a false one. The consequences to Saddam or any leader of using nuclear weapons are definite and undeniable; he could not possibly have used them without facing retaliation from Israel or the United States. And as reports since 2003 have indicated, his primary goal was state and regime survival, making nuclear use all the more unthinkable.[14]

Saddam also would not have been likely to transfer nuclear weapons to terrorists (his connections to Al Qaida were revealed to be almost nonexistent). Just as autocratic leaders should be loath to launch a nuclear weapon themselves, they should have no incentive to transfer one to an irresponsible and uncontrollable party. After assuming a great financial burden to acquire nuclear weapons (including the sanctions that accompanied that pursuit), Saddam would not have wanted to share his weapons with non-state actors. A nuclear detonation by a terrorist anywhere in the world would necessarily spark an energetic attribution effort, which could, in turn, unseat the leader who permitted the nuclear transfer. Once again, this was the last thing Saddam ever would have wanted.

Finally, experts, including Sagan, argue that less-developed, rogue regimes will be unable to control their own arsenals, leading to accidental detonations or nuclear theft. On the contrary, a nuclear arsenal in Saddam's possession would have been relatively safe. Hussein would not have developed more than a small cache, and ten or twenty weapons are relatively easy to keep track of as Saddam's Iraq was nothing if not highly centralized. As with many dictators, Saddam was obsessed with control, to a fault; an atomic heist would have been much easier to pull off in the former Soviet Union.

Since 2003, it has become clear that Saddam Hussein had not restarted the Iraqi nuclear program. In fact, Saddam deliberately created the impression that he was acquiring a deterrent although he was not. Interviews with Iraqi Generals and others close to Hussein have indicated that he hoped that shirking inspections and failing to cooperate on nuclear matters would suggest that he might have a serious WMO program. This would allow him to deter both Iran and the United States from invasion and secure his regime.[15] Although this dissembling ultimately served as the justification for the 2003 invasion, it is indicative of something broader—namely, that Saddam Hussein was seeking the deterrent power of nuclear weapons rather than the ability to use them.

In conclusion, there is little reason to believe that a nuclear-armed Iraq would have posed a serious threat to the United States, or that this threat warranted invasion. "Rogue states" under the rule of a dictator act in a very unitary and controlled fashion indeed. And post-2003, evidence suggests that like so many leaders before him, Saddam was interested in nuclear weapons for their deterrent capability.

North Korea

Despite the political and journalistic attention it has received, the newly nuclear North Korea is not more dangerous since

2006. North Korea has been a rambunctious nuisance for decades, dating back to the Korean War, when it almost pushed South Korea off the peninsula. The North was difficult to defeat in that conflict and was even more difficult in the making and enforcement of the cease-fire that followed. In the years that followed, North Korea seized every opportunity to do damage to South Korea and its interests—notably, the attempted assassination of the ROK president and the assassination of the president's wife and several South Korean cabinet members in 1974. North Korea's behavior has actually become more moderate or more effectively constrained over time. Periodically it lashes out with an isolated but destructive act like the March 26, 2010, sinking of the Cheonon or the November 2010 shelling of Yeonpeong. These acts are annoying, to be sure, but they are sporadic and largely symbolic. They aim to irk South Korea, the United States, and even Japan, and create uncertainties about North Korea's intentions and future plans. There is little reason to worry about North Korea's plans, however. Even with nuclear weapons, the country is not capable of much.

Despite having over a million men under arms, North Korea is not a militarily powerful country. The Democratic People's Republic of Korea (DPRK) does not have enough fuel or supplies to conduct basic training exercises.[16] The North has numerous tunnels that trench into South Korean territory, but it is hard to know what these will accomplish, especially with U.S. and ROK troops massed on the other side.[17] North Korea periodically shows an interest in negotiations with the South Korea government, but these seldom amount to more than familial exchanges for those separated by the DMZ. Tens of thousands of U.S. and ROK troops send a clear signal to the North: a second Korean War would be a bloody and losing endeavor.

Notwithstanding North Korea's inclination for isolated acts of aggression, the military and political status quo on the peninsula has been remarkably stable since 1953. Even in the absence of a true peace treaty, the post-war territorial status quo has held, and U.S.-ROK cooperation is strong. And for decades, it is clear that North Korea is only becoming weaker. Massive numbers of refugees flee each year to the considerable embarrassment of the government, and the DPRK cannot feed its own people.[18]

Between 1989 and 1991, North Korea's world dissolved with the disappearance of the Soviet Union, the isolation of Cuba, and China's weakening interest in assisting the DPRK. Other North East Asian countries, like Japan and the ROK, have seen their alliances remain quite strong. The United States continues to be keenly engaged in the region, and South Korea and Japan are well supported by this ally. The occasional acts of aggression by North Korea are more an indication of weakness than of strength. The shaky North Korean regime may well be trying to demonstrate to its own people that it has influence beyond its own borders. North Korea was remarkably successful at convincing its people that they were better off than citizens in South Korea or Japan, but this sham is steadily unraveling as information leaks into the country from the rest of the world. The regime's occasional acts of aggression must be understood in light of this unsteady position.

It was under these circumstances that North Korea tested its first nuclear weapon in 2006. The DPRK's interest in a nuclear capability was decades old, however, and the North's nuclear program began with assistance from the USSR in the 1950s. North Korea stepped up its longstanding efforts to acquire a nuclear capability after the demise of its closest communist allies, clearly a reaction of a profoundly insecure country. The DPRK's invigorated nuclear pursuits caused quite a panic in the early Clinton years, but the nuclear standoff on the peninsula appeared to be resolved in 1994.

The Agreed Framework provided North Korea with light water reactors and fuel in exchange for their promise to remain nonnuclear, but this agreement was not fulfilled by the United States.[19] Early George W. Bush administration policy abrogated the framework, and in due course North Korea found itself included in the "Axis of Evil." The following year, the DPRK removed itself from the NPT, ending inspections of its nuclear sites. Its first nuclear test came just three years later. It is not hard to surmise the lessons that the DPRK took from the first years of the Bush administration. American guarantees could not be trusted, nuclear aspirants would become targets, and the safest way to avoid Iraq's fate was to actually acquire a deterrent.

It is not hard to see why North Korea has decided to assemble a nuclear arsenal. The question is not why the DPRK would seek this capability but how serious of a threat the country is now that they have it. Readers will not be surprised to learn that I do not think that a nuclear North Korea is particularly dangerous. In fact, its actions can safely be attributed to its intense worries about its own security.

In this section I will present several arguments for why we should not be alarmed by North Korea's new nuclear status. First, North Korea has certainly been no more aggressive since acquiring nuclear weapons than it had been in the past, and the DPRK cannot and will not use nuclear weapons in the region. Second, while North Korea has shown a proclivity to transfer sensitive nuclear materials, this is a threat that is easily contained. Third, recent events suggest that North Korea's nuclear capability itself is probably quite feeble. Fourth, the possibility of the North Korean regime's collapse is much more worthy of international attention than its small nuclear arsenal. And fifth, U.S. alliance relations and a rising China all augur well and suggest a stable future for Northeast Asia.

First, there is little evidence that since 2006 North Korea has become any more aggressive than it was as a nonnuclear power. The 2010 sinking of the Cheonon and the shelling of Yeonpeong were surely disagreeable acts, but compared to the massive assassination efforts the DPRK pursued in the past, these register as annoyances rather than as serious belligerence. Like so many new nuclear countries before it, the North is clearly aware that nuclear acquisition makes it something of a target. Great powers like the United States, Russia, and China have been keenly engaged in the DPRK's dealings since it acquired this capability. And while the regime might occasionally choose to remind the world that it exists, it is unlikely to do much more than ruffle some feathers. Nuclear weapons discourage, rather than encourage, serious aggressive action.

Even if the North is predisposed to occasional misdeeds, this does not suggest that the Kims might actually *use* North Korea's nuclear capability. The sinking of a single ship or shelling of an island is in no way comparable to nuclear use. Even if tensions escalated on the peninsula, the DPRK would not resort to nuclear weapons, out of fear of a devastating and inevitable response from the United States. Nuclear weapons are unusable in war, no matter how bellicose the leader who possesses them.

Second, many worry that North Korea will transfer sensitive nuclear materials beyond its borders. The country is impoverished and isolated, giving it plenty of incentive to sell illicit technology. These concerns are valid indeed, as the North has proven willing to export sensitive goods in the past. But I believe this is a threat that can certainly be contained. There is strong evidence that the DPRK assisted Syria in building its Al-Kibar nuclear reactor. U.S. and Israeli intelligence caught this illicit transfer, and Israeli airstrikes leveled the facility in 2007.[20] North Korea is also known to have transferred missile technology to Myanmar. But the Proliferation Security Initiative, a multilateral maritime security effort, has interdicted illicit cargo on numerous occasions, proving that it is no simple task for the DPRK to export sensitive materials unnoticed.[21] United States' and international surveillance capabilities are excellent and have shown to be adept at containing North Korean export efforts.

A critic would surely argue that no intelligence effort is perfect. A few failed attempts to detect a North Korea transfer could result in serious international weapons proliferation. But the transfer of sensitive technology is an insufficient condition for the spread of nuclear weapons. That is, just because North Korea is willing to sell nuclear components, and it finds a customer, does not mean that customer will be able to make use of its acquisitions. Take the example of Libya's WMD program. Under Muammar Qaddhafi, Libya had a longstanding and very unsuccessful nuclear weapons program. Around the year 2000, Libya became a customer of A. Q. Khan—the leader of an illicit black-market nuclear network run out of Pakistan. Qaddhafi purchased everything from centrifuges to weapons designs from Khan. Yet when he gave up his weapons program in 2003, nothing had been assembled. It was clear that Libya could afford to *purchase* these nuclear components, but it still could not put them to use.[22] The same may well hold true for potential North Korean customers. Procuring technology absent the requisite know-how is not likely to be a fruitful endeavor.

Another reason to believe that a nuclear North Korea is not a serious threat is the shaky nature of its own weapons program. As I have mentioned, the North began its program in the 1950s but did not test a weapon until 2006. This is hardly speedy progress. Its first test of a plutonium bomb produced a yield of less than 1 kiloton. A test this small is often referred to as a "fizzle," and many speculated that a serious weapons design problem was to blame for the subpar performance. The North's 2009 test produced a larger yield, but one that was still much smaller than the early U.S. nuclear weapons.[23] Current estimates suggest that North Korea may possess eight or twelve nuclear weapons, but we know little about the nature of these weapons.[24] If North Korea is running into bomb design problems, this handful of weapons may not even work. We also do not know how large in size these weapons are. Are they mobile? Could the North even use them if it wanted to?

That the North's program is on shaky ground is supported by recent revelations that the DPRK has begun full-scale uranium enrichment. During a 2010 visit, North Korean officials chose to show its uranium enrichment facilities to former Los Alamos Director Siegfried Hecker. But why would the North pursue a uranium avenue if it had already mastered plutonium reprocessing? It may be because the DPRK is struggling with the design of its plutonium weapons, as revealed by its two small tests. Plutonium is the easier fissile material to extract, but it is a harder bomb to build. Uranium enrichment is a more difficult process, but the weapon design is a much simpler one. This dual course suggests that North Korea is not satisfied with its own technical progress.

The widespread fear of North Korea's nuclear capability and occasional aggressive acts has obscured the real worst-case scenario on the peninsula—that the regime itself might collapse. This is a regime that has been on its last gasps for a very long time. It is unable to feed its own people, unable to employ them productively, and increasingly incapable of isolating its populace from the outside world. The transfer of power from Kim Jong Il to Kim Jong Un appears to have gone smoothly so far, but this does not change the fact that the country has been weakening in recent years.

If North Korea collapsed, a major international effort would be required to secure it. Among the items on this agenda would be locating and securing the North's nuclear materials and missile technology, and the United States should plan for this contingency, with help from countries like China and Japan. The United States and partners in Northeast Asia will be capable of handling this worst-case scenario, but it deserves significant international attention.[25] North Korea, the United States, and the other countries of Northeast Asia all share an interest in insuring that the DPRK does not collapse violently. This, and not any specific episode of North Korean bellicosity, is the real danger, and all possible measures should be taken to manage this risk. As long as the North Korean state remains intact, we have little to fear from its nuclear weapons.

Finally, it is worth commenting more broadly on the current and future state of affairs in Northeast Asia. At present, many experts are worried that nuclear North Korea and a rising China could seriously destabilize the region. Will a declining United States be able to maintain its security commitments there? And if it cannot, will South Korea and Japan be tempted to go nuclear themselves? Alliance relations in the region have been stable since the 1950s. Both South Korea and Japan are quite capable of acquiring their own nuclear weapons but have declined to do so for fear of upsetting their security relationships with the United States. A significantly reduced U.S. commitment to either partner could cause them to rethink these decisions, but that will probably not occur in the near future.

Additionally, there is a reason to believe that China's rise might not be a bad thing where nuclear issues are concerned. The People's Republic of China (PRC) has historically been uninterested in interfering with smaller countries' affairs, including their nuclear weapons programs. As its power grows, however, its interest in these issues is likely to do the same. A rising China has every reason to want to see a stable Northeast Asia, and thus every reason to want a docile and cooperative North Korea. Recurrent efforts to resuscitate the Six Party Talks may give China an opportunity to take the lead on this issue. It is unlikely that North Korea will give up its nuclear arsenal (recall that NATO airstrikes on Libya caused a North Korean representative to publicly remark that Qaddhafi should have kept his nuclear program)—but this does not mean that we should expect strife in the region.[26] The past five years have proved that we can live with a nuclear North Korea, and, in fact, that we might prefer this DPRK to the more bellicose one of the past.

Iran

As they have so often in the past, Iran and the United States find themselves in a condition of conflict and mutual suspicion. Under the Shah, Iran aimed for regional hegemony and the United States was reasonably supportive of this goal. Iran's interests and ours often coincided, and the Shah served as an informal but quite reliable ally. With the Shah overthrown in 1979 and an unpredictable and shaky regime replacing him, dramatic events like the Hostage Crisis signaled that American-Iranian relations were at a nadir. Relations have not seen much improvement since they ran aground in 1979 and in many respects have worsened. One crucial reason for this is the past decade of U.S. foreign policy toward the Islamic Republic.

Directly following the September 11 attacks, Iran extended an olive branch of sorts to the United States, offering counter-terror assistance. In 2002, President Bush identified three countries in the Axis of Evil. In due course, one of them was invaded. The hostility and insecurity of Iran was guaranteed by the U.S.'s invasion of Iraq. Although their relations had hardly been friendly, Iran and Iraq had maintained a stable regional balance of power for decades. The United States appeared to Iran as a great power arbitrarily intruding into this regional dynamic. The United States possessed overwhelming power and a clear agenda to remake Iraq, and the fears of neighboring countries were naturally great.

To dissuade and deter the United States, no country can rely on conventional weaponry alone. Smaller powers who fear incursion naturally may seek an independent nuclear capability. Iraq lacked such capability and it suffered a consequent invasion. North Korea had its own nuclear weapons program and did not. Iran easily concluded that the DPRK had made itself immune from an American use of force. If Iran was to be able to deter America from interfering in its affairs, it would need to be able to acquire its own nuclear weapons capability.

The Iranian nuclear weapons program dates back to the Shah but has taken center stage since 2002. A 2007 National Intelligence Estimate declared that Iran had halted warhead production in 2003—an unsurprising fact given the U.S.'s invasion of its closest neighbor in that year.[27] But a halt is not cessation, and there is ample reason to believe that Iran has returned to its nuclear pursuits with great gusto. With the United States bogged down in Iraq, and American and Israeli threats against Iran continuing, it is hard to see why Iran would *not* want to acquire a nuclear capability.

Under these circumstances, any country, if it were able, would want to prevent interference by an overwhelmingly powerful foreign country. When it seemed that Iran was setting itself on a nuclear course, American journalists, officials, and academics worried that it was seeking nuclear means to pursue nefarious ends. We began to ask ourselves what a nuclear Iran might do in its neighborhood and beyond. Might it not use its weaponry to threaten its neighbors, support terrorists, or supply WMD to other parties? We must explore all of these possibilities.

An important factor to keep in mind as we ponder the future with a nuclear Iran is the degree to which this country is revisionist and has grand designs to remake the region. Iran has shown very little interest in expanding beyond its own borders, and there is no reason to believe that this will change. Its primary geographic concern is control of and stability in the Strait of Hormuz, and Iran can be considered a status quo power as far as territorial claims are concerned. Iran therefore fits the bill of a security-seeking state in its bid for nuclear acquisition. The history of U.S. relations in the region certainly suggests that Iran wants to deter, and Iran's own limited aims do nothing to undermine this judgment.

Nine countries now have nuclear military capabilities, and none has shown any ability to do anything with these weapons other than use them for deterrence. How might a new nuclear power hope to do anything with its nuclear weapons that countries with much greater capabilities have failed to do? Nuclear blackmail has often been a worry. It has perhaps occurred once, attempted by the United States during the Korean War, and scholars agree that nuclear coercion is very difficult to exact.[28] Iran will be no more able or likely to use nuclear weapons than any of the eight countries that have come before it. So why do we fear its nuclear development so?

Those who worry about the future with a nuclear Iran generally share some key concerns. First, Iran will wage proxy wars or support terrorism under its new nuclear shield. Second, Iran may transfer nuclear weapons to terrorists or otherwise lose control of its arsenal. Third, there may be an actual nuclear exchange with Israel. Fourth, Iranian proliferation will cause a chain reaction in the region. And fifth, Iranian nuclear acquisition will shatter the NPT and accompanying nonproliferation regime. I consider each of these arguments in turn. Some of these are overstated and some are unfounded. None suggests that we cannot live with a nuclear Iran.

First, consider the notion that Iran might become more rambunctious and use its nuclear shield for nefarious purposes. Nuclear alarmists suggest that Iran will use its capability to ramp up its support for terrorism in the Middle East. But this concern is at odds with the historical record since 1945. As countries acquire nuclear weapons they become conscious of their own vulnerability. They become acutely aware that nuclear weapons possession makes them a potential target in the eyes of major powers, and this discourages them from bold and aggressive action. Maoist China became much less rambunctious after acquiring nuclear weapons in 1964, and India and Pakistan have both become more cautious despite their longstanding rivalry. Even North Korea, the ultimate rogue in the eyes of many, can hardly be said to have become more tenacious since acquiring a nuclear capability.

Every new nuclear country discovers that nuclear weapons have only one conceivable purpose—deterrence—and there is no reason to believe Iran will be different. Even concerns about the stability-instability paradox are overstated. Theorists such as Glenn Snyder have suggested that the deterrent power of nuclear weapons may allow for the use of lower-level violence: succinctly, strategic stability breeds tactical instability.[29] But why should Iran be adventurous in the region, especially with a nuclear neighbor like Israel nearby? Such mischief does not serve Iran's security-seeking goals.

Another prominent concern is the idea that Iran will transfer nuclear weapons to terrorists or otherwise lose control of its arsenal. But again, the surveillance capabilities of the United States are awesome. No country can transfer weapons to third parties without running a great risk of being found out. This is especially true of terrorists, who have less ability to camouflage weapons and disguise their movements. Even countries or factions that may sponsor terrorism will not be able to control what they will do or predict the directions their efforts may take. Once a country like Iran acquires a nuclear capability, it has every reason to want to keep control over its arsenal. Transferring weapons to terrorists implies a complete loss of control over these weapons. Acquiring a nuclear capability is a costly investment. It makes little sense to transfer that investment to grounds that fundamentally cannot be trusted or controlled.

Critics worry that deterring terrorists is impossible without a return address. A terrorist group with nuclear weapons is therefore an extreme danger. But nuclear use by a terrorist group is a huge risk to any state actor who transfers weapons. If nuclear weapons were acquired and used by non-state actors (an extremely low probability event), we can be sure that the United States and others would make every effort to attribute that capability to the state that transferred it. This creates a strong disincentive to transfer in the first place. Given that ties between terrorist groups and states are fairly well known, this deterrent is all the stronger. If Hezbollah somehow managed to acquire and use a nuclear weapon, the world would of course look first to Iran. A state that hopes to survive, then, would be extremely unwise to relinquish control of its nuclear capability to a terrorist group.

Some worry that non-state actors are especially likely to acquire nuclear weapons from a country like Iran. Iran has multiple leaders (the president and the Ayatollah) and also has multiple military organizations. Among these is the Iranian Revolutionary Guard Corp (IRGC), which itself has been labeled a terrorist organization by the United States.[30] If Iran acquired nuclear weapons it might make the IRGC responsible for their control. But a single faction that controls nuclear weapons is in the same position as a unitary state actor. What can it do and what can it not do with this capability? Even non-state agents disposing of nuclear weaponry have not been able to think of anything that they can do with nuclear weapons except to use them for deterrence. It is hard to imagine that factions within Iran will be able to conceive of purposes that reach beyond deterrence. No one in possession of nuclear means has shown any disposition to share them with others, yet. If the IRGC wants to keep hold of its position in Iran and see its country survive it will be no different.

Another concern is the idea that Iran will actually use nuclear weapons once it has them. Nuclear alarmists suggest that the deterrent relationship between the United States and the USSR was fundamentally different than the one that might be obtained between Iran and Israel. A point that is often made is that the United States and the Soviet Union were separated by continents and large bodies of water; nuclear powers in close proximity are much more vulnerable and susceptible to miscalculation. But I see no reason why this should hold true. Iran and Israel are both relatively small countries, and this means that the use of even a few nuclear weapons could easily destroy either of them as viable nations. Both Iran and Israel would know that the use of a single nuclear weapon against its adversary could be suicidal. In strategic parlance, assured destruction is obtained even with very small nuclear arsenals in close geographic proximity. We should not expect Iran to have any inclination to use its nuclear weapons against Israel, just as India and Pakistan have exercised forbearance with their own arsenals. Given the inevitable retaliation that would follow, actual nuclear use is unthinkable.

A fourth prominent concern is that Iranian nuclear acquisition will cause a proliferation chain reaction in the region. Specifically, experts worry that Egypt, Saudi Arabia, and Turkey may all try to acquire independent nuclear capabilities in response. These concerns are not unfounded, but they should be qualified. Saudi Arabia is unlikely to want to acquire nuclear weapons over the protestations of the United States, given their strong political and economic ties. Like Taiwan and South Korea, Saudi Arabia is likely to feel that antagonizing a crucial security partner is unwise. Turkey, likewise, would risk disrupting its relations with the United States as well as with NATO. As a NATO member state, Turkey enjoys protection from the U.S. nuclear umbrella. While this may be insufficient to satisfy Turkey's nuclear appetite in the future, one can certainly envision deepening ties through the NATO framework to assuage Turkey's fears. Finally, Egypt has just undergone a major revolution, and it is simply too soon to tell what its foreign policy priorities will be. A nuclear Iran may feel threatening to Egypt, but Egypt is likely to be focused on getting its own house in order in the near term.

More generally, scholars and policymakers have often held fears that the nuclearization of one country will lead to a nuclear "tipping point." But this threshold thinking has never been born out. Despite fears among U.S. policymakers in the early 1960s, China's first nuclear test did *not* convince all of Asia to go nuclear. There is no reason to believe that a true tipping point would occur in the Middle East when it has not occurred before.[31] Although the term "proliferation" is used (including here), proliferation properly defined means a rapid and uncontrolled spread. Going from one nuclear power to nine over the course of sixty years can hardly be called proliferation. Iran may be part of the slow spread of nuclear weapons, but there is little reason to believe it will catalyze any sort of tipping point.

Experts also worry that a nuclear Iran will erode the fragile Nuclear Non-Proliferation Treaty and the accompanying nonproliferation regime. Post-NPT nuclear states like India, Pakistan, and Israel have refused to join the NPT in the first place. North Korea abrogated its commitments before testing its first nuclear device. At present, Iran is on track to become a nuclear weapons power while remaining inside of the NPT, and many are concerned that if it does so, this will spell disaster for the treaty.

The NPT is and always has been a voluntary commitment by member states that operates on consensus principles. Those 189 countries that are members have acceded because the treaty serves their interests or at least does not impinge upon them.

That the NPT may not have independent constraining power should not come as a surprise to us. No state that has been determined to acquire nuclear weapons has ever been stopped by it before. In his 2009 Prague speech, President Barack Obama emphasized the importance of the NPT and nonproliferation regime: "Rules must be binding. Violations must be punished. Words must mean something."[32] But in the international realm, rules are *not* binding, and violations are very hard to punish. So long as it remains an anarchic world, we cannot hope to enforce a treaty commitment on a state that is determined to shirk it. This has always been the case.

The forgoing arguments suggest that concerns about the dangers of a nuclear Iran are overstated. But there are more reasons to believe that we can safely and comfortably live with a nuclear Iran. Despite the fact that Iran is interested in holding a prominent regional position, there will be limits to what it can achieve. Sunni countries are unlikely to bandwagon with a nuclear Iran because of serious religious and cultural differences. States like Saudi Arabia are much more likely to seek protection from the United States than they are to join up with the Islamic Republic, with whom they have never been friendly. Recent events suggest just this pattern.

In 2010, the Israeli Defense Force ran a practice drill, simulating a preventive strike on Iran's nuclear facilities. Saudi Arabia cooperated with this drill, standing down its air defenses to allow the Israeli Air Force to pass safely.[33] While we cannot be certain that Saudi Arabia would be complicit with an actual preventive strike on Iran (and I do not recommend one), this suggests that other countries in the region are not eager to see Iran acquire nuclear weapons. They are therefore more likely to balance against it than bandwagon with it.

A newly nuclear Iran also does not require Israel to make major strategic changes in the region. Israel maintains a policy of "nuclear opacity"—it does not admit to having a nuclear capability—but its weapons status is widely known. And anyone who has such a capability, may, under the direst of circumstances, think of using it, which is enough to deter. Iran's nuclear quest does not mean that Israel must change its nuclear tune. Opacity serves as a perfectly good deterrent.

Furthermore, the relationship between Israel and Iran is not as fragile as many suggest. This dynamic is most nearly comparable to India and Pakistan, and is likely to be more stable and less fraught than that. Israel and Iran are neighbors, and do not share warm relations. But they also do not have major territorial or political conflicts, and their rivalry is largely a rhetorical one. Just as India and Pakistan have quickly established a stable deterrent relationship, Israel and Iran are likely to do the same. Since 1998, India and Pakistan have not gone to war, but moreover, their relationship has become markedly more peaceful. The two countries have agreed not to target each other's nuclear facilities, and have put in place other confidence-building measures and information exchanges to mitigate the uncertainty between them. If this age-old rivalry can be pacified by the presence of nuclear weapons, we should not expect the relationship between Iran and Israel to follow a different pattern. Iran knows that Israel has a nuclear capability. Israel knows that Iran may have an incipient one. That always has been and will remain enough to deter either country from inflicting serious damage on the other.

So what should U.S. policy be toward a nuclearizing Iran? The current economic sanctions against the Islamic Republic are unlikely to slow its progress or induce concessions. If Iran believes that its security depends on nuclear weapons, sanctions will not stay its hand. And if Iran had security concerns before, sanctions have only heightened this state of affairs. Scholars note very few cases of successful economic coercion, and in cases of WMD proliferation, it is hard to argue that sanctions have an independent effect. The United States was unaware of the efficacy of its sanctions against Iraq until it invaded. Likewise, the effects of sanctions against Libya were hard to determine until Qaddhafi gave up his nuclear weapons. These sanction packages did, however, have profound effects on Iraqi and Libyan citizens, whose quality of life was jeopardized by the loss of crucial imports.[34] Dropping the current sanctions against Iran might assuage its security concerns. Moreover, it will prevent Iranian citizens from bearing the brunt of an inefficacious policy.

If Iran is willing to come back to the negotiating table and consider giving up its nuclear aspirations, the United States should clearly welcome that. If not, it doesn't really matter. We can safely and comfortably live with a nuclear Iran.

THE REASONS TO WORRY

Scott D. Sagan

Nuclear weapons are not controlled by the abstract entities we call states, but rather by normal, imperfect individuals and normal, self-interested organizations within the state. To understand the effects of nuclear proliferation, therefore, one must pry open the black box of decision making inside states to look at who issues commands and who actually controls the nuclear weapons that are being built. Organization theory provides a useful lens to focus attention on how governments in different states are differently organized (and sometimes disorganized) and, therefore, how and why they might contemplate the use of nuclear weapons in different manners.

Over the past decade, the U.S. government and much of the international community have greatly feared the dangerous consequences should Iraq, North Korea, or Iran acquire nuclear weapons. Such fears have been and remain utterly warranted. Saddam Hussein, we now know, wanted to use nuclear weapons as a shield behind which to take aggressive action, and his decisions regarding launching wars in the past were marred by false information—even delusions—encouraged by his entourage of yes-men and sycophants. North Korea, the one member of the "Axis of Evil" that did get the bomb, is also a dangerous holder of nuclear weapons, but for somewhat different reasons. The North Korean communist government traditionally has maintained tight control over its military, but the stability of the country is tenuous and the extreme poverty of North Korea has encouraged the military and nuclear establishment to be willing to sell or barter anything to make ends meet, including nuclear technology. Finally, Iran would be the most dangerous proliferator of all, combining strongly aggressive tendencies like Saddam's Iraq with a lack of strong civilian leadership control over the ideologically radical military organization—IRGC—that manages the country's nuclear power and nuclear weapons programs. Each of these dangerous proliferators will be analyzed in turn.

Iraq

Soon after the March 2003 U.S. invasion of Iraq, American arms inspectors were startled to discover that the government of Saddam Hussein had in fact destroyed all Iraqi nuclear weapons facilities in the years following the 1991 Gulf War and had not restarted a covert program. The great secret that Saddam was hiding from international inspectors was not the existence of a covert nuclear, chemical, or biological weapons program; the great secret was that the Iraqis and international inspectors had in fact already dismantled all the nuclear, chemical, and biological WMD development facilities that Saddam had constructed prior to the 1991 war. Saddam Hussein did not want Iran and his own people to know that he had effectively disarmed under the cease-fire agreement and subsequent UN inspection system. He was clearly looking forward to restarting these programs in the future if UN sanctions were lifted against his regime, but that future fortunately never arrived.

We now know a great deal about Saddam's motivations to pursue nuclear weapons, and the reality is alarming. Saddam Hussein secretly taped many of his meetings with the cabinet and military officers, and his statements reveal that he was not primarily motivated by defensive security concerns vis-à-vis Iran or Israel. Instead, Saddam envisioned nuclear weapons as a strategic shield behind which Iraq would be able to engage in conventional aggression against Israel. Before the invasion of Kuwait in 1990, for example, Saddam predicted that Iraq would get nuclear weapons within five years and rhetorically asked his colleagues that "if the Arabs were to have a nuclear bomb, wouldn't they take the territories that were occupied after 1967?"[35] This was a long-standing theme for Saddam Hussein. For example, in the late 1970s, Saddam told other high-level Iraqi leaders that nuclear weapons would allow Iraq to engage in a war of attrition against Israel to reclaim the West Bank and Golan Heights. Iraqi nuclear weapons would counter Israeli nuclear weapons and thereby permit Iraq to launch a conventional war against the Zionist state without fear that Israel would, in desperation, retaliate with its nuclear arsenal. The transcript of Saddam's secret speech is chilling:

> We want, when the Israeli enemy attacks our civilian establishments, to have weapons to attack the Israeli civilian establishment. We are willing to sit and refrain from using it [a nuclear weapon], except when the enemy attacks civilian establishments in Iraq or Syria, so that we can guarantee the long war that is destructive to our enemy, and take at our leisure each meter of land and drown the enemy with rivers of blood. We have no vision of war that is any less than this. . . . We should consider losses in the thousands, thousands, so that we plan to be prepared to lose in those 12 months 50,000 martyrs and keep going.[36]

Proliferation optimists, like Kenneth Waltz, believe that nuclear weapons only serve a deterrent function for all states, but for Saddam Hussein, a nuclear deterrent was sought so that he could more safely engage in conventional aggression.

An additional frightening insight is apparent when one looks inside the Iraqi government's decision-making process: the tyrant created such a climate of fear that his subordinates wove an intricate web of lies and delusions to please him. Saddam Hussein tolerated no disagreements, spurned professional military advice, and trusted his own mystical intuition more than objective intelligence reports. Anyone who questioned Saddam's assumptions or decisions, or those of his brutal sons, was likely to be severely punished. That climate of fear produced constant exaggerations about Iraqi military capabilities and self-serving reports of interactions with foreign governments. He made virtually all of his major strategic decisions on his own and actively discouraged advisors from delivering intelligence or counsel that contradicted his wisdom and what he called his "politician's alertness." According to one taped conversation after the 1990 invasion of Kuwait, for example, Saddam told his colleagues: "I forbade the intelligence outfits from deducing from press and political analysis anything about America. . . . I said I don't want either intelligence organization to give me analysis—that is my specialty. . . . We agree to continue on that basis . . . which is what I used with the Iranians, some of it out of deduction, some of it through invention and connecting the dots, all without having hard evidence."[37]

Saddam compartmentalized strategic decision making and refused to let military commanders coordinate operational plans before conflicts, lest they challenge his authority or even prepare coup attempts. This produced remarkably poor military planning and operations. Before the 1980 invasion of Iran, Iraqi commanders received only days or weeks of warning to prepare and, according to Saddam's later testimony, neither the defense minister nor the army chief of staff was informed of the 1990 invasion of Kuwait prior to the attack.[38] Saddam's strategic decisions were made in a haze of delusions; in 1991, he insisted that the chemical weapons that Iraq had just developed were 200 times more powerful than those he used against the Kurds and Iranians and could "make fire eat up half of Israel"; he insisted after the 1991 Gulf War that Iraqi military forces had actually won the battle against the U.S.-led coalition forces due to their superior "fighting spirit"; and he insisted prior to the U.S. invasion in 2003 that Washington would not send forces all the way to Baghdad and would once again settle for a limited victory without imposing regime change.[39]

These observations about Saddam Hussein's pathological decision-making style are a warning sign that nuclear weapons would not have contributed to stable deterrence in the region had Iraq acquired them through the covert nuclear program which was uncovered after the 1991 Gulf War. Saddam without nuclear weapons attacked Iran in 1980. Saddam without nuclear weapons invaded Kuwait in 1990. Saddam without nuclear weapons launched missile strikes against Israel in 1991. It strains credibility to believe that Saddam with nuclear weapons would have behaved more cautiously.

This realistic view of the dangers of a nuclear Iraq does not in any way excuse the failures of intelligence that occurred in the United States before the 2003 war concerning the Iraqi WMD program, nor does it excuse the failure of the Bush administration to adequately plan for the post-war contingency operations after the fall of Baghdad. And we should not forget the hubris that led some American officials to believe that the Iraqi people would welcome the Americans with open arms and peacefully accept a Jeffersonian democracy in Baghdad. Clearly poor individual decision making and glaring organizational blind spots existed in the United States as well as in Iraq.

North Korea

The George W. Bush administration cannot be blamed for the DPRK government's initiation of a nuclear weapons program. That program began many years ago and was, after a tense crisis during the Clinton administration, significantly curtailed by the Agreed Framework Agreement under which the North Koreans dismantled their plutonium producing graphite reactor and permitted IAEA inspectors to verify that the reactor's fuel rods were kept in spent fuel pond storage at the Yongbyon facility. The Bush administration can, however, be at least partially blamed for the abandonment of the Agreed Framework— for when Bush administration officials confronted the DPRK in 2002 with evidence that Pakistan had helped Pyongyang develop a secret uranium enrichment program, North Korean officials abruptly withdrew from the NPT and reinvigorated their nuclear weapons program, separating plutonium from the fuel rods and then conducting nuclear weapons tests in 2006 and 2009.

Today, North Korea is estimated to have extracted enough plutonium from its now dismantled graphite reactor to build approximately eight nuclear weapons. We know that much because we know the amount of plutonium that was in the spent fuel coming out of the one North Korean reactor. What the U.S. government does not know is how much progress North Korea has made toward constructing small nuclear warheads that could be placed on the long-range missiles that it clearly has in abundance. Pyongyang officials have continued to insist that they need to increase the strength of their national deterrent given the perceived threats from the United States and South Korea. In 2010, they surprised both U.S. intelligence agencies and western scholars by taking Stanford professor and former Los Alamos National Laboratory Director Siegfried Hecker on a tour of what had until then been a secret uranium enrichment facility.[40] Once completed, this facility—jam-packed with centrifuges based on Pakistani designs—will give the North Koreans the ability to expand its nuclear arsenal significantly.

Kenneth Waltz argues that we have little to fear from these North Korean nuclear weapons developments, indeed claiming that we might come to prefer a DPRK with more nuclear weapons in the future to "the more bellicose one of the past." This optimistic view underestimates the degree of aggression exhibited by the DPRK in recent years, misestimates of the progress that North Korea can make in developing a more usable nuclear arsenal in the future, and presents an overly rosy assessment of the U.S. ability to deter, detect, and counter any North Korean shipments of nuclear materials and technology outside of its borders.

One slightly reassuring point about the DPRK should be acknowledged: the North Korean regime is an unusual mixture of a traditional Asian kingdom, passing down leadership from father to son and idolizing each new leader, and a strict communist government, in which communist party leaders make collective decisions and exert strong control of a subordinate military. This unusual mixture has led to a tight command and control system in which orders are obeyed without question. The organizational structure has permitted the North Korean leadership to probe and bluster and bluff quite often, but then back down when confronted with strong reactions. For example, in March 2010, the DPRK military took aggressive action in the Yellow Sea, sinking the South Korean warship the *Cheonon* with a torpedo. But then when the South Koreans mobilized their military forces, the DPRK government launched grand rhetorical threats against South Korea and U.S. "imperialists," yet cautiously refrained from ordering further military action. With its communist party discipline, collective decision making, and civilian control of the military, North Korea presents a different kind of challenge from the one we saw in Iraq and the one that is emerging in Iran. But it is a severe nuclear danger nonetheless for three related reasons.

First, why should we be optimistic that the DPRK, which has been quite aggressive when weak, will suddenly become more cautious when strong? Within months of the March 2010 North Korean sinking of the *Cheonon*, which killed forty-six South Korean seamen, the leadership in Pyongyang apparently ordered North Korean artillery units to shell the South Korean island of Yeonpyeong, an attack that killed two marines and two civilians and wounded nineteen others. It is true that these incidents occurred in disputed waters and that the North Koreans did not escalate the operations afterward, even though in the Yeonpyeong incident the South Koreans retaliated by shelling the artillery units on the North Korean mainland. But Waltz's reference to the incidents as "annoyances rather than serious belligerence" strikes me as a gross understatement. Indeed, Waltz contrasts these "annoyances" with what he calls the "massive assassination efforts" that North Korea attempted against the South Korean government in the past (Ch. 6, p. 187). The most massive of these actions, the 1968 Blue House raid, however, killed fewer South Korean soldiers (twenty-six) than the 2010 *Cheonon* attack (forty-six). I therefore see no reason for optimism in this regard about the effect of nuclear weapons on North Korean behavior and even less reason to predict increased caution once North Korea acquires a larger and more effective nuclear arsenal.

And this is the second reason to be worried. The DPRK seems determined to do exactly that—expand its nuclear arsenal, create smaller warheads that can fit on its existing missiles, and develop and deploy longer-range missiles capable of hitting the United States, as well as South Korea and Japan. This is the main explanation for North Korea's development of its new uranium enrichment facilities: after the dismantlement of their gas-graphite nuclear reactor, the DPRK lacks an ability to produce more plutonium, and the alternative Highly Enriched Uranium (HEU) route to making the bomb became far more attractive. Moreover, U.S. intelligence agencies discovered in 2003 that A. Q. Khan had sold the bomb blueprints of an HEU implosion device (based on a tested Chinese design) to Libya, and there is no reason not to assume that Khan included such blueprint designs in the package of materials and technology that he sold to North Korea. If that is the case, the North Koreans may actually prefer to use HEU for their emerging arsenal because using a proven design would make miniaturization of new warheads for long-range missiles significantly easier.[41] Finally, in October 2010, the North Koreans displayed a new road-mobile Intermediate Range Ballistic Missile (IRBM), reportedly based on a Russian submarine-launched missile, in a parade in Pyongyang, with an estimated range of 3,000 to 5,000 kilometers.[42]

These observations about how military technology imports are leading to enhanced North Korean nuclear capabilities lead us directly to the third, and I believe the most important, reason to be alarmed by a nuclear DPRK. North Korea is such a basket case economically that its government has been led to sell virtually anything to other nations that have cash available. Pyongyang started with production and smuggling of counterfeit currency, fake pharmaceuticals, and illicit drugs but has moved quickly into the even more lucrative missile and nuclear technology smuggling business. Smuggling is a tough business, however, and the need for covert and decentralized operations is leading to a shift away from the traditional North Korean reliance on centrally managed operations. Sheena Chestnut, in the most thorough study of the North Korean smuggling networks, notes a disturbing trend: "An examination of patterns in illicit activity, however, reveals that although North Korean criminal smuggling has been centrally inspired and sanctioned, it is not always centrally controlled; the state has shifted over time from using solely state agents and assets to contracting out transportation and distribution of smuggled goods to criminal partners over whom it has less control."[43] North Korea has been observed shipping missiles to Pakistan and Iran and is known to have sold nuclear materials or technology to Syria and Libya. Other deals with other countries are suspected. I hope that Kim Jong-Un maintains tight control over North Korean nuclear exports in the future, but that is only a hope, and not a confident expectation.

To his credit, Waltz recognizes that North Korea's nuclear smuggling activities are a problem. But he downplays its significance by asserting that the United States and its allies have excellent surveillance capabilities and have been "adept at containing North Korean export efforts." I am not so confident. To give the most dramatic example, U.S. intelligence agencies failed to discover that North Korea had been helping Syria build a secret nuclear reactor, camouflaged as the ruins of a Crusaders fort, starting in 2001 until Israeli intelligence notified the CIA about their suspicions in 2007.[44] The Israeli Air Force destroyed the Al-Kibar reactor facility that September, but the United States (and the IAEA that has been denied access to other Syrian sites) still cannot verify the location of a suspected plutonium reprocessing facility. In addition, there is still great uncertainty about the extent of North Korea's assistance to a suspected nuclear program in Burma, despite the U.S. government's efforts to focus intelligence on that cooperation activity between two of the world's most isolated nations. Finally, there are many reasons to suspect that Tehran and Pyongyang are cooperating as well—exchanging nuclear know-how and technology from Tehran for missile know-how and technology from North Korea—but U.S. intelligence agencies lack firm evidence to confirm or deny such allegations.[45]

The North Korean development of nuclear weapons has not produced the cascade of nuclear proliferation in East Asia that some pessimistic specialists predicted. At least, that is, not so far. But it also has not led to cautious North Korean international behavior as Waltz and other proliferation optimists predicted. Instead of welcoming North Korean nuclear developments as a force for stability, the United States should continue to use sanctions, negotiations, and deterrence to try to contain the DPRK nuclear threat and attempt to reverse it. But I am not optimistic that reversal is likely anytime soon.

Iran

This leads to the most recent and the most serious case of a state trying to acquire nuclear weapons: Iran.[46] The reasoning of scholars and officials struggling to deal with Iran's nuclear ambitions too often displays both creeping fatalism about the United States' ability to keep Iran from getting the bomb and excessive optimism about the United States' ability to contain Iran if it does become a nuclear power. Such proliferation fatalists argue that over the long term it may be impossible to stop Iran—or other states for that matter—from getting the bomb. Given the spread of nuclear technology and know-how, and the right of parties to the NPT to enrich uranium and separate plutonium, the argument goes, any foreign government determined to acquire nuclear weapons will eventually do so. Moreover, the 1981 Israeli attack on the Osirak nuclear reactor in Iraq may have delayed Iraq's progress, but similar air strikes today are unlikely to disable Iran's capacities completely, since its uranium enrichment facilities at Natanz are buried underground and many specialists suspect that there are covert facilities hidden elsewhere as well.

Given this pessimism about nonproliferation efforts, and Iran's development of significant amounts of Low Enriched

Uranium (LEU), it is understandable that many analysts are turning their attention to how best to deter a nuclear Iran. A Bush administration official in the executive branch anonymously told *The New York Times* in March 2006, "The reality is that most of us think the Iranians are probably going to get a weapon, or the technology to make one, sooner or later."[47] According to *The New York Times*, Obama administration officials have also discussed whether a nuclear-armed Iran is inevitable and, if so, how the United States should best provide deterrence and containment against Tehran.[48] But that analysis should be considered long-term contingency planning against an undesirable outcome, not an excuse for accepting that Iran's nuclear ambitions are acceptable or inevitable. Indeed, proliferation fatalism and deterrence optimism interact in a particularly diabolical manner; the more we think it inevitable that Iran is going to acquire nuclear weapons, the more we are tempted, through wishful thinking, to say, "Well, maybe it won't matter." And, the more we bolster our belief that it won't matter, the less we are willing to take the necessary diplomatic and strategic steps that could potentially stop Iran from getting nuclear weapons.

Waltz assumes that the Iranians will behave cautiously, the way that Cold War adversaries did once they got nuclear weapons. But Iran does not have the internal characteristics that communist China and the communist Soviet Union had: an ideology eschewing risks, centralized collective decision making, and tight civilian control of the military. Instead of using a Cold War analogy, we should look back at more recent cases of nuclear proliferation or attempted nuclear proliferation—Pakistan and Iraq—in order to predict the effects of a nuclear Iran. First, as I have already discussed in the case in Pakistan in 1999 and with Saddam Hussein in the 1990s, we should worry that Iranian leaders with nuclear weapons will see them as a shield behind which they can more safely engage in aggression against neighbors and the United States. Iran is a major arms supplier to Hezbollah, the Lebanese-based Shi'a militia, and supports its attacks against civilian and military targets inside

Israel. It has provided support for the 1996 Hezbollah bombing of the U.S. barracks at the Khobar Towers in Saudi Arabia and covertly armed and supported Iraqi Shi'a militia who were fighting U.S. troops combating the insurgency inside Iraq after 2003. Iranian leaders have called for revolutions against many Arab governments in the region and are already suspected by U.S. officials of having provided special artillery shells to Muammar Qaddafi's regime in Libya, which were then filled with mustard gas.[49]

If Iran acquires nuclear weapons, will it behave more or less aggressively in the Middle East? On the one hand, we have good insight from Kenneth Waltz: the United States and Israel would be more reluctant to attack Iran if it had nuclear weapons—and indeed I do believe that Tehran's concerns about forced regime change is its central motivation for wanting to acquire nuclear weapons. On the other hand, however, even if that is true, it is also likely that various Iranians, especially those in the IRGC, may feel that it is now safer for them to probe—to attack American troops in the region, to support terrorist attacks against Israel, and to attempt to destabilize Arab regimes in the neighborhood.

The second crucial question is who would control nuclear weapons in Iran: the mullahs, the elected politicians, the professional military, or the IRGC? The evidence suggests that the IRGC will be the guardians of the Iranian arsenal, for it is the IRGC, not the professional Iranian military, that has been covertly purchasing nuclear technology, guarding the nuclear facilities, conducting research on weapon delivery systems, and managing the nuclear weapons activities. And it is the IRGC leadership that has been responsible for running Iran's relationship with terrorist organizations in the Middle East. That is a deadly mixture—nuclear command and control responsibilities and terrorist ties in the same organization.

There is no reason to assume that, even if they wanted to, central political authorities in Tehran could completely control the details of nuclear operations by the Islamic Revolutionary Guard Corps. The IRGC recruits young "true believers" to join its ranks, subjects them to ideological indoctrination and—as the IAEA discovered when it inspected Iran's centrifuge facilities in 2003—gives IRGC units responsibility for securing production sites for nuclear materials. The IRGC also has ties with the most radical clerics in Iran, including some who have argued (in contrast to the views of many traditional Shiite clerics) that nuclear weapons acquisition and use is justified under Islamic law.[50]

Concerns about whether the IRGC can be controlled by the Tehran government is not just a theoretical proposition, for there have been numerous cases in the past decade of senior IRGC commanders acting aggressively on their own authority, without the apparent sanction of the central authorities. In January 2002, for example, the Israeli Navy intercepted a ship that was delivering weapons from Iran to the Palestinian territories, an operation that many Western officials believed was a rogue IRGC operation, launched without the knowledge or approval of the Iranian president Mohammad Khatami.[51] In September 2007, in a similar incident, IRGC-controlled naval vessels captured a group of British sailors, holding them hostage for two weeks claiming that they were in Iranian waters. British and American officials believed at the time that this capture was "probably not directed from the upper reaches government."[52] Finally, there are suspicions in the United States that the 2011 Iranian plot to assassinate the Saudi ambassador in Washington was a rogue operation: "It's a rogue plan or they're using very different tactics. We just don't know," a senior U.S. official told a reporter.[53]

For nuclear weapons to provide even a semblance of stability, the government must maintain tight command and control. These incidents are disturbing warnings that Iranian nuclear weapons operations would be dangerous in this regard. The central government in Tehran might not be in command; the IRGC might be out of control.

Some Western government officials resort to blind faith in deterrence when faced with this looming danger. In order to deter Tehran from giving nuclear weapons to terrorists, for example, the French government announced in 2006 that it would respond to nuclear terrorism with a nuclear strike of its own against any state that had served as the terrorists' accomplice. But this "attribution deterrence" posture glosses over the difficult question of what to do if the source of nuclear materials for a terrorist bomb is uncertain.

Moreover, then-French president Jacques Chirac took a line out of Kenneth Waltz's deterrence optimist's playbook, though the French government claimed afterward that the president was simply thinking out loud, in an off-the-record moment of rare French candor. As reported by *The New York Times*, Chirac said, "I would say what is dangerous about this situation is not the fact of having a nuclear bomb. One, maybe a second one a little later, well, that's not very dangerous. But what is very dangerous is the effects on proliferation."[54]

Indeed there is a real danger of further proliferation in the Middle East if Iran acquires nuclear weapons. For example, in June 2011 Prince Turki Al Faisal Bin Abdulaziz Al Saud of Saudi Arabia stated that, "Iran [developing] a nuclear weapon would compel Saudi Arabia . . . to pursue policies which could lead to untold and possibly dramatic consequences. . . . If they successfully pursue a military program, we will have to follow suit."[55]

Further proliferation in the region is therefore a real danger. But nuclear weapons in Iran are problematic enough. Indeed, saying that Iran's acquisition of nuclear weapons is worrisome because it encourages nuclear proliferation elsewhere is like telling your kid "Don't take heroin, because it could lead to stronger drugs."

Conclusion: Waltzing Past the Graveyard

Deterrence optimists are like individuals whistling past the graveyard. Indeed, they are often waltzing past the graveyard. The United States and regional powers may have to live with nuclear ambiguity in Iran in the future, but we should certainly not welcome it or celebrate it.

Given how far Iran has gone already with its nuclear program, some are tempted to advocate preventive air strikes, or even a preventive war, against Iran. But such a military option is unlikely to be completely successful, as former Secretary of Defense Robert Gates has said in Washington and former Mossad intelligence chief Meir Dagan has warned in Israel.[56] Continued pressure, through UN Security Council sanctions when possible and U.S. and allied nations' sanctions when necessary, is more attractive, and continued sabotage efforts, such as the Stuxnet computer virus attacks, are more promising. Greater support for government opposition forces inside Iran, to promote an Iranian Spring sometime, should be considered, and more vigorous trade embargoes, including embargoes on Iranian imports of refined petroleum, should be explored. The United States and the world community are not yet at the crucial crisis point when it faces only the horrible options of going to war with Iran or living with a nuclear-armed Iran. Our policy objective should be to push that horrendous day of reckoning as far as possible over the distant horizon to create time for these other options to be effective.

Chapter 7

IS NUCLEAR ZERO
THE BEST OPTION?

Scott D. Sagan and Kenneth N. Waltz

YES

Scott D. Sagan

Every time Barack Obama announces that he is in favor of a world free of nuclear weapons, the nuclear hawks descend. Soon after his inauguration, former Reagan administration Pentagon official Frank Gaffney proclaimed that the president "stands to transform the 'world's only superpower' into a nuclear impotent." After Obama promised in his 2009 Prague speech that "the United States will take concrete steps toward a world without nuclear weapons," former Secretary of Defense James Schlesinger declared that "the notion that we can abolish nuclear weapons reflects on a combination of American utopianism and American parochialism." And when the president won the 2009 Nobel Peace Prize, in part for his embrace of the disarmament vision, *Time Magazine* even ran an essay entitled "Want Peace? Give a Nuke the Nobel."

Obama is right to declare, loudly and often, that the United States seeks a world without nuclear weapons, and the administration is right to be taking concrete steps now toward that long-term goal. Indeed, by proclaiming that America seeks nuclear zero, Obama is simply reaffirming that we will follow our treaty commitments: states that joined the 1970 NPT agreed "to pursue negotiations in good faith on effective measures relating to cessation of the nuclear arms race at an early date and to nuclear disarmament." Since Article 6 of America's Constitution says that a treaty commitment is "the supreme Law of the Land," at a basic level, Obama is simply saying that he will follow U.S. law.

The abolition aspiration is not, however, based on such legal niceties. Instead, it is inspired by two important insights about the global nuclear future. First, the most dangerous nuclear threats to the United States today and on the horizon are from terrorists and potential new nuclear powers, not from our traditional Cold War adversaries in Russia and China. Second, the spread of nuclear weapons to new states, and indirectly to terrorist organizations, will be made less likely if the United States and other nuclear-armed nations are seen to be working in good faith toward disarmament.

Nuclear weapons may have been a dangerous necessity to keep the Cold War cold, but scholars and policy makers who are nostalgic for the brutal simplicity of that era's nuclear deterrence do not understand how much the world has changed. The choice we face is not between a nuclear-free world or a return to bipolar Cold War deterrence; it is between creating a nuclear weapons–free world or living in a world with many more states with nuclear arsenals. And if there are more nuclear nations, and more atomic weapons in global arsenals, there will be more opportunities for terrorists to steal or buy the bomb.

The threat of nuclear-armed terrorists is not new. In 1977, the Revolutionary Cells (RZ) in West Germany attacked a U.S. military base hoping to steal the tactical nuclear weapons there. The Aum Shinrikyo apocalyptic cult in Japan sought recruits in the Russian military in the 1990s to get access to loose nukes and only settled on using sarin-gas chemicals in the Tokyo subway when their nuclear efforts failed. Today's threat is even more alarming. It is well known that Osama bin Laden proclaimed that Islamic jihadis have a duty to acquire and to use nuclear weapons against the West. And Al Qaida is known to have recruited senior Pakistani nuclear scientists in the past and may now have "sleeper agents" in Pakistani laboratories to help in that effort.

The even more destructive danger of terrorists with nuclear weapons is looming on the horizon. Terrorists are not likely to be deterred by threats of retaliation. Stopping them from purchasing or stealing a nuclear weapon, or from getting the materials to make their own, is a much better strategy. If aspiring nuclear-arms states—such as Iran and Syria (and some suspect Burma)—get nuclear weapons in the future, the danger that terrorists will get their hands on one will clearly increase. And if the United States and other nuclear-weapons nations are seen to be hypocritical, by not following our NPT commitments and maintaining that we (but only we) are responsible enough to have them, it will reduce the likelihood of ensuring the broad international cooperation that is needed to reduce these proliferation risks.

Officials in the George W. Bush administration believed that there was no link between U.S. arsenal size or military posture and nonproliferation decisions made by nonnuclear states. The Obama administration's new Nuclear Posture Review maintains that the connection is strong, even if it is often indirect and hard to measure: "By demonstrating that we take seriously our NPT obligation to pursue nuclear disarmament, we strengthen our ability to mobilize broad international support for the measures needed to reinforce the nonproliferation regime and secure nuclear materials worldwide."[1]

There are now many signs that the Obama administration is correct in its assessment that progress in disarmament enables progress in nonproliferation. The April 2010 Nuclear Security Summit brought forty-six countries to Washington where they reached agreement on a number of concrete steps to better protect nuclear materials from terrorists. And in stark contrast to the Bush-era 2005 NPT Review Conference, which ended in failure, the May 2010 review took place in a cooperative atmosphere and produced a final document that called on all states to sign onto improved safeguards for their reactors and encouraged governments not in compliance with their treaty commitments to change their ways. The successful efforts to get additional rounds of sanctions against Iran in the UN Security Council can be credited, in part, to this new spirit of cooperation, including the progress on arms-control agreements between the United States and China, and the United States and Russia.

Severe challenges to global zero remain. It will be critical that all states have increased confidence that final disarmament agreements will be enforced and that any new nuclear proliferator will not be tolerated. Fortunately, in a nuclear-free world, the former nuclear states would have far stronger mutual incentives to punish and reverse any new state's decision to acquire atomic bombs. Ironically, it is precisely because nuclear states have such large arsenals today that they sometimes succumb to the temptation to accept new proliferators. In a disarmed world, such complacency would be more obviously imprudent, thus encouraging the once-nuclear-armed states to enforce nonproliferation.

Verification at zero (or at low numbers for that matter) is an obvious challenge. Even if better verification technology is created, there will remain the problem of what to do if an erstwhile nuclear nation is caught secretly preparing to re-arm. A way around this is to accept the fact that all former nuclear states will retain the option of reversing course. Ironically, this capability will be both reassuring and deterring—reassuring because it enables states to begin taking the final steps toward total nuclear disarmament even in the absence of complete confidence that the process will be successful, and deterring because each state will know that even if it can reverse its final disarmament steps, so can the others. In short, there will still be a latent form of nuclear deterrence even in a nuclear-disarmed world.

Finally, there is the question of ballistic missile defenses. During and immediately after the Cold War, many scholars and officials—including both of the authors of this book—saw these systems as "de-stabilizing" because as long as a government's nuclear security was dependent on the ability to retaliate with devastating force after an attack, if an adversary hitting first could use even limited defenses to reduce the effectiveness of second-strike retaliation, mutually assured destruction no longer held. I still hold that position regarding ballistic missile defenses against Russian or Chinese ICBMs. (Theater defenses against Iranian threats in Europe or Middle East nations are another matter.) But in a disarmed world, missile defense can play a very different and more stabilizing role. Managed mutual-missile-defense deployments in the future could, however, permit the final steps of disarmament to take place with less concern about cheating in the immediate term and could provide more confidence in the ability of governments to respond in a timely manner to successful rule breaking by another state.[2]

The nuclear-weapons-free world will not be a world free of conflicts of national interest; nor will it be a utopia in which governments never feel tempted to cheat on their international obligations. A world without nuclear weapons will not be a world without war. Indeed, the maintenance of global zero will require that conventionally armed major powers be prepared to enforce nuclear disarmament and nonproliferation commitments in a fair and vigorous manner. Potential proliferators may have to be "forced" to be free.

In medieval times, European mapmakers placed the words *hic sunt dracones* (here be dragons) at the edge of the known world. Disarmament critics today are like those medieval mapmakers, fearing that we are entering unknown territory fraught with hidden nuclear monsters. But these dragons are fantasies. The genuine strategic challenges we face in creating a secure nuclear-weapons-free world—adequate verification, enforcement of violations, and mutual-defense deployments—are challenges that can be met over time. And the world we are heading toward if we fail to find safe paths to mutual and verifiable disarmament—a world crowded with nuclear states and terrorist temptations—is even more fraught with danger.

NO

Kenneth N. Waltz

War may not pay, as British economist Norman Angell repeatedly claimed, but the lesson proved a hard one for states to learn. Even with the horrors of World War I fresh in their minds, European countries went into World War II just twenty-one years later. Until August of 1945, violent conflict punctuated the history of states, especially of those major and great.

When in short order the Soviet Union followed the United States into the nuclear-arms business with "man of steel" Stalin and in due course "we will bury you" Khrushchev at the helm, many in the Western world thought that all hell would break loose. President of the University of Chicago Robert Maynard Hutchins and Bertrand Russell, eminent in mathematics and rhetoric, proclaimed that in the nuclear age world government was the only alternative to world war. With nuclear weapons, war presumably meant that civilization would perish and we along with it. Instead, the alternative to world government proved to be nuclear deterrence, which has banished war among the world's major nations through the long years of the Cold War and ever since.

Certainly, violent conflict still exists, but it has been relegated to taking its course in the periphery of international politics. The United States, in particular, has been fond of beating up poor and weak states. In the twenty years dating from 1983, we invaded six of them, beginning and ending with Iraq. Yet since the end of World War II, states with nuclear weapons have never fought one another. Testing propositions against historical events has become a favorite indoor sport of social scientists—this is the only proposition that has passed every test. One might think that the best, or in fact the only, peacekeeping weapon that the world has ever known would gain many fans, but it does not seem to have done so.

We now have a president who wants to free us from our nuclear arsenal in the hope of making the world a safer place.

This "zero option" has intuitive appeal. Nuclear weapons are immensely destructive. No defense against them is possible. Why then should states not band together and agree to abolish them? Why is the zero option not the best choice?

Abolishing the weapons that have caused sixty-seven years of peace would certainly have effects. Such an action would, among other things, make the world safe for the fighting of World War III. Like any dominant power, America is a looming threat in the minds of many international leaders. When President George W. Bush identified Iraq, Iran, and North Korea as forming an axis of evil in January of 2002, and when he then ordered the invasion of one of them, what were the other two to think? It would make sense for them to believe that they might be next, and in that case to take steps to deter the United States from invading. But how can any state hope to deter a world-dominant power? Conventional defense and deterrence strategies have historically proven ineffective against the United States, so, logically, nuclear weapons are the only weapons capable of dissuading the United States from working its will on other nations.

To suggest to other states that America's willingness to shrink its nuclear arsenal should induce them to follow the example, or should persuade them to give up their efforts to become nuclear states, is fanciful. In spite of much rhetoric coming from the White House, the United States shows no intention of dropping its nuclear forces below the second-strike level. The president, speaking to the people of the Czech Republic, promised that we will "take concrete steps toward a world without nuclear weapons." However, he then followed that statement with this one: "Make no mistake: as long as these weapons exist, the United States will maintain a safe, secure, and effective arsenal to deter any adversary and guarantee that defense to our allies." That is, we will—as we should—continue to maintain forces able to launch a devastating retaliatory blow even if struck first. Nuclear arsenals may be reduced to very small numbers, but if they remain at or above the second-strike level, the military relations of states continue unchanged.

For decades, various factions in and out of the U.S. government have advocated the development of nuclear defenses that could protect the U.S. homeland from an incoming ICBM attack (known as National Missile Defenses). These have since been dropped in favor of thinner, more flexible area defenses. I am quite pleased that the U.S. government has abandoned its ill-advised pursuits at a National Missile Defense capability.[3] Nevertheless, Theater Missile Defenses are not much better and still doomed to failure.

Like their more ambitious National counterparts, Theater Missile Defenses are and will always be too easily overcome to promise an effective defense against nuclear weapons, as indeed, there is no such thing. In a conventional world, the effectiveness of defense varies with changes in technology and strategy; in a nuclear world, the offense will always dominate the defense. A billion dollars spent on defense against incoming missiles can be overcome by a fraction of that amount spent on offensive weaponry. An aggressor hoping to overwhelm a Theater Missile Defense System like THAAD or SM-3, need only launch more delivery vehicles than those systems can handle, or launch their weapons on a trajectory that confuses them. For example, inflatable balloon decoys could swamp these systems and render them useless.[4]

Beyond the many practical reasons for eschewing ballistic missile defense, there are also important theoretical considerations at play. Specifically, the nuclear revolution effectively serves to invert all prevailing wisdom about offense and defense.[5] While ICBMs or bombers are widely considered offensive technologies, I have noted many times that nuclear weapons are not useable as weapons of war. Their only use is as weapons of deterrence, and they must therefore be considered defensive. Missile defense, an alleged countermeasure to these weapons, then, must be considered offensive, as it aims to undercut the deterrent power of a nuclear capability. It is small wonder that countries like Russia and China remain vociferously opposed to U.S. missile defense deployments.[6] In addition to being fiscally irresponsible and technologically infeasible, they are also strategically unwise.

If somehow world leaders blundered into an agreement to pursue nuclear zero, then what would any nuclear country with sensible leaders do? The answer can be given in one word: cheat. Nuclear weapons are small and light; they are easy to hide and easy to move. Nuclear warheads can be placed in small vans or small boats and sent across borders or into harbors. Because a ban on all nuclear weapons would be impossible to police and enforce, countries would be tempted to break the rules. And because some might cheat, all would have a strong incentive to do so. Even worse, if the zero option were generally accepted, one state or another might eventually come to believe that it faced a threat to its very existence. A mad scramble to re-arm with nuclear weapons would then take place. As Thomas C. Schelling long ago wrote, "Short of universal brain surgery, nothing can erase the memory of weapons and how to build them."[7]

With the dawn of the nuclear age, peace has prevailed among those who have nuclear weapons or enjoy their protection. Those who like peace should love nuclear weapons. They are the only weapons ever invented that work decisively against their own use. Those who advocate a zero option argue in effect that we should eliminate the cause of the extensive peace that the nuclear world has enjoyed.

India and Pakistan provide an object lesson. When they tested their warheads in May of 1998, journalists, academics, and public officials predicted that war and chaos on the subcontinent would ensue. The result, as I expected, was to ensure a prolonged peace between countries that had fought three wars since independence and continued for a time to spill blood in the conflict over Kashmir.

That countries with nuclear capabilities do not fight wars against one another is a lesson we should have learned by now. The proposition has held exactly where the prospects for war seemed the brightest—for example, between the United

States and the Soviet Union, between the Soviet Union and the People's Republic of China, and between India and Pakistan. New nuclear states are often greeted with dire forebodings: Is the government stable? Are the rulers sensible? The answers may be disconcerting, yet every new nuclear nation, however bad its previous reputation, has behaved exactly like all of the old ones. The effect of having nuclear weapons overwhelms the character of the states that possess them. Countries with nuclear weapons, no matter how mean and irrational their leaders may seem to be, no matter how unstable their governments appear to be, do not launch major conventional attacks on other countries, let alone nuclear ones. Even conventional attacks can all too easily escalate out of control and lead to an exchange of nuclear warheads. With conventional weapons, countries worry about winning or losing. With nuclear weapons, countries worry about surviving or being annihilated. Nuclear weapons induce caution all around; think of the Cuban missile crisis, or think of the external behavior of China during the frightful decade of the Cultural Revolution.

These days, everyone favors transparency. On the nuclear front the United States is transparent enough. Transparently, it is in America's interest to get would-be nuclear states to foreswear the capability. Transparently, it is in America's interest to get presently nuclear states to reduce or, better yet, eliminate their warheads. We are, after all, the world's dominant conventional power and have been for years. Are we willing to reduce the number of our nuclear weapons? Sure; we have far more warheads than deterrence requires. Would we be willing to reduce the number of our strategic warheads below what we think is necessary for a second-strike capability? Obviously not. We are transparent on that point as well.

SAGAN RESPONDS

Kenneth Waltz served in the U.S. Army in World War II, became a leading proponent of realist "balance of power" theory during the Cold War, and has consistently maintained since then that new proliferators will also behave cautiously if they acquire the bomb. It is therefore not surprising to learn that Waltz fears that nuclear disarmament would "make the world safe for the fighting of World War III (Ch. 7, p. 221)". He further believes that the atomic bomb is the best "peacekeeping weapon" ever invented, and deduces that the Obama administration must, despite the president's grand rhetoric, really have no intention of moving toward global zero. What is surprising is that Waltz exaggerates the peace-inducing effect of nuclear weapons, displays a strangely apolitical perspective on the causes of war, completely ignores the risks of nuclear terrorism, and misrepresents Barack Obama's statements about nuclear disarmament. Let me address these point by point.

Waltz claims that "states with nuclear weapons have never fought one another (Ch. 7, p. 220)". Wrong. India and Pakistan, after testing nuclear weapons in 1998, fought the 1999 Kargil War, in which over one thousand soldiers died. Moreover, the Kargil War occurred not despite Pakistan developing nuclear weapons but rather because Pakistan got the bomb. Pakistani generals thought that their new nuclear arsenal was a shield behind which they could safely sneak Pakistani soldiers into Indian-controlled Kashmir without triggering a war. They were wrong, dangerously wrong.

Waltz also notes that "even with the horrors of World War I fresh in their minds, European countries went into World War II (Ch. 7, p. 220)". This is apolitical political science. Didn't Hitler and the Nazi Party's ambition to create Lebensraum and gain mastery of Europe have something to do with the outbreak of war? Poland, England, and France did not just stumble into war in 1939 and 1940; they were attacked by an expansionist power led by a megalomaniac leader who did not fear the consequences of war. (Indeed, by 1945 Hitler thought the German people should be destroyed because they had proven themselves unworthy of his leadership.) If the United States faced an aggressive leader like Hitler today, I would certainly advocate the maintenance of a U.S. nuclear arsenal for

the sake of deterrence. But we do not now face that kind of
threat in Russia and China. And the possibility of leaders like
Iran's Ahmadinejad getting nuclear weapons is precisely why
the United States should work with others to pressure would-
be proliferators and prevent the spread of nuclear weapons.

It is revealing that the word "terrorism" does not appear
in Waltz's essay. He may believe that terrorists' interests in getting the bomb are exaggerated or that governments can easily
protect their arsenals from insider or outsider threats. But he is
incorrect on both counts. Islamic jihadis, left-wing radicals,
and apocalyptic cults have all tried to obtain nuclear weapons.
Further proliferation will increase their chances of success. No
wonder Waltz ignores this issue—he has no credible way to
address it.

Waltz cites Obama's Prague speech about America keeping nuclear weapons as long as others possess the same capability as evidence that we are not serious about disarmament.
Wrong again. Obama was in fact emphasizing that the United
States will not disarm unilaterally and that the process will
take a significant amount of time. But if we can negotiate multilateral arms-reduction agreements and create new verification
technology, safe and secure disarmament is possible. Waltz
misinterprets Obama's nod toward realism as hypocrisy.

Nuclear weapons have not been the best things since
sliced bread. They have been a mixed blessing and a dangerous deterrent. The Cold War witnessed many close calls; new
nuclear states will be even more prone to deterrence failures.
Living with nuclear weapons was a perilous necessity in the
past. It should not be repeated. Celebrating this dangerous condition is misguided.

WALTZ RESPONDS

In 1963 President John F. Kennedy famously speculated that by
1970 ten countries would be able to deploy nuclear weapons
and by 1975, fifteen to twenty countries would have followed

suit.[8] In fact, the number of nuclear states peaked at ten when some of the successor states to the Soviet Union were born nuclear, then the number dropped to seven, and now it stands at nine with Pakistan and North Korea having joined what remains the world's most exclusive club.

Why have nuclear weapons spread so slowly? The answer is found not in the Nuclear Non-Proliferation Treaty but in the fact that most countries feel sufficiently secure without adding nuclear weapons to their conventional arsenals. If a country believes that its security depends on nuclear weapons, then preventing it from acquiring them becomes almost impossible. President George W. Bush, among others, announced that North Korea becoming a nuclear state would be "unacceptable." Yet when North Korea developed a nuclear military capability, we quietly acquiesced. The alternative to acceptance would have been to attack North Korea's nuclear facilities, and that would surely have been unacceptable.

Sagan emphasizes that verification and enforcement of an agreement to create a nuclear-free world would be required. If for a moment we imagine that Sagan's hoped-for world without nuclear weapons could be realized, what would anyone do if a major state revealed that it had secretly rebuilt a considerable nuclear arsenal? Would someone then attack the reborn nuclear state using the only weapons it would have, that is, conventional ones? I think not.

Sagan, having rejected "legal niceties," would instead rely on international pieties. If other countries believe that America is on the road to nuclear disarmament, they will presumably jump on the bandwagon. The problem is that no road leads from a world with a small number of nuclear states to a world with none. Sagan believes that if the world does not become nuclear-weapons free it will soon be a world of many nuclear states. One wonders why. Many more states can make nuclear weapons than do. Why should one now expect a large number of new nuclear states to join the hitherto-exclusive club? The old answer was that states seek the prestige that members of the club enjoy. Little prestige, however, attaches to new nuclear states when countries like Pakistan and North Korea already have them. Strong states—the old Soviet Union and China—are no longer seen as threats. Sagan would have us transfer our worries to puny new nuclear states and terrorists. We used to worry about the strong; now we should worry about the weak.

Sagan emphasizes the perils that attend a world with many more nuclear states, thus increasing the chances that terrorists would be able to steal or buy nuclear devices. To find good words to say about terrorists is difficult. Terrorists are a big annoyance and may occasionally do a fair amount of damage. We all know about the attacks on the Twin Towers and the Pentagon in which upwards of three thousand people perished. One thought, however, gives comfort: terrorists are incapable of rending the fabric of society and of occupying and administering territory. We should all heave a sigh of relief that strong adversaries have been replaced by weak ones.

NOTES

CHAPTER 1

1. The Maginot line was a string of fortifications built before World War II to protect the eastern borders of France.

2. Richard Smoke, *War: Controlling Escalation* (Cambridge, Mass.: Harvard University Press, 1977), pp. 175–88.

3. Glenn H. Snyder, *Deterrence and Defense* (Princeton, N.J.: Princeton University Press, 1961), p. 44; Stephen Van Evera, "Primed for Peace: Europe After the Cold War," *International Security* 15, no. 3 (Winter 1990–91).

4. Snyder, *Deterrence and Defense*, pp. 37, 49, and 79–82; Bernard Brodie, *Escalation and the Nuclear Option* (Princeton, NJ: Princeton University Press, 1966), pp. 74–78; Robert Jervis, "Why Nuclear Superiority Doesn't Matter," *Political Science Quarterly* 94 (Winter 1979–80); Shai Feldman, *Israeli Nuclear Deterrence: A Strategy for the 1980s* (New York: Columbia University Press, 1982), passim.

5. Bernard Brodie, *War and Politics* (New York: Macmillan, 1973), p. 321.

6. Georg Simmel, "The Sociology of Conflict, I", *American Journal of Sociology* 9 (January 1904), p. 501.

7. George Sansom, "Japan's Fatal Blunder," in Robert J. Art and Kenneth N. Waltz, eds., *The Use of Force* (Boston: Little, Brown, 1971), pp. 208–9.

8. Cf. Lewis A. Dunn, "Nuclear Proliferation and World Politics," in Joseph I. Coffey, ed., *Nuclear Proliferation: Prospects, Problems, and Proposals* (Philadelphia: The Annals of the American Academy of Political Science, March 1977), pp. 102–7. For a recent elaboration see Lewis A. Dunn, *Containing Nuclear Proliferation*, Adelphi Paper 263 (London: International Institute for Strategic Studies, 1991).

9. Feldman, *Israeli Nuclear Deterrence*, p. 163.

10. *The Middle East and North Africa, 1994*, 40th ed. (London: Europa Publications, 1993), pp. 363, 810.

11. For brief accounts, see S. E. Finer, *The Man on Horseback* (London: Pall Mall Press, 1962), pp. 106–8; and Roy Medvedev, "Soviet Policy Reported Reversed by SALT II," *Washington Star*, July 7, 1979, p. 1.

12. Cf. Kenneth N. Waltz, "America's European Policy Viewed in Global Perspective," in Wolfram F. Hanreider, ed., *The United States and Western Europe* (Cambridge, Mass.: Winthrop, 1974), p. 31; Richard K. Betts, *Soldiers,*

Statesmen, and Cold War Crises (Cambridge, Mass.: Harvard University Press, 1977), appendix A. For a revised version of this book with additional evidence from the Reagan and Carter administrations, see Betts, Soldiers, Statesmen and Cold War Crises, 2d ed. (New York: Columbia University Press, 1991).

13. Cf. John J. Weltman, "Nuclear Devolution and World Order," World Politics 32 (January 1980), pp. 190–92.

14. Cf. Dunn, "Nuclear Proliferation," p. 101.

15. The distinction between prevention—striking to prevent a state from gaining nuclear-military capability—and preemption—striking to destroy weapons before they can be used—is discussed in Chapter 3, pp. 94–95.

16. Walter H. Waggoner, "U.S. Disowns Matthews Talk of Waging War to Get Peace," New York Times, August 27, 1950, p. 1.

17. William B. Bader, The United States and the Spread of Nuclear Weapons (New York: Pegasus, 1968), p. 96.

18. E.g., David M. Rosenbaum, "Nuclear Terror," International Security 1 (Winter 1977), p. 145.

19. See Kenneth N. Waltz, "Nuclear Myths and Political Realities," American Political Science Review 84, no. 3 (September 1990).

20. Geoffrey Kemp, Nuclear Forces for Medium Powers: Part I: Targets and Weapons, Adelphi Paper 196 (London: International Institute for Strategic Studies, 1974).

21. Justin Galen (pseud.), "US Toughest Message to the USSR," Armed Forces Journal International (February 1979), p. 31.

22. Cf. Paul H. Nitze, "Assuring Strategic Stability in an Era of Detente," Foreign Policy 54, no. 2 (Winter 1976–77), pp. 207–32; James R. Schlesinger, "U.S.-U.S.S.R. Strategic Policies," Hearing before the Subcommittee on Arms Control, International Law and Organizations of the Committee on Foreign Relations, U.S. Senate, 93rd Cong., 2d sess., March 4, 1974, in Robert J. Pranger and Roger P. Labrie, eds., Nuclear Strategy and National Security: Points of View (Washington, D.C.: American Enterprise Institute, 1977), p. 105; Colin Gray, "Nuclear Strategy: A Case for a Theory of Victory," International Security 4 (Summer 1979), pp. 67–72.

23. Thomas C. Schelling, The Strategy of Conflict (New York: Oxford University Press, 1963), pp. 187–203.

24. Glenn H. Snyder, "Crisis Bargaining," in C. F. Hermann, ed., International Crises: Insights from Behavioral Research (New York: Free Press, 1972), p. 232.

25. John G. Stoessinger, Henry Kissinger: The Anguish of Power (New York: W. W. Norton, 1976), ch. 8.

26. Feldman, Israeli Nuclear Deterrence, pp. 29–32.

27. Steven J. Rosen, "Nuclearization and Stability in the Middle East," in Onkar Marwah and Ann Schultz, eds., Nuclear Proliferation and the Near-Nuclear Countries (Cambridge, Mass.: Ballinger, 1975), p. 173.

28. Frederic J. Brown, "Chemical Warfare: A Study in Restraints" (1968) in Art and Waltz, The Use of Force, p. 183.

29. William T. R. Fox, "International Control of Atomic Weapons," in Bernard Brodie, ed., The Absolute Weapon (New York: Harcourt, Brace, 1946), p. 181.

30. Donald A. Quarles, "How Much Is Enough?" *Air Force* 49 (September 1956), pp. 51–52.

31. Harold Brown, Department of Defense, *Annual Report, FY 1980* (Washington, D.C.: GPO, 1980), pp. 75–76.

32. "Part II of the Press Conference by Valéry Giscard d'Estaing, President of the French Republic" (New York: French Embassy, Press and Information Division, February 15, 1979).

33. Eldon Griffiths, "The Revolt of Europe," *Saturday Evening Post* 263 (March 9, 1963), p. 19.

34. International Institute for Strategic Studies, *Strategic Survey* (London: Brassey's, various years).

35. Brodie, "War in the Atomic Age" in Brodie, *The Absolute Weapon*, p. 74.

36. Patrick Morgan, *Deterrence: A Conceptual Analysis* (Beverly Hills, Calif.: Sage, 1977), p. 116.

37. Thomas C. Schelling, *Arms and Influence* (New Haven: Yale University Press, 1966), p. 22.

38. Richard Pipes, "Why the Soviet Union Thinks It Could Fight and Win a Nuclear War," *Commentary* 64, no. 1 (July 1977).

39. Joseph Nye, "Maintaining a Non-Proliferation Regime," *International Organization* 35 (Winter 1981).

40. Feldman, *Israeli Nuclear Deterrence*, ch. 5.

41. Interviews by the author, December 1978.

42. Norman Angell, *The Great Illusion* (London: William Heinemann, 1914).

Chapter 2

1. References to Chapter 1 will appear in the text in parentheses (e.g., Ch.1, p. x). References to Waltz's earlier work will appear in endnotes.

2. Bruce Bueno de Mesquita and William H. Riker, "An Assessment of the Merits of Selective Nuclear Proliferation," *Journal of Conflict Resolution* 26, no. 2 (June 1982), p. 283.

3. John J. Mearsheimer, "Back to the Future: Instability in Europe after the Cold War," *International Security* 15, no. 1 (Summer 1990), pp. 5–56 (quote at p. 20); Mearsheimer, "The Case for a Ukrainian Nuclear Deterrent," *Foreign Affairs* 72, no. 3 (Summer 1993), pp. 50–66. Mearsheimer's position on Japan was expressed on National Public Radio's "Morning Edition" on June 21, 1993. NPR Transcript, June 21, 1993, p. 21.

4. Stephen Van Evera, "Primed For Peace: Europe After the Cold War," *International Security* 15, no. 3 (Winter 1990/91), p. 54; Sumit Ganguly, "India's Pathway to Pokhran II," *International Security* 23, no. 4 (Spring 1999), p. 176; Peter Lavoy, "Civil-Military Relations, Strategic Conduct, and the Stability of Nuclear Deterrence in South Asia," in *Civil-Military Relations and Nuclear Weapons* (Stanford Center for International Security and Arms Control, June 1994); Martin van Creveld, *Nuclear Proliferation and the Future of Conflict* (New York: Free Press, 1993); Shai Feldman, *Israeli Nuclear*

Deterrence: A Strategy for the 1980s (New York: Columbia University Press, 1982), pp. 142–75, 238.

5. Important pessimistic appraisals include: Lewis A. Dunn, *Containing Nuclear Proliferation*, Adelphi Paper 263 (London: International Institute of Strategic Studies, 1991); Steven E. Miller, "The Case Against a Ukrainian Nuclear Deterrent," *Foreign Affairs* 72, no. 3 (Summer 1993), pp. 67–80; Paul Bracken, "Nuclear Weapons and State Survival in North Korea," *Survival* 35, no. 3 (Autumn 1993), pp. 137–53; and Peter D. Feaver, "Proliferation Optimism and Theories of Nuclear Operations," *Security Studies* 2, no. 3–4 (Spring/Summer 1993), pp. 159–91.

6. See, for example, the symposium on rational deterrence theory in *World Politics* 41, no. 2 (January 1989), pp. 143–224.

7. Kenneth N. Waltz, "Nuclear Myths and Political Realities," *American Political Science Review* 84, no. 3 (September 1990), pp. 731, 734. One measure of Waltz's influence on this issue is the fact that this article won the Heinz Eulau award for the best article published in the *APSR* in 1990.

8. Kenneth N. Waltz, "The Origins of War in Neorealist Theory," in Robert I. Rotberg and Theodore K. Rabb, eds., *The Origin and Prevention of Major Wars* (Cambridge, U.K.: Cambridge University Press, 1988), pp. 50, 51. Also see Waltz, "The Emerging Structure of International Politics," *International Security* 18, no. 2 (Fall 1993), pp. 51–55.

9. Ibid. and Kenneth N. Waltz, "Response to My Critics," in Robert O. Keohane, ed., *Neorealism and Its Critics* (New York: Columbia University Press, 1986), p. 331.

10. Waltz, "Nuclear Myths and Political Realities," p. 739.

11. The classic text is James G. March and Herbert Simon, *Organizations*, 2d ed. (Cambridge, Mass.: Basil Blackwell, 1993). For valuable reviews of relevant scholarship see Charles Perrow, *Complex Organizations*, 3rd ed. (New York: Random House, 1986), pp. 119–56; and Jonathan Bendor and Thomas H. Hammond, "Rethinking Allison's Models," *American Political Science Review* 86, no. 2 (June 1992), pp. 301–22.

12. March and Simon, *Organizations*, p. 186. On goal displacement see Robert K. Merton, "Bureaucratic Structure and Personality," in Merton et al., eds., *Reader in Bureaucracy* (Glencoe, Il.: Free Press, 1952), pp. 365–66; Herbert Simon, "Bounded Rationality and Organizational Learning," *Organizational Science* 2, no. 1 (February 1991), pp. 125–34; and Charles Perrow, "Goals in Complex Organizations," *American Sociological Review* 26, no. 6 (December 1961), pp. 854–65.

13. The seminal works on conflict in organization theory are James G. March, "The Business Firm as a Political Coalition," *Journal of Politics* 24, no. 1 (February 1962), pp. 662–78; Richard M. Cyert and James G. March, *A Behavioral Theory of the Firm*, 2d ed. (Cambridge, Mass.: Basil Blackwell, 1992); and Philip Selznick, *TVA and the Grassroots* (Berkeley: University of California Press, 1949). For valuable recent perspectives, see Terry Moe, "Politics and the Theory of Organization," *Journal of Law, Economics, and Organization* 7 (special issue 1991), pp. 106–29; Jeffrey Pfeffer, *Power in Organizations* (Cambridge, Mass.: Ballinger, 1981); and James Q. Wilson, *Bureaucracy: What Government*

Agencies Do and Why They Do It (New York: Basic Books, 1991), especially pp. 179–95.

14. Perrow, *Complex Organizations*, p. 132.

15. See Graham T. Allison, *Essence of Decision* (Boston: Little Brown, 1971); John D. Steinbruner, *The Cybernetic Theory of Decision* (Princeton: Princeton University Press, 1974); Morton H. Halperin, *Bureaucratic Politics and Foreign Policy* (Washington, D.C.: Brookings Institution, 1974); Barry R. Posen, *The Sources of Military Doctrine* (Ithaca, N.Y.: Cornell University Press, 1984); Scott A. Snook, *Friendly Fire* (Princeton, N.J.: Princeton University Press, 2000); Bruce G. Blair, *The Logic of Accidental Nuclear War* (Washington, D.C.: Brookings Institution, 1993); and Scott D. Sagan, *The Limits of Safety: Organizations, Accidents and Nuclear Weapons* (Princeton, N.J.: Princeton University Press, 1993).

16. For discussions of preventive war see Jack S. Levy, "Declining Power and the Preventive Motivation for War," *World Politics* 40, no. 1 (October 1987), pp. 82–107; and Randall L. Schweller, "Domestic Structure and Preventive War," *World Politics* 44, no. 2 (January 1992), pp. 235–69.

17. Waltz, *The Spread of Nuclear Weapons*, p. 12; Richard K. Betts, *Soldiers, Statesmen, and Cold War Crises*, 2d ed. (New York: Columbia University Press, 1991).

18. Samuel P. Huntington, *The Soldier and the State* (Cambridge, Mass.: Harvard University Press, 1957), p. 65; Alfred Vagts, *Defense and Diplomacy: The Soldier and the Conduct of Foreign Relations* (New York: Crown Point Press, 1956), p. 263. For empirical support see John P. Lovell, "The Professional Socialization of the West Point Cadet," in Morris Janowitz, ed., *The New Military* (New York: Russell Sage, 1964), p. 129; and Bengt Abrahamsson, "Military Professionalization and Estimates on the Probability of War," in Jacques van Doorn, ed., *Military Profession and Military Regimes* (The Hague: Mouton, 1969), pp. 35–51.

19. See Jack Snyder, *The Ideology of the Offensive* (Ithaca, N.Y.: Cornell University Press, 1984), pp. 26–30; and Posen, *The Sources of Military Doctrine*, pp. 47–50.

20. It is important to note, however, that Truman's military advisers tended to focus on tactical, military reasons for not using the bomb (such as the lack of suitable targets in Korea or the need to retain weapons for targets in the USSR), while civilians more often emphasized political factors (such as the effects on allied governments or U.S. public opinion). See John Lewis Gaddis, "The Origins of Self-Deterrence: The United States and the Non-Use of Nuclear Weapons, 1945–1958," in Gaddis, *The Long Peace: Inquires into the History of the Cold War* (New York: Oxford University Press, 1987), pp. 115–23; and Roger Dingman, "Atomic Diplomacy During the Korean War," *International Security* 13, no. 3 (Winter 1988/89), pp. 65–69.

21. The best source is Marc Trachtenberg's essay, "A 'Wasting Asset,' American Strategy and the Shifting Nuclear Balance, 1949–1954," in Trachtenberg, *History and Strategy* (Princeton: Princeton University Press, 1991), pp. 100–152.

22. SWNCC 282, "Basis for the Formulation of a U.S. Military Policy," September 19, 1945, reprinted in Thomas H. Etzold and John Lewis Gaddis, *Containment: Documents on American Policy and Strategy, 1945–1950* (New

York: Columbia University Press, 1978), p. 42. Significantly, the State Department's response to the report rejected the specific military recommendations that appeared "preventive in purpose." SC169b, "Action on Joint Chiefs of Staff Statement on United States Military Policy," November 16, 1945, in ibid., p. 47.

23. Text of Truman's " 'Report to Nation' on Korea War," *New York Times*, September 2, 1950, p. 4. Truman made similar comments in private conversations. For example, he told Admiral Leahy in May 1948 that the American people would never accept the bomb being used "for aggressive purposes." See David Alan Rosenberg, "American Atomic Strategy and the Hydrogen Bomb Decision," *Journal of American History*, vol. 66, no. 1 (June 1979), p. 67. Also see Harry S. Truman, *Years of Trial and Hope* (Garden City, N.Y.: Doubleday, 1956), vol. 2, pp. 359, 383.

24. NSC-68, in *Foreign Relations of the United States* (hereinafter *FRUS* followed by year and volume), 1950, vol. 1, National Security Affairs, pp. 281–82. According to General Nathan Twining, the moral issue was the most important factor in NSC-68's rejection of preventive war. Nathan F. Twining, *Neither Liberty nor Safety* (New York: Holt, Rinehart and Winston, 1966), p. 49.

25. Anderson stated, "Give me the order to do it and I can break up Russia's five A-bomb nests in a week. . . . And when I went up to Christ—I think I could explain to Him that I had saved civilization." Austin Stevens, "General Removed over War Speech," *New York Times*, September 2, 1950, p. 8.

26. See Trachtenberg, "A 'Wasting Asset,' " pp. 106–7 and p. 123; and *USAF Basic Doctrine*, October 1951, K239.71605-1, Air Force Historical Research Center, Maxwell AFB, AL, p. 3.

27. Project Control suggested the following might be an appropriate definition of "aggression" calling for a U.S. military response after issuing the ultimatum: "Any nation that persists in the development and production of military force capable of threatening the existence of the Free World and whose political actions and stated national intent leaves no doubt that she intends to use military force to conquer or subjugate free countries should be considered as an aggressor who is preparing to commit an aggressive act against the United States." Quoted in Tami Davis Biddle, "Handling the Soviet Threat: 'Project Control' and the Debate on American Strategy in the Early Cold War Years," *The Journal of Strategic Studies* 12, no. 3 (September 1989), p. 287.

28. Ibid., pp. 291–92.

29. Matthew Ridgway, memorandum for the record, May 17, 1954, historical records file 1/15–6/30, Box 30, Ridgway papers, U.S. Army Military History Institute. Originally cited in David Alan Rosenberg, "The Origins of Overkill: Nuclear Weapons and American Strategy, 1945–1960," *International Security* 7, no. 4 (Spring 1983), p. 34.

30. Memorandum by the Chief of Staff, U.S. Air Force, to the JCS on The Coming National Crisis, (August 21, 1953), Twining Papers, series 2, topical series, nuclear weapons 1952–1961 folder, USAF Academy, Colorado Springs, CO.

31. Memorandum of Discussion, NSC meeting, November 24, 1954, *FRUS*, 1952–54, vol. 2, National Security Affairs, part 1, p. 792.

32. Eisenhower wrote in a top secret memorandum to Dulles in September 1953, the U.S. "would have to be constantly ready, on an instantaneous basis, to inflict greater loss upon the enemy than he could reasonably hope to inflict on us. . . . This would be a deterrent—but if the contest to maintain this relative position should have to continue indefinitely, the cost would either drive us to war—or into some form of dictatorial government. In such circumstances, we would be forced to consider whether or not our duty to future generations did not require us to *initiate* war at the most propitious moment that we could designate." Memorandum by the President to the Secretary of State, September 8, 1953, ibid., p. 461 (emphasis in original).

33. Robert H. Ferrel, ed., *The Diary of James C. Hagerty* (Bloomington, Ind.: Indiana University Press, 1983), p. 69. Also see Trachtenberg, "A 'Wasting Asset,'" p. 141; and McGeorge Bundy, *Danger and Survival: Choices about the Bomb in the First Fifty Years* (New York: Random House, 1988), p. 140.

34. When the U.S. preventive-war advocates presented their views in 1954, U.S. intelligence estimates of Soviet nuclear capabilities were highly uncertain, but nonetheless significant: estimates of the Soviet nuclear stockpile ranged from 188 to 725 nuclear weapons; and an estimated 300 Soviet bomber aircraft could be launched in a first strike, or possibly launched upon warning, of a U.S. attack, "200 to 250 of which might reach their targets [in the U.S.]." NIE 11-4-54 (August 28, 1954), Declassified Documents Reference System, 1981, No. 283A; and Memorandum by the Acting Special Assistant to the Secretary of State for Intelligence to the Acting Secretary of State, (March 1, 1954), *FRUS* 1952–54, vol. 2, National Security Affairs, part 1, p. 634.

35. Although advocacy of preventive war diminished within the U.S. military in the late 1950s, common organizational proclivities continued to influence military thinking about nuclear war. Goal displacement was especially pronounced in the early integrated war plans which enabled the JCS to argue, as late as 1961, that the United States would "prevail in the event of general nuclear war," even if the USSR struck first. "Prevail in this context" did *not* mean avoiding massive U.S. casualties, however; it simply meant achieving the damage expectancy war aims set out in the guidance given to war planners. See Scott D. Sagan, "SIOP-62: The Nuclear War Plan Briefing to President Kennedy," *International Security* 12, no. 1 (Summer 1987), p. 36.

36. This paragraph is based on William Burr and Jeffrey T. Richelson, "Whether to 'Strangle the Baby in the Cradle': The United States and the Chinese Nuclear Program, 1960–1964," *International Security*, 25, no. 3 (Winter 2000/2001) pp. 54–99.

37. Memorandum by the Joint Chiefs of Staff, "A Strategic Analysis of the Impact of the Acquisition by Communist China of a Nuclear Capability," June 26, 1961, in *FRUS* 1961–63, vol. 22, pp. 84–85.

38. *FRUS* 1964–68, vol. 30, p. 24, no. 7.

39. The best source is Victor M. Gorbarev, "Soviet Policy Toward China: Developing Nuclear Weapons 1949–1969," *Journal of Slavic Military Studies* 12, no. 4 (December 1999), pp. 37–39. Also see Bruce G. Blair, *The Logic of Accidental Nuclear War* (Washington, D.C.: Brookings Institution, 1993), p. 25; and

Raymond L. Garthoff, *Détente and Confrontation* (Washington, D.C.: Brookings Institution, 1985), p. 209.

40. Arkady N. Shevchenko, *Breaking with Moscow* (New York: Knopf, 1985), p. 1965.

41. For analysis of the American policy, see William Burr, "Sino-American Relations, 1969: The Sino-Soviet Border War and Steps Toward Rapprochement," *Cold War History* 1, no. 3 (April 2001), pp. 73–112. On the U.S. alert, see Scott D. Sagan, "Correspondence: Proliferation Pessimism and Emerging Nuclear Powers," *International Security* 22, no. 2 (Fall 1997), p. 197.

42. Stephen P. Cohen, *The Pakistan Army* (Berkeley, Calif.: University of California Press, 1984), p. 112.

43. On the preventive motivations for Pakistan's 1965 attack, see *ibid.*, p. 139; Gowher Rizvi, "The Rivalry Between India and Pakistan," in Barry Buzan and Gowher Rizvi, eds., *South Asian Insecurity and the Great Powers* (Basingstoke, U.K.: Macmillan, 1986), pp. 107–8; and Sumit Ganguly, *The Origins of War in South Asia* (Boulder, Colo.: Westview Press, 1986), pp. 57–95.

44. The paragraph is based on Gregory F. Giles, "The Islamic Republic of Iran and Nuclear, Biological and Chemical Weapons," in Peter R. Lavoy, Scott D. Sagan, and James J. Wirtz, eds., *Planning the Unthinkable: How New Powers Will Use Nuclear, Biological, and Chemical Weapons* (Ithaca, N.Y.: Cornell University Press, 2000), pp. 79–103.

45. Waltz, "Nuclear Myths and Political Realities," p. 732.

46. Ibid., p. 731; Waltz, "Origins of War in Neorealist Theory," p. 51.

47. Halperin, *Bureaucratic Politics and Foreign Policy*, p. 28.

48. See Henry S. Rowen and Richard Brody, "The Development of U.S. Nuclear Strategy and Employment Policy," in Andrew W. Marshall et al., eds., *On Not Confusing Ourselves* (Boulder, Colo.: Westview Press, 1991), p. 32; and Fred Kaplan, *The Wizards of Armageddon* (New York: Simon and Schuster, 1983), p. 99.

49. Bruce L. R. Smith, *The RAND Corporation* (Cambridge, Mass.: Harvard University Press, 1966), pp. 222–23.

50. Ibid., p. 226.

51. Harvey M. Sapolsky, *The Polaris System Development* (Cambridge, Mass.: Harvard University Press, 1972), p. 15.

52. Ibid., pp. 17–18. Opposition also existed because another navy tradition—that ships should only have one commanding officer—was also challenged by the development of ballistic missile submarines which used two commanders and crews, so that replacements could take over immediately after a lengthy patrol at sea.

53. Ibid., p. 35.

54. Ibid., p. 18. Also see Vincent Davis, *The Politics of Innovation: Patterns in Navy Cases*, University of Denver Monograph Series in World Affairs 4, no. 3 (1966–67), p. 23.

55. Edmund Beard, *Developing the ICBM* (New York: Columbia University Press, 1976), p. 8.

56. Robert Frank Futrell, *Ideas, Concepts, Doctrine: A History of Basic Thinking in the United States Air Force* (Maxwell AFB, Ala.: Air University, 1971), p. 257; Beard, *Developing the ICBM*, p. 85.

57. Graham Allison and Philip Zelikow, *Essence of Decision* (New York: Longman, 1999), p. 208; Dino A. Brugioni, *Eyeball to Eyeball: The Inside Story of the Cuban Missile Crisis* (New York: Random House, 1990), pp. 277–88 and picture 22; Ernst R. May and Philip D. Zelikow, eds., *The Kennedy Tapes: Inside the White House During the Cuban Missile Crisis* (Cambridge, Mass.: Harvard University Press, 1997), p. 79.

58. Dino A. Brugioni, "The Art and Science of Photo Reconaissance," *Scientific American*, 274, no. 3 (March 1996), pp. 78–85.

59. The paragraph is based on Sherry Sontag and Christopher Drew, *Blind Man's Bluff: The Untold Story of American Submarine Espionage* (New York: Public Affairs, 1998), pp. 158–230. The United States was not immune to such organizational snafus either. When the Soviets pulled up the secret cable-recording device, they had no problem identifying its source since U.S. navy personnel had left the inscription "Property of the United States Government" on one piece of equipment inside the pod. *Ibid.*, p. 231.

60. See John Wilson Lewis and Hua Di, "China's Ballistic Missile Programs: Technologies, Strategies, and Goals," *International Security* 17, no. 2 (Fall 1992), pp. 18–19 and p. 28.

61. Chong-Pin Lin, *China's Nuclear Weapons Strategy* (Lexington, Mass.: Lexington Books, 1988), p. 64; He Chiang, "PRC Ballistic Missiles: A Preliminary Survey," *Conmilit* 2, no. 7 (August 1978), p. 12, as quoted in *Ibid.*, p. 63.

62. Lewis and Hua, "China's Ballistic Missile Programs," p. 24.

63. *Ibid.*, pp. 12, 27.

64. Nadav Safran, *From War to War* (New York: Pegasus, 1969), p. 319.

65. *New York Times*, May 26, 1967, p. 16. Also see Anthony Nutting, *Nasser* (New York: E. P. Dutton, 1972), p. 398.

66. Edgar O'Ballance, *The Third Arab-Israeli War* (Hamden, Conn.: Archon Books, 1972), p. 65. This is not an uncommon problem. Despite assurances to the contrary, U.S. aircraft at bases in Florida were discovered to be deployed wing-tip to wing-tip at the height of the Cuban missile crisis. See Allison, *Essence of Decision*, p. 139; and *Chronology of JCS Decisions Concerning the Cuban Crisis*, Historical Division, Joint Chiefs of Staff, December 21, 1962 (National Security Archives, Washington, D.C.), pp. 31–32 and pp. 40–41.

67. O'Ballance, *The Third Arab-Israeli War*, p. 63; and Safran, *From War to War*, p. 321.

68. David Albright, "How Much Plutonium Does North Korea Have?" *Bulletin of Atomic Scientists* 50, no. 5 (September/October 1994), p. 48.

69. The best examples of "high reliability theory" are Joseph G. Morone and Edward J. Woodhouse, *Averting Catastrophe: Strategies for Regulating Risky Technologies* (Berkeley: University of California Press, 1986); Todd R. La Porte and Paula M. Consolini, "Working in Practice But Not in Theory: Theoretical Challenges of 'High Reliability Organizations,'" *Journal of Public Administration Research and Theory* 1, no. 1 (January 1991), pp. 19–47; Karlene H. Roberts, ed., *New Challenges to Understanding Organizations* (New York: Macmillan, 1993); Aaron Wildavsky, *Searching For Safety* (New Brunswick, N.J.: Transaction Books, 1988); and Jonathan B. Bendor, *Parallel Systems: Redundancy in Government* (Berkeley: University of California Press, 1985).

70. Charles Perrow, *Normal Accidents: Living with High-Risk Technologies* (New York: Basic Books, 1984), passim.

71. These ideas and the examples that follow are discussed in more detail in Sagan, *The Limits of Safety.*

72. For further discussion see Scott D. Sagan, "Toward a Political Theory of Organizational Reliability," *The Journal of Contingencies and Crisis Management* 2, no. 4 (December 1994).

73. *Report on the Unauthorized Movement of Nuclear Weapons,* The Defense Science Board Permanent Task Force on Nuclear Weapons Surety (February 2008). www.defense.gov/npr/docs/DSB%20TF%20on%20NWS%20Welch %20Feb%202008.pdf

74. Gary Milhollin, "Building Saddam Hussein's Bomb," *New York Times Magazine,* March 8, 1992, p. 32.

75. See Itty Abraham, *The Making of the Indian Atomic Bomb* (London: Zed Books, 1998).

76. David Albright, "South Africa's Secret Nuclear Weapons," *ISIS Report* (Institute for Science and International Security) 1, no. 4 (May 1994), p. 10.

77. FBIS-NEW-90-076, April 17, 1990, p. 7. The best analyses of Iraqi pre-delegation policy are Amatzia Baram, "An Analysis of Iraqi WMD," *Nonproliferation Review* 8, no. 2 (Summer 2001), pp. 34–37; and Timothy V. McCarthy and Jonathan B. Tucker, "Saddam's Toxic Arsenal: Chemical and Biological Weapons and Missiles in the Gulf War," in Lavoy, Sagan, and Wirtz, eds., *Planning the Unthinkable,* pp. 73–76.

78. Eliot A. Cohen, *Gulf War Air Power Survey,* vol. 2, part 1 (Washington, D.C.: U.S. Government Printing Office, 1993), p. 281.

79. ITV News Bureau, Ltd., "A Psy-Ops Bonanza in the Desert," April 18, 1991; Douglas Waller, "Secret Warriors," *Newsweek,* June 19, 1991, p. 24.

80. William Potter, "Nuclear Threats from the Former Soviet Union," Center for Security and Technology Studies, Lawrence Livermore National Laboratory, March 16, 1993, p. 6.

81. See Leonard S. Spector, *Going Nuclear* (Cambridge, Mass.: Ballinger, 1987), pp. 25–32.

82. John Wilson Lewis and Xue Litai, *China Builds the Bomb* (Stanford: Stanford University Press, 1988), pp. 202–3.

83. See especially Hans J. Morgenthau, *Defending the National Interest* (New York: Knopf, 1951); and George F. Kennan, *American Diplomacy* (Chicago: University of Chicago Press, 1951).

84. Kenneth N. Waltz, *Theory of International Politics* (New York: Random House, 1979), p. 118. In his 1986 essay Waltz similarly argued that the international system is a competitive one in which the less skillful must expect to pay for their ineptitude. The situation provides enough incentive to cause *most of the actors* to behave sensibly. Waltz, "Response to My Critics," p. 331 (emphasis added).

85. Waltz, "Response to My Critics," p. 331.

86. For example see the discussions of Waltz and Mearsheimer in Ravi Shastri, "Developing Nations and the Spread of Nuclear Weapons," *Strategic Analysis* (New Delhi), 11, no. 12 (March 1988), pp. 1379–91; and "Kiev and the

Bomb: Ukrainians Reply," *Foreign Affairs* 72, no. 4 (September/October 1993), pp. 183–86.

87. A detailed discussion of U.S. nuclear weapons safety mechanisms appears in Sidney Drell and Bob Peurifoy, "Technical Issues of a Nuclear Test Ban," *Annual Review of Nuclear and Particle Science* 44 (December 1994), pp. 294–313.

CHAPTER 3

1. Bertolt Brecht, *Mother Courage and Her Children: A Chronicle of the Thirty Years War*, trans. Eric Bentley (New York: Grove Press, 1966), p. 76.

2. C. P. Snow, "Excerpts from Snow's Speech to American Scientists," *New York Times*, December, 28, 1960, p. 14.

3. John Deutch, "Think Again: Terrorism," *Foreign Policy* 108 (Fall 1997), p. 10.

4. Larry Johnson, "The Declining Terrorist Threat," *New York Times*, July 10, 2001, p. A19.

5. Bruce G. Blair and Henry W. Kendall, "Dismantle Armageddon," *New York Times*, May 21, 1994, p. 21. Also see Scott D. Sagan, *The Limits of Safety: Organizations, Accidents, and Nuclear Weapons* (Princeton, N.J.: Princeton University Press, 1993), pp. 225–49.

6. Bruce G. Blair and Henry W. Kendall, "Accidental Nuclear War," *Scientific American* 263, no. 6 (December 1990), p. 53; and Sagan, *The Limits of Safety*, pp. 275–77.

7. Walter Millis, ed., *The Forrestal Diaries* (New York: Viking Press, 1951), pp. 492–530; and Warner R. Schilling, "Conclusions," in Warner R. Schilling, Paul Y. Hammond, and Glenn H. Snyder, eds., *Strategy, Politics and Defense Budgets* (New York: Columbia University Press, 1962), p. 217.

8. David Alan Rosenberg, "A Smoking, Radiating Ruin at the End of Two Hours: Documents of American Plans for Nuclear War with the Soviet Union, 1954–1955," *International Security*, vol. 6 (Winter 1981/82).

9. Stephen E. Ambrose, *Eisenhower: Soldier and President* (New York: Simon and Schuster, 1990), p. 543.

10. "The No-Cities Doctrine," in Robert J. Art and Kenneth N. Waltz, *The Use of Force: Military Power and International Politics*, 4th ed. (Lanham, Md.: University Press of America, 1993), p. 376.

11. See, for example, Schilling's discussion of Medaris, Taylor, Gavin, and Ridgway, in *Strategy, Politics and Defense Budgets*, pp. 229 and 242–43. On Taylor, see Colonel James A. Donovan, *Militarism, U.S.A.* (New York: Scribner, 1970), pp. 119–20; General Maxwell Taylor, *The Uncertain Trumpet* (New York: Harper and Brothers, 1960); General Matthew Ridgway, *Soldier* (New York: Harper and Brothers, 1956); Major General J. B. Medaris, *Countdown for Decision* (New York: Paperback Library, 1961).

12. Alfred Vagts, *A History of Militarism: Civilian and Military* (New York: Free Press, 1959), p. 165.

13. Elaine Sciolino, "Clinton's Haiti Problem: What Price Democracy?" *New York Times*, July 7, 1994, p. A8.

14. Richard H. Kohn, "Out of Control," *The National Interest*, no. 35 (Spring 1994), pp. 12–13, 17.

15. Michael R. Gordon, "Powell Delivers a Resounding No on Using Limited Forces in Bosnia," *New York Times*, September 28, 1992, p. A1; Ed Vulliamy, "Bosnia: The Secret War/America's Big Strategic Lie," *Guardian* (London), May 20, 1996, p. 12.

16. Kenneth N. Waltz, "A Necessary War?" in Harry Kreisler, ed., *Confrontation in the Gulf* (Berkeley, Calif.: Institute of International Studies, 1992), pp. 59–65.

17. The German armies in the west in 1940 had 136 divisions against 156 French, British, Belgian, and Dutch divisions. The Germans had 2,800 tanks and faced more than 4,000. Klaus Knorr, *The War Potential of Nations* (Princeton, N.J.: Princeton University Press, 1963), pp. 30–31.

18. Bernard Brodie, *Strategy in the Missile Age* (Princeton, N.J.: Princeton University Press, 1959), p. 275

19. William J. Broad, "Book Says Britain Bluffed about Its H-Bombs," *New York Times*, March 24, 1994, p. A4.

20. Kenneth N. Waltz, "Nuclear Myths and Political Realities," *American Political Science Review* 84, no. 3 (September 1990).

21. Robert McNamara, "Reducing the Risk of Nuclear War: Is Star Wars the Answer?" *Millennium: Journal of International Studies* 15, no. 2 (Summer 1986), p. 137.

22. Cited in Robert L. Gallucci, "Limiting U.S. Policy Options to Prevent Nuclear Weapons Proliferation: The Relevance of Minimum Deterrence," Center for Technical Studies on Security, Energy and Arms Control, Lawrence Livermore National Laboratory, February 28, 1991, p. 6.

23. Waltz, "Nuclear Myths and Political Realities."

24. Henry Kissinger, *For the Record: Selected Statements, 1977–1980* (Boston: Little, Brown, 1981), p. 18.

25. Sagan has managed to find three, not all of which are unambiguous: *Limits of Safety*, p. 263. Michael Howard has found none: *The Causes of War and Other Essays* (Cambridge, Mass.: Harvard University Press, 1983), p. 12.

26. David E. Sanger, "Missile Shield Point Man Does Not Shy From Tough Sell," *New York Times*, June 11, 2001, p. A10.

27. James Dao, "Skeptical Senators Question Rumsfeld on Missile Defense," *New York Times*, June 22, 2001, p. A14.

28. Robert S. McNamara, Speech delivered before the editors of the United Press International, San Francisco, September 18, 1967. Excerpted in Robert J. Art and Kenneth N. Waltz, *The Use of Force* (Boston: Little, Brown, 1971), pp. 503ff.

29. James Dao, "Rumsfeld Calls on Europe to Rethink Arms Control," *New York Times*, June 11, 2001, p. A8.

30. Thom Shanker, "Missile Defenses Need More Tests, Key Senator Says," *New York Times*, June 1, 2001, p. A1.

31. Sha is director of arms control and disarmament in China's Foreign Ministry.

32. Dennis M. Gormley, *Dealing with the Threat of Cruise Missiles* (London: International Institute for Strategic Studies, 2001). Adelphi Paper 339, pp. 74–76.

33. Powell, cited in Richard Cohen, "Political Science," *Washington Post*, May 3, 2001, p. A21.

34. Schultz, quoted in Frances FitzGerald, "The Poseurs of Missile Defense," *New York Times*, June 4, 2000, sec. 4, p. 19.

35. Patrick E. Tyler, "Putin Says Russia Would Add Arms to Counter Shield," *New York Times*, June 19, 2001, p. A1.

36. Excerpts from President Bush's Speech, *New York Times*, May 2, 2001, p. A10.

37. FitzGerald, "The Poseurs of Missile Defense."

38. Steven Lee Meyers, "Study Said to Find U.S. Missile Shield Might Incite China," *New York Times*, August 10, 2000, p. A1.

39. "Three Propositions for a New Era Nuclear Policy," Commencement Address, Massachusetts Institute of Technology, June 1, 1992. Published in *Tech Talk* by the MIT News Office, Cambridge, Mass., June 3, 1992, p. 2. Available online at web.mit.edu/newsoffice/tt/1992/jun03/ 26094/html.

40. Quoted in Samuel P. Huntington, "The Lonely Superpower," *Foreign Affairs* 78, no. 2 (March/April 1999), p. 42.

41. Thom Shankar and David E. Sanger, "White House Wants to Bury Pact Banning Test of Nuclear Arms," *New York Times*, July 7, 2001, p. A1; William J. Broad, "U.S. Plan Shows New Design Work on Nuclear Arms," *New York Times*, August 18, 1997, p. A1.

42. Kanti Bajpai, "The Fallacy of an Indian Deterrent," pp. 179, 150; Butler quoted in James Carroll, "War Inside the Pentagon," *The New Yorker*, August 18, 1997, p. 59.

43. "Palladium's Favorite Quotes," *Palladium*, 1996, www.home.earth link.net/~jdpierce/palladium/quotes.htm.

44. Michael Mandelbaum, "Lessons of the Next Nuclear War," *Foreign Affairs* 74, no. 2 (March/April 1995), p. 24; Eliot Cohen's comment excerpted in Mitchell Reiss, "The Future that Never Came," *Wilson Quarterly* 19, no. 2 (Spring 1995), p. 65. Cohen regrets that "the days of Osirak-type raids on a single, easily located and above-surface nuclear facility are over."

45. Desmond Ball concludes that with strategic warheads a war could not be sustained beyond the shooting of weapons numbered in the tens: "Counterforce Targeting: How New? How Viable?" *Arms Control Today* 11, p. 9.

46. Blair and Kendall, "Accidental Nuclear War," p. 53; Cf. Frank Von Hippel et al., "How to Avoid Nuclear War," *Bulletin of the Atomic Scientists* 46, no. 5 (June 1990), pp. 35–36.

Chapter 4

1. For detailed analyses of the nuclear revolution see Charles L. Glaser, *Analyzing Strategic Nuclear Policy* (Princeton, N.J.: Princeton University Press, 1990); and Robert Jervis, *The Meaning of the Nuclear Revolution* (Ithaca,

N.Y.: Cornell University Press, 1989). During the Cold War, I argued that it was possible and desirable to develop a "second-strike counterforce" capability to enhance deterrence at an organizational level, by preventing Soviet military planners from achieving their targeting war aims, and thus not even achieve their narrow definition of victory. I argued, however, that such a capability could be smaller in size, safer in operations, and slower in arrival than the U.S. arsenal developed in the 1980s. See Scott D. Sagan, *Moving Targets: Nuclear Strategy and National Security* (Princeton, N.J.: Princeton University Press, 1989), pp. 58–97.

2. Brian M. Jenkins, "International Terrorism: A New Mode of Conflict" in David Carlton and Carlo Shaerf, eds., *International Terrorism and World Security* (London: Croom Helm, 1975), p. 15. Also see Brian M. Jenkins, "Will Terrorists Go Nuclear?" *Orbis* 29, no. 112 (Fall 1998), pp. 116–18.

3. For other optimistic assessments see Bruce Hoffman, "The American Perspective" *Survival* 42, no. 2 (Summer 2000), pp. 161–66; and Paul R. Pillar, *Terrorism and American Foreign Policy* (Washington, D.C.: Brookings Institution, 2001), pp. 21–23.

4. David E. Kaplan, "Aum Shinrikyo (1995)," in Jonathan Tucker, ed., *Toxic Terror: Assessing Terrorist Use of Chemical and Biological Weapons* (Cambridge, Mass.: MIT Press, 2000).

5. Jessica Eve Stern, *The Ulimate Terrorists* (Cambridge, Mass.: Harvard University Press, 1999), p. 72; Stern, "The Covenant, the Sword, and the Arm of the Lord (1985)" in Tucker, ed., *Toxic Terror,* p. 146.

6. As quoted in Jessica Eve Stern, "Terrorist Motivations and Unconventional Weapons," in Peter R. Lavoy, Scott D. Sagan, and James J. Writz, eds., *Planning the Unthinkable: How New Powers Will Use Nuclear, Biological, and Chemical Weapons* (Ithaca, N.Y.: Cornell University Press, 2000), p. 215.

7. See Jessica Eve Stern, "Larry Wayne Harris 1998," in Tucker, ed., *Toxic Terror,* pp. 227–46.

8. FBI Field Intelligence Groups: 9 December 2008 Discovery of Radiological Dispersal Device Components, Literature, and Radioactive Material at the Maine Residence of an Identified Deceased US Person. www.bangordailynews.com/external/cummings/cummings2.pdf

9. abcnewsgo.com/sections/world/DailyNews/transcript_binladen 1 _98228.html

10. abcnews.go.com/sections/world/DailyNews/miller_binladen_ 980609.html

11. Ibid.

12. Ibid.

13. David Carlisle, "Dhiren Barot: Was He an Al-Qaeda Mastermind or Merely a Hapless Plotter?" *Studies in Conflict & Terrorism,* vol 30: no. 12 (December 2007), pp. 1057–71.

14. "Rough Presentation for Gas Limos Project," *The NEFA Foundation.* www.nefafoundation.org/miscellaneous/Barot/GasLimos.pdf

15. Ibid.

16. www.ceip.org/files/projects/npp/resources/Conference%202002/ sattar.htm

17. Kamran Khan and Molly Moore, "Leader Purges Top Ranks of Military, Spy Service," *Washington Post*, October 8, 2001, p. 1; Sanjay Singh, "Indian Intelligence Inputs Behind ISI Chiefs Exit," *Statesmen*, October 9, 2001; John F. Burns, "Pakistan Atom Experts Held Amid Fear Of Leaked Secrets," *New York Times*, November 1, 2001, p. 1.

18. See Greg Myre, "US wants to Advise Pakistan on Nukes," *Associated Press*, November 2, 2001.

19. Ibid. The earlier quote comes from David Albright, "Securing Pakistan's Nuclear Weapons Complex," October 2001, www.isisonline.org/publications/terrorism/stanleypaper.html.

20. David E. Sanger, *The Inheritance: The World Obama Confronts and the Challenges to American Power* (New York: Harmony Books, 2009), p. 220.

21. See the evidence presented in Joseph G. Morone and Edward J. Woodhouse, *The Demise of Nuclear Energy?* (New Haven, Conn.: Yale University Press, 1989); and Joseph V. Rees, *Hostages to Each Other: The Transformation of Nuclear Safety Since Three Mile Island* (Chicago: University of Chicago Press, 1994).

22. On the organizational roots of the space shuttle Challenger accident, see Diane Vaughan, *The Challenger Launch Decision: Risk, Culture, and Deviance at NASA* (Chicago: University of Chicago Press, forthcoming); Cf. Larry Heimann, "Understanding the *Challenger* Disaster: Organizational Structure and the Design of Reliable Systems," *American Political Science Review* 87, no. 2 (June 1993), pp. 421–35; and William H. Starbuck and Francis J. Milliken, "*Challenger*: Fine-Tuning the Odds until Something Breaks," *Journal of Management Studies* 25, no. 4 (July 1988), pp. 319–40.

23. See Scott D. Sagan, "Toward a *Political* Theory of Organizational Reliability," *Journal of Contingencies and Crisis Management* 2, no. 4 (December 1994); and James F. Short and Lee Clarke, eds., *Organizations, Uncertainties, and Risk* (Boulder, Colo.: Westview Press, 1992).

24. See Bruce G. Blair, *The Logic of Accidental Nuclear War* (Washington, D.C.: Brookings Institution, 1993); Paul Bracken, *Command and Control of Nuclear Forces* (New Haven, Conn.: Yale University Press, 1983); Peter Douglas Feaver, *Guarding the Guardians: Civilian Control of Nuclear Weapons in the United States* (Ithaca, N.Y.: Cornell University Press, 1992); and Scott D. Sagan, *The Limits of Safety: Organizations, Accidents, and Nuclear Weapons* (Princeton, N.J.: Princeton University Press, 1993).

25. For valuable discussions of the trade-offs between actions designed to increase the certainty of deliberate use and those designed to decrease the risks of accidents and unauthorized use, see Peter D. Feaver, "Command and Control in Emerging Nuclear States," *International Security* 17, no. 3 (Winter 1992–93), pp. 160–87; and Bradley A. Thayer, "The Risk of Nuclear Inadvertence: A Review Essay," *Security Studies* 3, no. 3 (Spring 1994), pp. 428–93.

26. This alert was reported by Seymour M. Hersh in *The Samson Option: Israel's Nuclear Arsenal and American Foreign Policy* (New York: Random House, 1991), p. 231. U.S. knowledge of the Israel alert was confirmed by a former National Security Council official, William B. Quandt, in his review essay, "How Far Will Israel Go," *Washington Post Book World*, November 24, 1991.

27. For reports that Israel alerted its nuclear arsenal during the 1991 Gulf War see Hersh, *The Samson Option*, p. 318 and Bill Gertz, "Israel Deploys Missiles for a Possible Strike at Iraq," *Washington Times*, January 28, 1991, p. B7. Other sources have claimed, however, that the United States did not receive any intelligence on an Israeli nuclear weapons alert. See "Special Report: The Secret History of the War," *Newsweek*, March 18, 1991, p. 36.

28. The estimates are from the National Resources Defense Council. See Robert S. Norris, "The Soviet Nuclear Archipelago," *Arms Control Today* (January/February 1992), p. 25.

29. On the United States sharing, see Richard H. Ullman, "The Covert French Connection," *Foreign Policy*, no. 75 (Summer 1989), pp. 3–33. On China's assistance to Pakistan, see David Albright and Mark Hibbs, "Pakistan's Bomb: Out of the Closet," *Bulletin of Atomic Scientists* 48, no. 6 (July/August 1992), pp. 42–43.

30. See Scott D. Sagan, "SIOP-62: The Nuclear War Plan Briefing to President Kennedy," *International Security* 12, no. 1 (Summer 1987), p. 36.

31. As quoted in Samuel P. Huntington, *The Soldier and the State* (Cambridge, Mass.: Harvard University Press, 1957), p. 69.

32. Sweeney is quoted in Robert S. McNamara, "Notes on October 21, 1962 Meeting with the President," October, 21, 1962, Cuban Missile Crisis 1962 Documents Collection (Alexandria, Va.: Chadwick-Healy, 1990), microfiche 1372-00738, p. 2. Moreover, the 90 percent success rate referred only to the thirty-six *known* missile sites; U.S. intelligence agencies estimated that there were four additional missile sites in Cuba that had not yet been found on October 21. Ibid.

33. Chronology of JCS Decisions Concerning the Cuban Crisis, Historical Division, Joint Chiefs of Staff (Freedom of Information Act Request), pp. 23, 49. The latter recommendation was not unanimous: "Chairman of the Joint Chiefs, General Maxwell Taylor, recommended against taking the decision to execute now" and wanted instead to maintain a readiness to launch the air strike and invasion with a twelve-hour notice. Ibid.

34. Bernard Brodie, *War and Politics* (London: Cassel, 1974), p. 496.

35. See Roberta Wohlstetter, *Pearl Harbor: Warning and Decision* (Stanford, Calif.: Stanford University Press, 1962), pp. 10–11, 73–74; and Gordon W. Prange, *At Dawn We Slept* (New York: McGraw-Hill, 1991), pp. 411–12.

36. D. Clayton James, *The Years of MacArthur: Volume II, 1941–1945* (Boston: Houghton Mifflin, 1975), pp. 3–15; Louis Morton, *The Fall of The Philippines* (Washington, D.C.: GPO, 1953), pp. 79–90.

37. R. V. Jones, *The Wizard War: British Scientific Intelligence 1939–1945* (New York: Coward, McCann and Geoghegan, 1978), pp. 360–64; Basil Collier, *The Battle of the V-Weapons, 1944–1945* (Morley, Yorkshire: Elmfield Press, 1976), pp. 23–41.

38. Jones, *The Wizard War*, p. 246.

39. *The Military Balance* (London: International Institute for Strategic Studies, 1991), p. 108.

40. Shamir, speech of August 9, 1990, as quoted in Shai Feldman, "Israeli Deterrence and the Gulf War," in Joseph Alpher, ed., *War in the Gulf* (Boulder, Colo.: Westview Press, 1992), p. 197.

41. See Jose Goldemberg and Harold A. Feiveson, "Denuclearization in Argentina and Brazil," *Arms Control Today* 24, no. 2 (March 1994), pp. 10–14.

42. See David Albright, "South Africa's Secret Nuclear Weapons"; Darryl Howlett and John Simpson, "Nuclearisation and Denuclearisation in South Africa," *Survival* 35, no. 3 (Autumn 1993), pp. 154–73; and J. W. de Villers, Roger Jardine, and Mitchell Reiss, "Why South Africa Gave Up the Bomb," *Foreign Affairs* 72, no. 5 (November/December 1993), pp. 98–109.

CHAPTER 5

1. These and subsequent estimates are from Michael Clodfelter, *Warfare and Armed Conflict: A Statistical Reference*, vol. 2 (London: McFarland & Co., 1992).

2. Stephen P. Cohen, *India: An Emerging Power* (Washington, D.C.: Brookings Institution, 2001), p. 146.

3. Peter D. Feaver, *Guarding the Guardians: Civilian Control of Nuclear Weapons in the United States* (Ithaca, N.Y.: Cornell University Press, 1992).

4. See Julian Schofeld, "Militarized Decision-Making for War in Pakistan: 1947–1971," *Armed Forces and Society* 27, no. 1 (Fall 2000); Scott D. Sagan, "The Perils of Proliferation: Organization Theory, Deterrence Theory, and the Spread of Nuclear Weapons," *International Security* (Spring 1994); and Sumit Ganguly, *The Origins of War in South Asia* (Boulder, Colo.: Westview Press, 1986).

5. See George Perkovich, *India's Nuclear Bomb* (Berkeley: University of California Press, 1999), pp. 303, 306–13; Michell Reiss, *Bridled Ambition* (Washington, D.C.: Woodrow Wilson Center Press, 1995), pp. 183–220; and *From Surprise to Reckoning: The Kargil Review Committee Report* (New Delhi: Sage, 2000), pp. 66–67.

6. See Whegru Pal Singh Sidhu, "India's Nuclear Use Doctrine," in Peter R. Lavoy, Scott D. Sagan, and James J. Wirtz, eds., *Planning the Unthinkable* (Ithaca, N.Y.: Cornell University Press, 2000), pp. 132–34; Kanti P. Bajpai, P. R. Chari, Pervaiz Iqbal Cheema, Stephen P. Cohen, and Sumit Ganguly, *Brasstacks and Beyond: Perception and Management of Crisis in South Asia* (New Delhi: Manohar, 1995), pp. 9–10; and Perkovich, *India's Nuclear Bomb*, pp. 239–44.

7. This interpretation of Brasstacks was first presented as a speculative argument based on organization theory predictions in Scott D. Sagan, "Correspondence: Proliferation Pessimism and Emerging Nuclear Powers," *International Security* 22, no. 2 (Fall 1997), p. 195.

8. See Bajpai et al., *Brasstacks and Beyond*, pp. 28–40, 127–28; and Devin T. Hagerty, *The Consequences of Nuclear Proliferation* (Cambridge, Mass., MIT Press, 1998), pp. 91–116.

9. Hagerty, *The Consequences of Nuclear Proliferation*, pp. 92, 106. Also see Bajpai et al., *Brasstacks and Beyond*, pp. 100–103.

10. Raj Chengappa, *Weapons of Peace: The Secret History of India's Quest to Be a Nuclear Power* (New Delhi: HarperCollins Publishers, 2000), pp. 322–23; P. N. Hoon, *Unmasking Secrets of Turbulence* (New Delhi: Manas Publications, 2000), p. 102.

11. Hoon, *Unmasking Secrets of Turbulence*, p. 102.

12. Bajpai et al., *Brasstacks and Beyond*, pp. 41–42.

13. Perkovich, *India's Nuclear Bomb*, p. 208.

14. Hagerty, *The Consequences of Nuclear Proliferation*, p. 184.

15. John Lancaster, "Kashmir Crisis Was Defused on Brink of War," *Washington Post*, July 26, 1999, p. A1; Thomas W. Lippman, "India Hints at Attack in Pakistan," *Washington Post*, June 27, 1999, p. A26.

16. Bradley Graham and Nathan Abse, "U.S. Says Pakistan Will Withdraw," *Washington Post*, July 5, 1999, p. A15. That Clinton's statement on Kashmir was merely a political cover for the withdrawal was later made clear when Clinton revealed that he had told Sharif that he could not come to Washington unless he was willing to withdraw the troops back across the line of control. See "Pak troops withdrew from Kargil at my insistence," *The Times of India*, June 3, 2001, www.timesofindia.com/030601/03worl6.htm.

17. See *From Surprise to Reckoning*, p. 77; and Maleeha Lodhi, "The Kargil Crisis: Anatomy of a Debacle," *Newsline* (July 1999), p. 1.

18. Ihtashamul Haque, "Peace Linked to Kashmir Solution," *Dawn Wire Service*, June 26, 1999.

19. Sharif later claimed that he was not informed of the operation until just before it began in May 1999. See "Sharif Blames Musharraf for Kargil," *Reuters*, June 13, 2000, www.timesofindia.com/2000/06/13/blame.html. Also see "Army Rejects Sharif Claim," *BBC News*, June 13, 2000, news.bbc.co.uk/hi/English/world/south_asia/newsid_787000/787795.stm.

20. Pamela Constable, "Pakistan Aims to 'Avoid Nuclear War,'" *Washington Post*, July 13, 1999, p A14; "U.S. Involvement Essential: PM," *Dawn Wire Service*, July 10, 1999.

21. Foreign Secretary Shamshad Ahmad, for example, proclaimed in May 1999 that Pakistan "will not hesitate to use any weapon in our arsenal to defend our territorial integrity." See "Any weapon will be used, threatens Pak," *The Hindu*, June 1, 1999.

22. Bruce Riedel, "American Diplomacy and the 1999 Summit at Blair House," Policy Paper Series 2002, Center for Advanced Study of India, University of Pennsylvania; Raj Chenagappa, "Pakistan Tried Nuclear Blackmail," *The Newspaper Today*, January 12, 2000, www.thenewspapertoday.com/interview/index.phtml?INTERVIEW-INT_PADCOUNT.

23. Molly More and Karam Khan, "Pakistan Moves Nuclear Weapons," *Washington Post*, November 11, 2001, p. A1; Manoj Joshi, "Pak May Have Relocated Nukes to Gilgit," *Times of India*, November 14, 2001, p. 1; Bill Gertz, "India, Pakistan Prepare Nukes, Troops for War," *Washington Times*, December 31, 2001 p. A1.

24. See, for example, Seymour M. Hersh, "Watching the Warheads," *The New Yorker*, November 11, 2001.

25. "Army Ready for War, Says Chief," *The Statesmen* (India), January 12, 2002.

26. Celia W. Dugger, "Indian General Talks Bluntly of War and a Nuclear Threat," *New York Times*, January 12, 2002, p. A1.

27. N. Prasannan, "Spark of Hope," *The Week*, September 28, 1997.

28. See John Diamond, "Satellite Shows Pakistan's March Toward Nuclear Capability," *Chicago Tribune*, March 16, 2000, p. 10.

29. Richard Sisson and Leo E. Rose, *War and Secession: Pakistan, India, and the Creation of Bangladesh* (Berkeley: University of California Press, 1990), pp. 199, 225 (also see p. 309, fn. 45).

30. Asoka Raina, *Inside RAW: The Story of India's Secret Service* (New Delhi: Vikas Publishing House, 1981), pp. 60–61.

31. Shisher Gupta, "Major's Diary Exposes Pak's Involvement," *Hindustan Times*, July 10, 1999, p. 1; "1st Definite Proof of Pak Army Role," soniagandhi.org/asian30b.htm; and *From Surprise to Reckoning*, pp. 21, 97.

32. The whole transcript is available at www.ipcs.org/documents/1999/2-apr-jul.htm#Tapes.

33. Chengappa, "Pakistan Tried Nuclear Blackmail"; Gertz, "India, Pakistan Prepare Nukes, Troops for War."

34. The paragraph is based on the following sources, "Doubts over BDL Safety Norms," *The Hindu*, January 9, 2001; "One Killed as Missile Fires Accidentally," *The Hindu*, January 5, 2001; and "One Killed as Missile Fires During Demonstration," *The Times of India*, January 5, 2001; and Lalita Iyer, "In House Strike," *The Week*, January 21, 2001, at www.the-week.com/21/ jan21/events6 .htm. Similar rocket explosions have occurred with other nuclear powers. For example, in 1960, the commander of the Soviet Union's Strategic Rocket Forces was killed, along with many others, when a space rocket exploded while being inspected prior to launch. See James E. Oberg, *Uncovering Soviet Disasters* (New York: Random House, 1988), pp. 177–83.

35. See Yossi Melman, "The Coming Mideast Nuclear-Arms Race," *Los Angeles Times*, June 7, 1998, part M, p. 2; "Pakistan Probably a Stronger Country than Most Pakistanis Think—U.S. Ambassador," *Dawn Magazine*, July 19, 1998; and Shahid-Ur-Rehman, *Long Road the Chagai* (Islamabad: Print Wise Publications, 1999), pp. 115–16.

36. Christopher Walker and Michael Evans, "Pakistan Feared Israeli Attack," *The Times*, June 3, 1998; Shahid-Ur-Rehman, *Long Road the Chagai*, p. 116.

37. Muhammad Yousaf and Mark Adkin, *The Bear Trap: Afghanistan's Untold Story* at www.afghanbooks.com/beartrap/ and Samina Ahmed and David C. Courtright, "Going Nuclear: The Weaponization Option," in Ahmed and Courtright, eds., *Pakistan and the Bomb*, p. 96.

38. John F. Burns, "Pakistan Arrests 40 Officers, Islamic Militant Tie Suspected," *New York Times*, October 17, 1995.

39. Tim Lister and Aliza Kassim, "Arrest of Pakistani Officer Revives Fears of Extremism within Military," *CNN World*, June 22, 2011.

40. "Punjab Governor Salman Taseer Assassinated in Islamabad," *BBC News*, January 4, 2011.

41. Zahid Hussain, *Frontline Pakistan: The Struggle with Militant Islam* (New York, NY: Columbia University Press, 2007), prologue.

42. Peter Vincent Pry, *War Scare: Russia and America on the Nuclear Brink* (Westport, Conn.: Praeger, 1999), pp. 217–20.

43. Raj Chengappa, "Missiles: Boom for Boom," *India Today International*, April 26, 1999, p. 28–30.

44. Chengappa, "Pakistan Threatened India."

45. David E. Sanger, *The Inheritance: The World Obama Confronts and the Challenges to American Power* (New York, NY: Harmony Books, 2009), pp. 220–24.

46. Neil Joeck, "The Kargil War and Nuclear Deterrence," in Sumit Ganguly and S. Paul Kapur, eds., *Nuclear Proliferation in South Asia: Crisis Behavior and the Bomb* (London: Routledge, 2008), pp. 117–43.

47. For further analysis see Scott D. Sagan, "The Evolution of Pakistani and Indian Nuclear Doctrine," in Scott D. Sagan, ed., *Inside Nuclear South Asia* (Stanford, CA: Stanford University Press, 2009), pp. 219–63.

48. Steven Erlanger, "India's Arms Race Isn't Safe Like the Cold War," *New York Times*, July 12, 1998, section 4, p. 18.

49. David E. Jeremiah, quoted in Tim Weiner, "The World: Naivete at the CIA: Every Nation Just Another US." (James Woosley made the same point earlier.) *Proliferation Threats of the 1990s*, Hearing before the Committee on Governmental Affairs, United States Senate, 103rd Congress, First Session, February 24, 1998, p. 134; and Michael Krepon quoted in John Kifner, "Pakistan Army at Ease, Even in Nuclear Choice," *New York Times*, June 23, 1998, p. A3.

50. Quoted in Erlanger, "India's Arms Race Isn't Safe Like the Cold War."

51. K. Subrahmanyam, "Nuclear Force Design and Minimum Deterrence Strategy," in Bharat Karnad, ed., *Future Imperiled: India's Security in the 1990s and Beyond* (New Delhi: Viking, 1994), pp. 190, 194. Both sides mention different numbers at different times. The important point is that all of them are low, running around one hundred warheads.

52. Cf. Peter D. Feaver, "Neooptimists and the Enduring Problem of Nuclear Proliferation," *Security Studies* 6, no. 4 (Summer 1997), pp. 105–20.

53. Strobe Talbott, "Dealing with the Bomb in South Asia," *Foreign Affairs* 78, no. 2 (March/April 1999), p. 117.

54. Claudia Dreifus, "Benazir Bhutto," *New York Times Magazine*, May 15, 1994, p. 39; K. Shankar Bajpai, "Nuclear Exchange," *Far Eastern Economic Review*, June 24, 1993, p. 24; Shamshad Ahmad, "The Nuclear Subcontinent: Bringing Stability to South Asia," *Foreign Affairs* 78, no. 4 (July/August 1999), p. 125.

55. John F. Burns, "War-Weary Kashmiris Contemplate the Price of Peace," *New York Times*, July 11, 2001, p. A3.

56. Quoted in Jonathan Spence, "Kissinger and the Emperor," *New York Review of Books*, March 4, 1999, p. 21.

57. Cf. K. Subrahmanyam, "India's Dilemma," in K. Subrahmanyam, ed., *Nuclear Myths and Realities* (New Delhi: ABC Publishing House, 1981), pp. 218–19; Perkovich, *India's Nuclear Bomb* p. 170.

58. Amitabh Mattoo, "India's Nuclear Policy in an Anarchic World," in Mattoo, ed., *India's Nuclear Deterrent: Pokhran II and Beyond* (New Delhi: Har-Anand, 1999), p. 22.

59. George Fernandes, quoted in John F. Burns, "Indian Defense Chief Calls U.S. Hypocritical," *New York Times*, June 18, 1998, p. A6.

60. Kanti Bajpai, "The Fallacy of an Indian Deterrent," in Amitabh Mattoo, ed., *India's Nuclear Deterrent*, p. 183. China does not recognize Arunachal Pradesh or Sikkim as parts of India.

61. Quoted in Erlanger, "India's Arms Race Isn't Safe Like the Cold War."

62. Albert Carnesale, Paul Doty, Stanley Hoffman, Samuel P. Huntington, Joseph S. Nye, Jr., and Scott Sagan, *Living with Nuclear Weapons* (Cambridge, Mass.: Harvard University Press, 1983) p. 44.

63. See, e.g., Mirza Aslam Beg, *Development and Security: Thoughts and Reflections* (Rawalpindi: Friends, 1994), p. 189; and K. Sundarji cited in Devin T. Hagerty, "Nuclear Deterrence in South Asia: The 1990 Indo-Pakistani Crisis," p. 109.

64. Raja Menon, *A Nuclear Strategy for India* (New Delhi: Sage, 2000), p. 116.

65. Karl Kaiser, "Nonproliferation and Nuclear Deterrence," *Survival* 31, no. 2 (March/April, 1989), p. 125; Arthur G. Rubinoff, "The failure of nuclear deterrence in South Asia," *Toronto Globe and Mail*, June 1, 1998, p. A17.

66. See Kenneth N. Waltz, "Thoughts about Virtual Nuclear Arsenals," *Washington Quarterly* 20, no. 3 (Summer 1997), p. 158.

67. Quoted in Celia W. Dugger and Barry Bearak, "You've Got the Bomb. So Do I. Now I Dare You to Fight," *New York Times*, January 16, 2000, sec. 4, p. 1.

68. Menon, *A Nuclear Strategy for India*, p. 293.

69. Ibid., p. 197.

70. Dugger and Bearak, "You've Got the Bomb."

71. James Bamford, "The Dangers of Spy Planes," *New York Times*, April 5, 2001, p. A21.

72. Pry, *War Scare*, pp. 33–43. Pry tells other hair-raising tales about provocative action by both sides.

73. Subrahmanyam, "Nuclear Force Design," p. 192.

74. Ibid., p. 186.

75. This time the commentator is Sam Gardiner, Colonel, USAF, retired. See his "It Doesn't Start in Kashmir, and It Never Ends Well," *Washington Post*, January 20, 2002, p. B1.

76. The analyst is Commodore Uday Bhaskar, deputy directory of the Institute for Defense Studies and Analysis, quoted in Rajiv Chandrasekaran, "For India, Deterrence May Not Prevent War," *Washington Post Foreign Service*, January 17, 2002, p. A1.

77. See, e.g., Walter C. Ludwig III, "A Cold Start for Hot Wars? The Indian Army's New Limited War Doctrine," *International Security*, vol. 32, no. 3 (Winter 2007–08), pp. 1589–90; Vipin Narang, "Posturing for Peace? Pakistan's Nuclear Postures and South Asian Stability," *International Security*, vol. 34, no. 3 (Winter 2009/10), pp. 38–78.

78. See, e.g., Paul Staniland, "Improving India's Counterterrorism Policy After Mumbai," *CTC Sentinel*, April 2009, vol. 2, Issue 4, 2.

79. Narang, "Posturing for Peace?," 63–64.

80. Colin Freeze, "Accused in India Massacre Claims Ties to Pakistan's Secret Service," *The Globe and Mail*, April 11, 2011, www.theglobeandmail.

com/news/world/americas/accused-in-india-massacre-claims-ties-to
-pakistani-secret-service/article1981052/

81. Paul Staniland, "Improving India's Counterterrorism Policy After Mumbai," 1–3.

82. Adrian Blomfield, "Syria Enlisted the Help of 'Father' of Pakistan's Bomb," *The Daily Telegraph*, November 1, 2011, www.telegraph.co.uk/news/ worldnews/middleeast/syria/8863416/Syria-enlisted-help-of-father-of-Pak-istans-atom-bomb.html

83. "AQ Khan Nuclear Chronology," Issue Brief: Nonproliferation, *Carnegie Endowment for International Peace*, vol VIII, no. 8, September 7, 2005, 7.

CHAPTER 6

1. George W. Bush, "State of the Union Address," Washington, D.C., January 29, 2002.

2. For an insightful analysis of the 2002 intelligence failure by the senior State Department intelligence official who wrote the dissenting footnote about the Iraqi nuclear program, see Thomas Fingar, *Reducing Uncertainty: Intelligence Analysis and National Security* (Palo Alto, CA: Stanford University Press, 2011).

3. Department of Defense, *Casualty Report*, April 10, 2012. www.defense .gov/news/casualty.pdf [date accessed: April 10, 2012].
Iraq Body Count, April 10, 2012. http://www.iraqbodycount.org/, [Date Accessed: April 10, 2012].

4. Korean Central News Agency. "Statement of FM spokesman blasts UNSC's discussion of Korean nuclear issue," April 6, 2003. www.kcna.co.jp/ item/2003/200304/news04/07.htm [date accessed: June 13, 2011].

5. This summary is based on the excellent analysis in Siegfried S. Hecker, "Lessons Learned from the North Korean Nuclear Crises," *Daedalus* 139, no. 1 (Winter 2010), pp. 44–56.

6. Greg Bruno, "Iran's Nuclear Program," *CFR Backgrounder*, March 10, 2010. www.cfr.org/iran/irans-nuclear-program/p16811 [date accessed: June 13, 2011].

7. Sonny Efron, "War with Iraq/Diplomacy: Looking Past Baghdad to the Next Challenge," *Los Angeles Times*, April 6, 2003.

8. The Director General, "Implementation of the NPT Safeguards Agreement and relevant provisions of Security Council resolutions in the Islamic Republic of Iran," *International Atomic Energy Agency*, November 8, 2011. http://graphics8.nytimes.com/packages/pdf/world/2011/ IAEA-Nov-2011-Report-Iran.pdf?ref=world [date accessed: November 17, 2011].

9. David Albright, et al. "ISIS Analysis of IAEA Iran Safeguards Report," *Institute for Science and International Security*, February 24, 2012. www.isisnucleariran.org/assets/pdf/ISIS_Analysis_IAEA_Rerport _24Feb2012.pdf [date accessed: April 9, 2012].

10. "War with Iraq is Not in America's National Interest," *New York Times,* September 26, 2002.

11. 2002 National Security Strategy of the United States.

12. "DCI Special Advisor Report on Iraq's WMD," Annex D, Iraq Economic Data, 1989–2003, The Central Intelligence Agency, www.cia.gov/library/reports/general-reports-1/iraq_wmd_2004/chap2_annxD.html

13. "Fiscal 2003 Year Budget," Center for Defense Information, www.cdi.org/issues/budget/FY03Highlights-pr.cfm

14. Kevin Woods et al., "The Iraqi Perspectives Project: A View of Operation Iraqi Freedom from Saddam's Senior Leadership," The Joint Center for Operational Analysis and Lessons Learned, US Joint Forces Command, 2008.

15. Woods et al., pp. 91–95.

16. "The Korean People's Army: Training," Global Security.org, www.globalsecurity.org/military/world/dprk/army.htm

17. "North Korea's Capital Has Secret Tunnels - Defector," *BBC News,* December 9, 2009, http://news.bbc.co.uk/2/hi/8403217.stm.

18. "Strangers at Home: North Koreans in the South," *The International Crisis Group,* Asia Report Number 208, July 14, 2011.

19. Joel S. Wit, Daniel Poneman, and Robert L. Gallucci, *Going Critical: The First North Korean Nuclear Crisis* (Brookings Institution Press, 2005).

20. Fiona Simpson, "The IAEA's Dilemma with Syria's Al Kibar Nuclear Site," *Bulletin of the Atomic Scientists,* May 6, 2008, www.the-bulletin.org/web-edition/features/the-iaeas-dilemma-with-syrias-al-kibar-nuclear-site

21. David E. Sanger, "US Said to Turn Back North Korean Missile Shipment," *New York Times,* June 12, 2011, www.nytimes.com/2011/06/13/world/asia/13missile.html

22. Wyn Q. Bowen, "Libya and Nuclear Proliferation: Stepping Back from the Brink," *Adelphi Paper,* Routledge, 2006.

23. Victor Cha, "What Do They Really Want? Obama's North Korea Conundrum," *The Washington Quarterly* 32, no. 4 (October 2009), p. 122.

24. Robert S. Norris and Hans M. Christensen, "Global Nuclear Weapons Inventories 1945–2010," *Bulletin of the Atomic Scientists* 66, no. 77 (July–August 2010), p. 82.

25. Bruce W. Bennett and Jennifer Lind, "The Collapse of North Korea: Military Missions and Requirements," *International Security* 36, no. 2 (Fall 2011), p. 84.

26. Christine Kim, "Libya Should Have Kept Its Nukes Says Pyongyang," *Korea JoonAng Daily,* March 24, 2011, http://koreajoongangdaily.join-smsn.com/news/article/article.aspx?aid=2933884

27. "Iran: Nuclear Intentions and Capabilities—Key Judgments," National Intelligence Estimate, National Intelligence Council, November 2007, p. 6.

28. Richard K. Betts, *Nuclear Blackmail and Nuclear Balance* (Washington, D.C.: The Brookings Institution, 1987).

29. Glenn Snyder, "The Balance of Terror and the Balance of Power," in Paul Seabury, ed., *The Balance of Power* (Chandler: San Francisco, 1964), 184–201.

30. "Country Reports on Terrorism, 2008," Publication Office of the Coordinator for Counterterrorism, United States Department of State, Released April 2009, p. 10.

31. Francis J. Gavin, "Blasts from the Past: Proliferation Lessons from the 1960s," *International Security* 29, no. 3 (Winter 2004–05), pp. 100–35.

32. U.S. President Barack Obama in Prague, Czech Republic, April 5, 2009.

33. Hugh Tomlinson, "Saudi Arabia Gives Israel Clear Skies to Attack Iranian Nuclear Sites," *The London Times*, June 12, 2010.

34. Gary C. Hufbauer, Jeffrey J. Schott, Kimberly Ann Elliot, and Barbara Oegg, *Economic Sanctions Reconsidered* (Washington, D.C.: Petersen Institute for International Economics, 2007), p. 12.

35. Hal Brands and David Palkki, "Saddam, Israel, and the Bomb: Nuclear Alarmism Justified?" *International Security* 36, no. 1 (Summer 2011), p. 156.

36. David D. Palkki, Mark E. Stout, and Kevin M. Woods, *The Saddam Tapes* (New York, NY: Cambridge University Press, 2011), pp. 223–24.

37. Kevin M. Woods, et al., *The Iraqi Perspectives Report* (Annapolis, MD: Naval Institute Press, 2006), p. 12.

38. Brands and Palkki, "Saddam, Israel, and the Bomb," pp. 152–53.

39. See *The Saddam Tapes*, pp. 211, 238, 240, and *The Iraqi Perspectives Report*, p. 31.

40. Siegfried S. Hecker, "A Return Trip to North Korea's Yongbyon Nuclear Complex," *CISAC*, November 20, 2010. http://cisac.stanford.edu/publications/north_koreas_yongbyon_nuclear_complex_a_report_by_siegfried_s_hecker/ [date accessed: November 22, 2011]; and Robert Carlin and Siegfried Hecker, "2011: North Korea's Countdown to Kim Il-Sung's Centenary," *Bulletin of the Atomic Scientists*, forthcoming 2012.

41. Carlin and Hecker, "2011: North Korea's Countdown to Kim Il-Sung's Centenary."

42. See Joshua Pollack, "North Korea Debuts an IRBM," *Arms Control Wonk*, October 10, 2010. http://pollack.armscontrolwonk.com/archive/3351/north-korea-debuts-an-irbm [date accessed: November 22, 2011].

43. Sheena Chestnut, "Illicit Activity and Proliferation: North Korean Smuggling Networks," *International Security* 32, no. 1 (Summer 2007), p. 81.

44. Leonard S. Spector and Deborah R. Berman, "The Syrian Nuclear Puzzle," in William C. Potter and Gaukhar Mukhatzhanova, eds., *Forecasting Nuclear Proliferation in the 21st Century* (Stanford, CA: Stanford University Press, 2010), pp. 100–28. Also see George W. Bush, *Decision Points* (New York: Crown Publishers, 2010), pp. 420–22.

45. Fredrik Dahl, "West fears possible Iran-North Korea nuclear links," *Reuters*, September 17, 2011. www.reuters.com/article/2011/09/17/us-nuclear-iran-northkorea-idUSTRE78G2HD20110917 [date accessed: November 22, 2011].

46. This section builds upon Scott D. Sagan, "How to Keep the Bomb from Iran," *Foreign Affairs* (September/October 2006), pp. 45–59.

47. David E. Sanger, "Suppose We Just Let Iran Have the Bomb?" *The New York Times*, March 19, 2006. www.nytimes.com/2006/03/19/weekinreview/19sanger.ART0.html?pagewanted=all [date accessed: November 22, 2011].

48. David E. Sanger, "Debate Grows on Nuclear Containment of Iran" *The New York Times*, March 13, 2010. www.nytimes.com/2010/03/14/weekinreview/14sanger.html [date accessed: November 22, 2011].

49. R. Jeffrey Smith, et al., "Iran May Have Sent Libya Shells for Chemical Weapons," *The Washington Post*, November 20, 2011. www.washington post.com/world/national-security/iran-may-have-sent-libya-shells -for-chemical-weapons/2011/11/18/gIQA7RPifN_print.html [date accessed: November 23, 2011].

50. Safa Haeri and Shahram Rafizadeh, "Iranian Cleric Okays Use of Nuclear Weapons," Iran Press Service, February 20, 2006. www.iran-press -service.com/ips/articles-2006/february-2006/iran_nuke_20206.shtml [date accessed: November 17, 2011]. For analysis of this and other statements see Shmuel Bar, "Can Cold War Deterrence Apply to a Nuclear Iran?" *Strategic Perspectives*, November 7, 2011. www.jcpa.org/text/cold_war_ deterrence_nuclear_iran.pdf [date accessed: November 17, 2011].

51. Annie Samuel and Daniel Tavana, "Going Rogue in Iran?" *CNN. com*, October 14, 2011. http://belfercenter.ksg.harvard.edu/publication/ 21402/going_rogue_in_iran.html?breadcrumb=%2Fexperts%2F2320 %2Fdaniel_tavana [date accessed: November 17, 2011].

52. David E. Sanger, "No Diplomatic Change After Britons' Release," *The New York Times*, April 6, 2007. www.nytimes.com/2007/04/06/washing-ton/06policy.html [date accessed: November 17, 2011].

53. Charlie Savage and Scott Shane, "Iranians Accused of a Plot to Kill Saudis' U.S. Envoy," *The New York Times*, October 11, 2011. www.nytimes.com/ 2011/10/12/us/us-accuses-iranians-of-plotting-to-kill-saudi-envoy.html ?pagewanted=all [date accessed: November 17, 2011].

54. Elaine Sciolino and Katrin Bennhold, "Chirac Unfazed By Nuclear Iran, Then Backtracks," *The New York Times*, February 1, 2007.

55. Jason Burke, "Saudi Arabia worries about stability, security and Iran," *The Guardian*, June 29, 2011. www.guardian.co.uk/world/2011/jun/29/ saudi-arabia-prince-turki-arab-spring-iran [date accessed: November 3, 2011].

56. David Blair, "Robert Gates: Bombing Iran Would Not Stop Nuclear Threat," *The Telegraph*, May 1, 2009. www.telegraph.co.uk/news/worldnews/ middleeast/iran/5257343/Robert-Gates-bombing-Iran-would-not-stop -nuclear-threat.html [date accessed: November 23, 2011]; Boaz Fyler, "Dagan: Iran Strike—Only as Last Resort," *Ynet News*, June 1, 2011. www.ynetnews. com/articles/0,7340,L-4077239,00.html [date accessed: November 23, 2011].

CHAPTER 7

1. *U.S. Nuclear Posture Review Report*, Department of Defense, April 2011. www.defense.gov/npr/

2. Dean A. Wilkening, "Nuclear Zero and Ballistic Missile Defense," *Survival* 52, no. 6, 2010.

3. "2010 Ballistic Missile Defense Review Fact Sheet," March 3, 2010, Department of Defense. www.defense.gov/bmdr/

4. Yousaf Butt, "The Delusion of Missile Defense," *New York Times*, September 20, 2011. www.nytimes.com/2011/09/21/opinion/21iht-edbutt21.html

5. See Robert Jervis, *The Meaning of the Nuclear Revolution: Statecraft and the Prospect of Armageddon* (Ithaca: Cornell University Press, 1989).

6. Steve Gutterman, "Russia Criticizes Latest US Missile Defense Deal," *Reuters*, October 16, 2011. www.reuters.com/article/2011/10/06/us-russia-usa-missiles-idUSTRE7951R620111006

7. Thomas C. Schelling, "The Role of Deterrence in Total Disarmament," *Foreign Affairs* 40, no. 3 (April 1962), p. 392.

8. Arthur M. Schlesinger Jr., *A Thousand Days: John F. Kennedy in the White House* (Boston: Houghton Mifflin, 1965).

INDEX

States with Nuclear Weapons

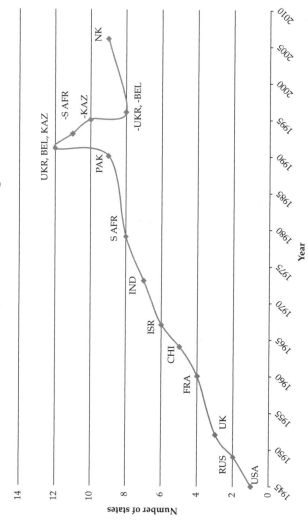

Nuclear weapons proliferation. This figure is based on multiple sources cited in Scott D. Sagan. 2011. "The Causes and Consequences of Nuclear Weapons Proliferation." *Annual Review of Political Science* 14: 225–244.

States that Explored or Pursued Nuclear Weapons

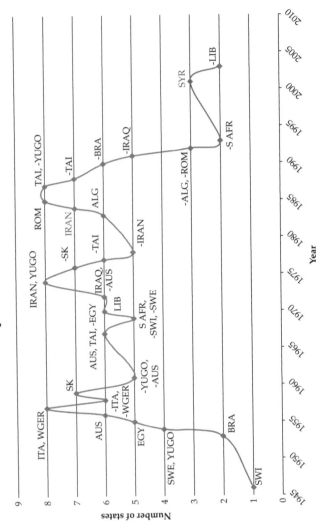

Nuclear exploration, programs, and reversal. This figure is based on multiple sources cited in Scott D. Sagan. 2011. "The Causes and Consequences of Nuclear Weapons Proliferation." *Annual Review of Political Science* 14: 225–244.